Nov. 24, 2014

For George Coyne, S.J.,
With much gratitude for his
help with this volume —

John O'Malley, S.J.

JESUIT MAPMAKING IN CHINA

D'ANVILLE'S *NOUVELLE ATLAS DE LA CHINE* (1737)

EARLY MODERN CATHOLICISM AND THE VISUAL ARTS SERIES, VOL. 11

JESUIT MAPMAKING IN CHINA

D'ANVILLE'S *NOUVELLE ATLAS DE LA CHINE* (1737)

EDITED BY

Roberto M. Ribeiro

with

John W. O'Malley, S.J.

SAINT JOSEPH'S UNIVERSITY PRESS

PHILADELPHIA

ISBN 978-0-91610-181-7

Library of Congress Cataloging-in-Publication Data

Jesuit mapmaking in China : D'Anville's Nouvelle atlas de la Chine (1737)
/ edited by Roberto M. Ribeiro ; with John W. O'Malley, S.J.
    pages cm.—(Early modern Catholicism and the visual arts series ; volume 11)
    Includes bibliographical references.
    ISBN 0-916101-81-9
    1. Anville, Jean Baptiste Bourguignon d', 1697-1782. Nouvel atlas de la Chine,
    de la Tartarie chinoise et du Thibet. 2. Jesuits—Missions—China—History—
    18th century—Maps. 3. Cartography—China—History—18th century.
    4. Cartography—China—Early works to 1800. I. Ribeiro, Roberto M., editor.
    II. O'Malley, John W. III. Title: D'Anville's Nouvelle atlas de la Chine (1737).

    G2306.E4J4 2014
    912.51—dc23
                            2014032562

Book design by Tim Durning, Scribe Inc., Philadelphia

Published by
Saint Joseph's University Press
5600 City Avenue
Philadelphia, PA 19131
www.sjupress.com

Saint Joseph's University Press is a member of the
Association of American University Presses
and the Association of Jesuit University Presses

TABLE OF CONTENTS

Preface: Friendship and Science   1
Roberto M. Ribeiro

Illustrations   5

Imperial China and the Jesuit Mission   25
R. Po-chia Hsia

Jean-Baptiste Bourguignon d'Anville and
the *Nouvelle atlas de la Chine*   37
Mario Cams

Cartography during the Times of the Kangxi Emperor:
The Age and the Background   51
Han Qi

Reproduction of the Original Title Page and Translation
of the Foreword of the *Nouvelle atlas de la Chine*   63

List and Order of the Maps   71

Facsimile of the Maps   73

List of Contributors   163

Index   165

Matteo Ricci and Xu Guangqi (see below Figure 1)

FRIENDSHIP AND SCIENCE

Everything begins with Matteo Ricci. When the Jesuit missionary entered the city of Beijing in 1601, a new style of dialogue and cultural exchange for Christianity gained momentum. This model, called "il modo soave" by Alessandro Valignano, Visitator of the Society of Jesus to the Far East and creator of the new strategy first implemented in Japan and then in China, insisted on knowledge of the local language and culture as the basis for further religious activities. Ricci will be the champion of this new paradigm. Dr. R. Po-chia Hsia, author of the text that opens our volume, summarizes the story of the Jesuit mission from the time of Matteo Ricci through the reign of Emperor Kangxi.

With Ricci, a bond of friendship and mutual appreciation was formed between members of the Society of Jesus and their Chinese counterparts. Friendship became the vehicle of exchange for many cultural resources between these men from the West and their Chinese hosts. Scientific knowledge then became a central piece of the history of the Jesuit mission in China, beginning with the translation of the "Elements" of Euclid into Chinese by the convert Paul Xu Guangqi, and Matteo Ricci, followed by the astronomical work of Adam Schall von Bell and Ferdinand Verbiest, and the cartographic achievements of the Italian Jesuit missionary Martino Martini, who in 1655 was the first person to publish a Chinese Atlas in Europe.

While Martini's maps will be a milestone for the geographical knowledge of China, the maps were essentially a European version of Chinese maps brought to the continent by Martini after the fall of the Ming dynasty in 1644. Only half a century later, after a request by Emperor Kangxi, a group of European Jesuit geographers were assembled to conduct a new topographical survey. This time the French Jesuits will be engaged, and they will for the first time use the scientific knowledge from the West to complete the task. Dr. Han Qi's (a member of the Chinese Academy of Sciences) contribution to this volume explains the intricacies and conundrums of the communication between the two very different cultures in fields as objective as cartography and topography. The translation of the traditional Chinese measurements, for instance, will remain for decades a point of controversy.

The atlas based on the survey of the French Jesuits was first published in Chinese, but it remained restricted to Imperial use. Only in 1735 did Jean-Baptiste du Halde, the Jesuit editor of the "*Lettres édifiantes et curieuses,*" finally publish the findings of the missionaries in China in the "*Description géographique,*" a monumental collection of four folio volumes. The researcher Mario Cams, Katholieke Universiteit Leuven (KU Leuven), guides us through the travels of the maps from China to France and, finally, to the Low Countries, where the volumes were printed, pirated and re-printed, before being again reprinted in Paris by Grosier in 1785.

We hesitated about keeping d'Anville's name as the author of this atlas. Since the maps we reproduce here are the fruit of an unauthorized print, we could have made the choice of respecting the distance between the original author of these pieces, M. d'Anville, and a printing that happened without his supervision. However, our choice was to honor the creator beyond the damage that may have been done to him with such an unauthorized publication. Indeed, the paradox here is that, because it was a much simpler print, this map was of lesser quality; yet, being cheaper, it contributed to the spread of the knowledge it contained and, most likely, to the fame of its author. Be that as it may, for our purpose here it is necessary to signal the importance of the work of this talented cartographer who, in cooperation with Jesuits in China and Europe, produced the most important China map of the eighteenth and nineteenth centuries.

In today's Beijing, the founder of The Beijing Center for Chinese Studies, Dr. Ronald J. Anton S.J., soon perceived the importance of the books attesting to the value of friendship as a model for us today. Dr. Anton began developing a small but outstanding collection of *Jesuitica Sinica,* a collection of Jesuit texts that includes the *Nouvel atlas de la Chine* here reprinted. It was under his leadership that this project began, mentored by the late Jesuit scholar Dr. John Witek, S.J. (of Georgetown University), who unfortunately was not able to see the project to completion.

As I was asked to succeed Dr. Anton at The Beijing Center for Chinese Studies in 2009, I was also given the assignment to complete this publication. Many circumstances interfered to delay it a number of times, not the least being John Witek's death in 2011.

Besides the authors of the contributions in this volume, with a particular thanks to Dr. Mario Cams for his help regarding some delicate decisions, many other scholars have contributed to its completion. On behalf of The Beijing Center, I wish to manifest my most sincere gratitude to Dr. Jean-Paul Wiest, Dr. Nicolas Standaert, S.J. (KU Leuven), Dr. Gianni Criveler (Holy Spirit Study Centre, Hong Kong), Dr. Eugenio Menegon (Boston University), Dr. Jeremy Clark, S.J. (Boston College), Dr. George Coyne, S.J. (former Director of the Vatican Observatory), and Dr. Thierry Meynard, S.J., who recently succeeded me at The Beijing Center for Chinese Studies, just to mention those most directly involved in the actual preparation of this volume. Moreover, I am deeply grateful to Mr. Chengyong Ge, Editor-in-Chief of the Cultural Relics Press, State Administrator of Cultural Heritage, Beijing, for seeing to the excellent photographing of the maps for use in *Jesuit Mapmaking in China* and to Mr. Hua Zheng, who carried out the actual photographing.

This project, though, is only possible thanks to the generous and patient support of Saint Joseph's University Press. The professionalism and wisdom of the editors at the Press confirm the reputation of this excellent house. My gratitude goes out in particular to Mr. Carmen Robert Croce, Director of Saint Joseph's University Press, and most especially to Dr. John W. O'Malley, S.J., general editor of this series, Early Modern Catholicism and the Visual Arts. Dr. O'Malley was of crucial assistance to me in ways great and small throughout the whole process of publication.

As I take the final steps for this publication, I am aware of how much could yet be done to make it better. Just as d'Anville was not completely satisfied with his final print, I wish the constraints of circumstances beyond our power had enabled us to achieve an even better result. Nevertheless, this publication has the merit of giving to the public the opportunity to participate in this piece of history still in play today. As in times past, scientific exchange remains an expression of friendship and mutual appreciation.

Roberto M. Ribeiro

São Paulo, 30 December 2013.

ILLUSTRATIONS

FIGURE 1.   Matteo Ricci and Xu Guangqi, frontispiece of *China Illustrata* by Athanasius Kircher.

(Courtesy Jesuitana Collection, Burns Library, Boston College)

ex iis , quæ humanâ potentiâ extructa sunt , jure suo maximum ; Ità autem res habet.

Murus Sinensis.

Murus Chinensis.

De quo ita Atlas Sinicus. *Hujus,* inquit , *muri celebris quidem , sed adhuc obscura , uti video, apud eos fama est ; is non unam sed quatuor omninò provincias , seu potiùs Regna ambitu suo cingit , quamquam mihi qui-*

Longitudo.

dem hactenus de eximia ejus existimata longitudine semper aliquid demendum visum est : nec enim, quod trecentas leucas Germanicas superet invenio, ex quibus 15. uni Gradui pares ; tota enim illius longitudo à Sinici ma-

ris , in quem Yalo *fluvius ex* Tartaria *Orientali influit, ad usque* Kin *civitatis montes , propè ripas* Crocei *fluminis , non excedit gradus viginti, licet illud , quod deesse ob parallelorum coarctationem videtur , abundè suâ inflexione & curvitate compenset. Nusquam interrupta ejus continua series , præterquam ad Boreales partes Urbis* Siuen *provinciæ* Pequing *, ubi exiguum spatium tenent horridi & inaccessi montes, qui firmissimum murum nectunt , & ubi* Croceum *fluvium ad se fauces admittit: reliqua flumina minora ; ab exteris subingredientia regionibus arcubus hinc inde fornicibusque super extructis adinstar pontis admittit , cætera totus sibi constans ac ferè uniformis non per planitiem*

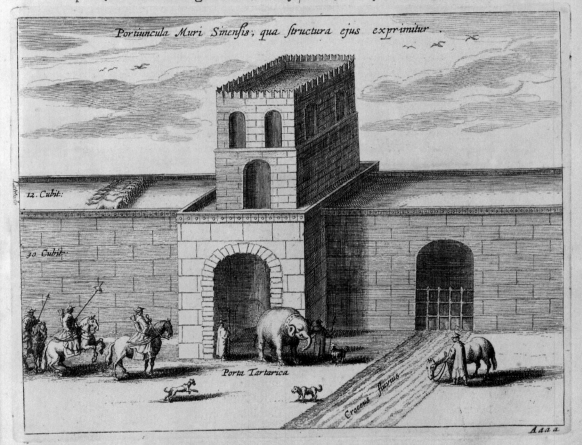

Portiuncula Muri Sinensis ; qua structura ejus exprimitur .

12. *Cubit:*

30 *Cubit:*

Porta Tartarica

Croceus fluvius

Aaaa

modo , quæ in hisce partibus rarior est , nec per montium crepidines tantum , sed &

qua ipsos montes transcendit ; certis intervallis altiores habet turres , portas etiam

E e

quasdam

FIGURE 2.   Section of the Great Wall, as illustrated in Athanasius Kircher, S.J., *China Illustrata*, 1667.

CONFUCIUS
SINARUM
PHILOSOPHUS,
SIVE
SCIENTIA SINENSIS
LATINE EXPOSITA.

Studio & Opera { *PROSPERI INTORCETTA,* *CHRISTIANI HERDTRICH,* *FRANCISCI ROUGEMONT,* *PHILIPPI COUPLET,* } *Patrum Societatis* JESU.

JUSSU

LUDOVICI MAGNI

Eximio Missionum Orientalium & Litterariæ Reipublicæ bono

E BIBLIOTHECA REGIA IN LUCEM PRODIT.

ADJECTA EST TABULA CHRONOLOGICA SINICÆ MONARCHIÆ AB HUJUS EXORDIO AD HÆC USQUE TEMPORA.

PARISIIS,
Apud DANIELEM HORTHEMELS, viâ Jacobæâ, sub Mæcenate.

M. DC. LXXXVII.
CUM PRIVILEGIO REGIS.

FIGURE 3. Title page of the *Confucius Sinarum Philosophus*, 1687, by Prospero Intorcetta, Christian Herdtrich, Philippus Couplet, and Franciscus de Rougemont, all Jesuits.

(Courtesy Jesuitica Sinica Collection, The Beijing Center for Chinese Studies)

FIGURE 4.   Portrait of Confucius, in the *Confucius Sinarum Philosophus* Prospero Intorcetta, Christian Herdtrich, Philippus Couplet, and Franciscus de Rougemont.

(Courtesy Jesuitica Sinica Collection, The Beijing Center for Chinese Studies)

CONFUCIUS
The celebrated Chinese Philosopher.

FIGURE 5.   Confucius the great philosopher, from the frontispiece of an English translation of Louis Le Comte, S.J., *Memoirs and Observations about China*, 1697.
(Courtesy Jesuitana Collection, Burns Library, Boston College)

FIGURE 6. Ancient observatory, Beijing, showing astronomical instruments designed by Ferdinand Verbiest, S.J.
(Photo by Jeremy Clarke, S.J., used with permission)

FIGURE 7.　Catholic cemetery, Hangzhou, where Martino Martini, S.J., Zhong Mingren, S.J. and other 17th-century Jesuits were buried.
(Photo by Jeremy Clarke, S.J., used with permission)

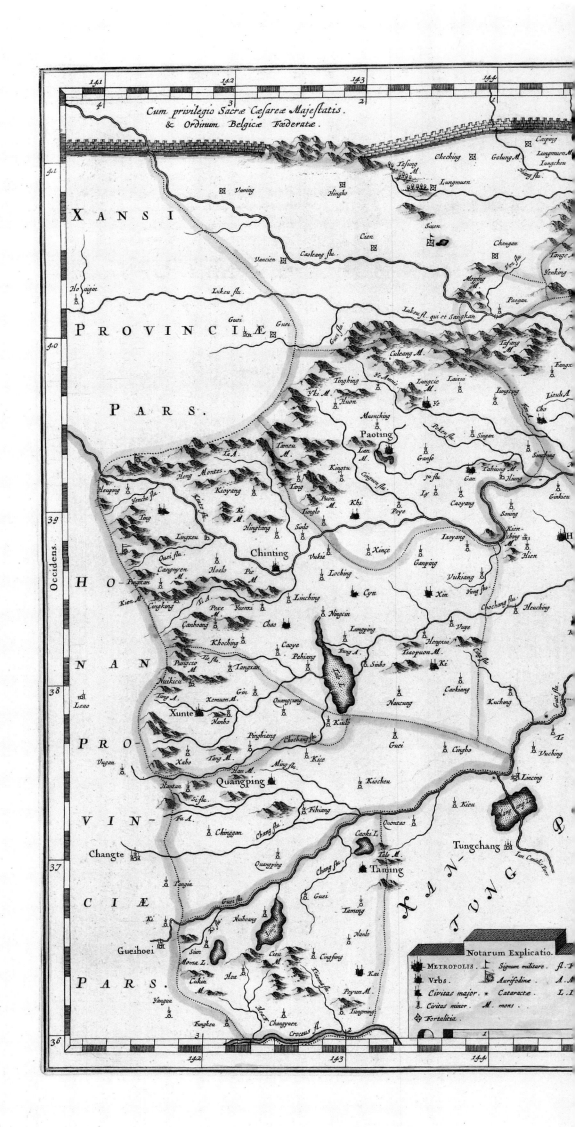

FIGURE 10.

Map of the province of Henan
from the *Novus Atlas Sinensis* by
Martino Martini.

(Courtesy Jesuitica Sinica Collection,
The Beijing Center for Chinese
Studies)

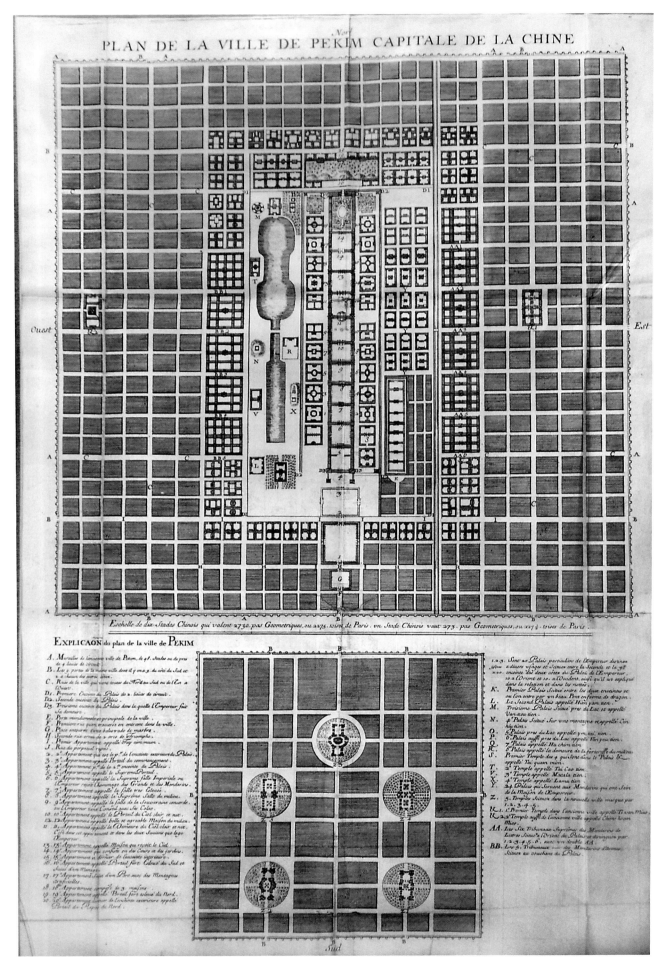

FIGURE 11. *Plan de la ville de Pekim Capitale de la China* (Map of the City of Beijing, Capital of China), folding map [scale 1:13000 ap., dimensions 44x66 cm], from Gabriel de Magalhães, S.J., *Nouvelle relation de la Chine* (Paris: chez Claude Barbin, 1688). [Lust 57; Cordier, Sinica, 36].

(Courtesy Jesuitica Sinica Collection, The Beijing Center for Chinese Studies) "The Portuguese original existed only in manuscript and was brought back by Father Couplet to Rome and presented to Cardinal César d'Estrées, to whom this edition is dedicated. The Cardinal was supposed to have been particularly interested in Beijing, which may explain the presence of the plan of that city." (http://www.bloomsburyauctions.com/detail/35857/240.0, access on December 19, 2012).

DESCRIPTION
GEOGRAPHIQUE
HISTORIQUE, CHRONOLOGIQUE,
POLITIQUE, ET PHYSIQUE
DE L'EMPIRE DE LA CHINE
ET
DE LA TARTARIE CHINOISE,

ENRICHIE DES CARTES GENERALES ET PARTICULIERES de ces Pays, de la Carte générale & des Cartes particulieres du Thibet, & de la Corée, & ornée d'un grand nombre de Figures & de Vignettes gravées en Taille-douce.

Par le P. J. B. DU HALDE, *de la Compagnie de* JESUS.

TOME QUATRIE'ME.

A. Humblot del.   Baquoy Sculp.

A PARIS,

Chez P. G. LE MERCIER, Imprimeur-Libraire, rue Saint Jacques, au Livre d'Or.

M. DCC. XXXV.

AVEC APPROBATION ET PRIVILEGE DU ROY.

FIGURE 12. Title page of Jean-Baptiste du Halde, S.J., *Description géographique, historique, chronologique, politique et physique de l'Empire de la Chine*, Vol. 4 (Paris, 1735).

(Courtesy Jesuitica Sinica Collection, The Beijing Center for Chinese Studies)

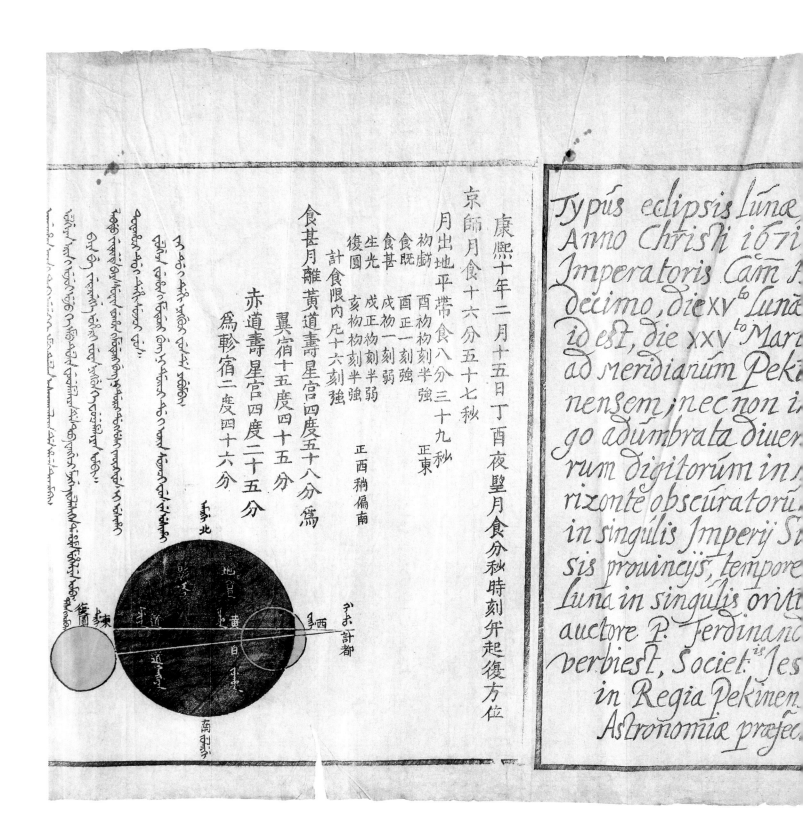

FIGURE 13. Ferdinand Verbiest, S.J. (1623–88), *Typus eclipsis lunae* (Beijing, 1971).

Source: Universiteitsbibliotheek Leuven - http://aleph08.libis.kuleuven.be:1801/view/action/nmets.do?DOCCHOICE=1113015.xml&dvs=1355945577162~567&locale=en_US&search_terms=&usePid1=true&usePid2=true (Accessed on December 19, 2012).

康熙十年二月十五日丁酉夜望月食圖

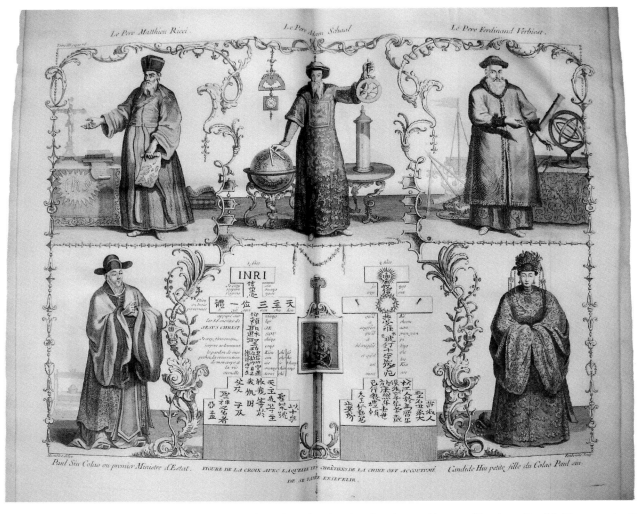

FIGURE 14. *Jesuit Missionaries* (Matteo Ricci, Adam Schall, Ferdinand Verbiest) and Paul Xu and his granddaughter, Candide Xu, engraving from Jean-Baptiste du Halde, *Description géographique, historique, chronologique, politique et physique de l'Empire de la Chine,* Vol. 3 (Paris, 1735).

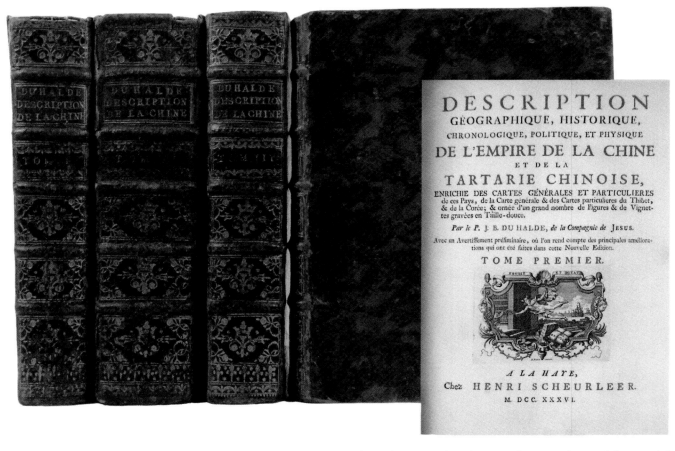

FIGURE 15. Jean-Baptiste du Halde, S.J. (1674–1743), *Description géographique, historique, chronologique, politique, et physique de l'Empire de la Tartarie Chinoise,* The Hague: Henri Scheurleer, 1736.
(Courtesy of Arader Galleries)

DESCRIPTION
GÉOGRAPHIQUE, HISTORIQUE,
CHRONOLOGIQUE, POLITIQUE, ET PHYSIQUE
DE L'EMPIRE DE LA CHINE
ET DE LA
TARTARIE CHINOISE,

ENRICHIE DES CARTES GÉNÉRALES ET PARTICULIERES
de ces Pays, de la Carte générale & des Cartes particulieres du Thibet,
& de la Corée; & ornée d'un grand nombre de Figures & de Vignettes gravées en Taille-douce.

Par le P. J. B. DU HALDE, *de la Compagnie de* JÉSUS.

Avec un Avertiſſement préliminaire, où l'on rend compte des principales améliora-
tions qui ont été faites dans cette Nouvelle Edition.

TOME PREMIER

A LA HAYE,
Chez HENRI SCHEURLEER.
M. DCC. XXXVI.

FIGURE 16.

Title page of the *Description géographique, historique, chronologique, politique, et physique de l'Empire de la Tartarie Chinoise*, by Jean-Baptiste du Halde, S.J. (1674–1743), The Hague: Henri Scheurleer, 1736.

IMPERIAL CHINA AND THE JESUIT MISSION

R. Po-chia Hsia

Laying the foundations

Without interruption, Beijing, the imperial capital of the Ming (1368–1644) and the Qing (1644–1911) dynasties, welcomed the presence of the Society of Jesus between 1601 and 1773. The first date refers to the securing of a permanent residence by the Italian missionary Matteo Ricci (1552–1610) and the second to the dissolution of the Old Society of Jesus by papal order.

The Italian Ricci left Europe in the midst of an intensifying conflict between Protestants and Catholics. And even though the new religious order, the Society of Jesus, contributed significantly to stemming the Protestant tide and the restoration of Catholic fortunes, its aim, according to the intentions of the original founder, St. Ignatius of Loyola (1491–1556), was evangelization and the salvation of souls. A generation of Jesuit missionaries had already followed the footsteps of St. Francis Xavier (1506–52), one of the original companions of St. Ignatius, and betook themselves to Asia in the ships of Portuguese merchants to harvest souls in lands that had not heard of the Christian gospels. Ricci was one of those who heard the calling. In 1583, he joined Michele Ruggieri (1543–1607) in the first Jesuit foothold in inland China, venturing forth from the Portuguese enclave of Macao. In 1601, after a long period of struggle and frustration, Ricci crowned his gradual ascent in the ladder of social success in Ming China by reaching the imperial capital of Beijing, where he was received as a foreign envoy bearing gifts for the emperor Wanli. Ricci received an imperial stipend and upon his death in 1610 was honored by an imperial grant of land for his burial. In spite of Ricci's success, the Jesuits had not yet gained a foothold in the imperial court. That would come in the next generation.

Under the patronage of the high mandarin (Paul) Xu Guangqi (1562–1633), a convert and close friend of Ricci, the first Jesuits were summoned to the court of emperor Chongzhen in 1629 and served in the newly created Calendar Office for the emendation of the Imperial Calendar. Three Jesuits—Johann Schreck (1576–1630), Giacomo Rho (1592–1638), and Johann Adam Schall von Bell (1592–1666)—collaborated with Chinese mandarins, many of whom became converts, in presenting their astronomical work to the emperor. This was known as the *Chongzhen Calendar Compendium*, which synthesizes Chinese and European methods of date calculations. Thanks to this effort, the Jesuits succeeded in maintaining their position when the capital city fell in 1644, first to a peasant rebel army, and then to the conquering Manchu, a people from the Northeast beyond the Great Wall. The German Schall, the only surviving member of the Jesuit mathematicians, was confirmed in his appointment at the new Directorate of Astronomy, placed under the Ministry of Rites, one of the six ministries of the central imperial administration.

Science and conversion in China

From the beginning of their mission, the Jesuits were well known in China as men of learning, especially as scientists. They owed their prestige, advancement, and patronage to their scientific expertise. Expanding from their first engagement in astronomy, later generations of Jesuits also worked as civil and military engineers, musicians, painters, engravers, physicians, clockmakers, geographers, and cartographers; the achievements of the last groups are amply demonstrated by this volume. Regularly called upon for imperial service, the Jesuits themselves often lamented the distraction from their evangelization. Nevertheless, the consensus within the Jesuit China Mission was that the security of Christianity itself depended on the favors of emperors, and that science represented a perfectly legitimate handmaiden for the true religion.

Nowhere is this better illustrated than in the book, *European Astronomy* (1687), written by the Belgian Jesuit Ferdinand Verbiest (1623–88), the successor to Schall as Director of the Directorate of Astronomy. In this book, Verbiest did not narrate so much the introduction of western astronomy to China, but rather the political triumph of the Jesuits over their enemies, thanks to the superiority of European science. As Director of the Directorate of Astronomy between 1644 and 1666, Schall was the first Jesuit in China to achieve a mandarin office, and a very high one. The elderly German became a confidant and friend of the first Manchu emperor, Shunzhi, who had lost his father as a young man, and who looked upon the westerner, with his formidable white beard, as a kindly and authoritative figure. In 1660 Schall called the young Verbiest to assist him in Beijing, thus launching the career of another Jesuit-astronomer, whose brilliance eventually rivaled his own.

At the height of his influence, Schall fell from power when Shunzhi died in 1661. The close and personal relationship between emperor and Jesuit, and Schall's high mandarin appointment, stirred up enormous ill will and jealousy. In the ensuing political struggles during the minority reign of the emperor Kangxi, the son of Shunzhi, Schall came under attack, for alleged inaccurate prognostications and the introduction of heterodox western/Christian teachings. The old astronomer, Verbiest, and other Jesuits in Beijing were arrested; all western missionaries were rounded up and taken to Guangdong province in the south in preparation for eventual expulsion; and it seemed Christianity was doomed. The two leading opponents of the Jesuit astronomers were the Confucian scholar and mandarin Yang Guangxian, who resented the alien influence of the westerners, and Wu Mingxuan, a Chinese Muslim astronomer, who first raised the charge of false astronomical readings against Schall. By being involved in a tangled web of factional and political interests, the so-called Calendar Case had significance beyond rival astronomical and intellectual systems. Its resolution to the advantage of the Jesuits, however, would hinge on the superior astronomical knowledge of Schall's successor, the Belgian Verbiest.

In 1664, the young emperor took charge. Kangxi ordered the rival astronomers to make predictions of the sun's position. By observation of the sun using the gnomon and by meticulous calculations, Verbiest awed the court by three successful demonstrations. His opponents, failing to match his skills, were imprisoned. The Imperial Calendar was entrusted to Verbiest, and, over strong opposition, he succeeded in amending the Chinese Lunar Calendar by the deletion of an intercalary month. Appointed as Director of the Directorate of Astronomy with charge over 160 officials, Verbiest was elevated in rank and showered with imperial honors, the only other Jesuit to have achieved the same high mandarin status as his mentor Schall. In the years of service after the restitution of Christianity, Verbiest worked tirelessly both to serve his master, the Kangxi emperor, and to promote Christianity. The key, for Verbiest, was western science: astronomy had saved the faith, and in her wake, the other muses—mathematics, geometry, hydraulics, music, meteorology, ballistics—labored to entice the Chinese emperor to lend his ears to the true faith. All this work was put to paper around 1678, in Latin, compiled and edited from Verbiest's extensive scientific publications in Chinese, and eventually published in 1687 in Europe.

The Jesuit mission: a cross-sectional view

Under Kangxi's reign, the Jesuit China Mission reached its apogee in the years between 1665 and 1705. The first date saw the triumph of the Jesuits over their accusers at court in the Calendar Case; the second refers to the formal prohibition of Christian evangelization by Kangxi as a result of the Chinese Rites Controversy, on which more will be said. The number of Jesuits in China reflects the fortunes of the Jesuit China Mission. In 1590, when Ricci was still struggling to get recognized in Guangdong province, there were only four Jesuits in China. That number rose to twenty-three, on the eve of the Society's breakthrough at the imperial court, and fluctuated little until the 1664–65 Calendar Case. Old age and death reduced the Jesuit number to twenty-one by 1679, despite the reversal of adverse political fortunes. The publication of Verbiest's *European Astronomy* helped to initiate a major recruitment campaign among the Jesuit colleges in Europe. Its success is reflected in the steady flow of new Jesuit missionaries to China, raising the strength to thirty-three in 1690, forty-five in 1696, sixty-seven in 1700, reaching the high tide of eighty-two Jesuits in 1701, prior to the gradual ebbing following the Chinese Rites Controversy between Rome and Beijing. For the period up to 1720, the Society of Jesus furnished more than two-thirds of all European missionaries sent to China. Between 1583 and 1723, a total of 563 Jesuits left Europe for China: a few perished en route, some eventually worked in India, Southeast Asia, or Japan, leaving a final and minimum figure of 288 European Jesuits active in the China Mission in this period.[1]

From their exclusive role in the China field in the beginning, the Society had to share their harvest of souls after the 1630s with other religious orders: the mendicant orders began arriving in the 1630s; the Paris Foreign Missions and priests from the Congregation for the Propagation of Faith joined the effort after the 1670s. Nonetheless, the Society of Jesus constituted the single most important religious order in the China mission, constituting approximately 50% of all Catholic clergy between 1582 and 1800.

The Jesuits differed from the other religious orders in one major aspect: theirs was the only truly international order. Based in the Spanish Philippines, the mendicant orders had an overwhelming Spanish presence, while the Paris Foreign Missions (MEP), as the name suggests, was exclusively French, and the Propaganda Fidei priests were mostly Italian by origins. In contrast, Jesuit missionaries in China were recruited from all Catholic countries in Europe: they came from Portugal, Spain, France, Italy, Spanish Netherlands (today Belgium), Catholic Germany (with heavy representations from the Rhineland and Bavaria), Austria, Bohemia, and Poland. The three largest nations were the Portuguese, French, and Italians, although the small numbers of Germans and Belgians belied the significant role these fathers would play in the scientific and cultural accomplishments of the Jesuit Mission.

The previous paragraphs have made clear the importance of Jesuit courtiers in Beijing: through imperial service, these Jesuit scientists provided protection for the other Jesuit residences in the vast Chinese empire. Prior to 1705, the Jesuit China Mission was to some extent distinguished between capital and province, science and evangelization. Superiors of the Mission were careful to call for trained scientists to be selected from the Jesuit missionary candidates, in order to ensure a steady pool of talent for imperial service. Life in the Jesuit residences in the provinces, however, would focus more on the routine tasks of evangelization and ministry, which often assumed heroic dimensions, given the enormous ratio between clergy and neophytes. The administration of sacraments often entailed almost incessant travel as a result of the ecclesiastical geography of the Chinese Church. Except for the larger urban centers such as Shanghai, Beijing, and Hangzhou, Christian communities tended to be widely dispersed, the more so in rural areas and in the mountainous interior provinces. Based on the ratio of clergy to the laity, the workload of the individual Catholic missionary was between ten and forty times of that of his counterpart in the urbanized regions of seventeenth-century Catholic Europe.

Jesuit writings in China

The Jesuit Mission produced an enormously impressive corpus of works, a direct result of the intensive language training of the Society. By 1700 Jesuit authors and translators had produced more than 200 scientific, liturgical, catechistic, theological, spiritual, humanistic, and geographical works in classical and colloquial Chinese. In addition, as a direct result of their studies of the *Four Books*, and the accumulative effort of several generations of Jesuit scholars, the Confucian canon was introduced to Europe by the *Sapientia Sinica* (1662), compiled and translated by Inácio da Costa (1603–66) and Prospero Intorcetta (1625–96), and the *Confucius Sinarum Philosophus* (1687), compiled mainly by Philippe Couplet (1622–93), based on the work of previous Jesuits.

The list of Jesuit Chinese titles dwarfs the other religious orders: in 1707 the Jesuit printing press in Beijing had published 212 Chinese books composed or translated by the fathers (123 titles in religious subjects, and 89 in secular subjects); Jesuit presses in the residence of Fuzhou had published 51 titles, in Hangzhou another 40.[2]

Translations on religion, for example, included prayers, liturgical texts (missal, breviary), works of theology, hagiographies, catechisms, rules of confraternities, and devotional texts. Scientific translations covered astronomy, geometry, arithmetic, hydraulics, weaponry, anatomy, optics, falconry, and musicology. Finally, there are a handful of texts that introduced fragments of Greco-Roman texts to Chinese readers of the seventeenth- century.

Religious texts included translations from the Roman liturgy for the use of the Chinese Church (special Chinese language liturgy was authorized in 1615 by the papacy but later rescinded in the late seventeenth century). Works translated included the *Missale Romanum* (1670), *Breviarium Romanum* (1674), and the *Manuale ad sacramenta ministranda juxta ritum S. Romae Ecclesiae* (1675), all translated by Ludovico Buglio (1606–82). Prayer translations and accompanying commentaries included the Lord's Prayer, the Rosary, and the Credo. A compilation of Christian prayers, the *Tianzhu shengjiao nianjing zongdu*, published by the Jesuits in 1628, contained the usual daily prayers in addition to many texts by the sixteenth-century Spanish spiritual author Luís de Granada.[3] The most important theological work to be translated were parts of Thomas Aquinas' *Summa Theologica*. In addition to works introducing the lives of the Virgin Mary and St. Joseph (the patron saint of China), Jesuits also published saints' lives and separate hagiographies on St. Josephat, St. John Nepomok, St. Francis Borgia, St. Francis Xavier, St. Stanislas Kostka, and St. Aloysius Gonzaga. These texts were based on European originals, although the precise texts still need to be established. Devotional texts included Thomas à Kempis' *Imitatio Christi*, translated by the Portuguese Jesuit Emmanuel Diaz in 1640 and aphorisms by St. Teresa of Avila and St. Bernard.

In the translations of scientific texts, the most important works were in the fields of astronomy and mathematics, all completed before 1640, during the early decades of the Jesuit Mission. The first six books of Euclid's *Geometry* was the earliest text to be translated, the product of the close collaboration between Ricci and Xu Guangqi; it was well received by Chinese mathematicians into the eighteenth century.

Under the Qing emperor Kangxi (reigns 1662–1722), several Jesuits served as imperial tutors. Although several European mathematical texts were translated for the instruction of the emperor, they were never published. The second period of the Jesuit Mission saw few scientific translations. One exception was in the theory of painting: the Jesuit painter Giuseppe Castiglione (1688–1766) collaborated with Nian Xiyao to translate the *Perspectiva pictorum* (1706) by the Jesuit artist Andrea Pozzo; the Chinese work, *Shixue*, appeared in 1729 and contributed to the reception of perspectival painting in eighteenth-century China.

Only a very small fragment of the Greco-Roman textual corpus was translated into Chinese. These texts, based on the humanistic curriculum of the *Ratio Studiorum*, familiar to all Jesuit missionaries, could further be divided into the genres of rhetoric and philosophy. Ricci's highly successful *Jiaoyou lun* (1595) or *De Amicitia* was based on Andreas Eborensis' *Sententiae et Exempla*, an aphoristic collection from the writings of Cicero, Seneca, and other classical authors.[4] Another of Ricci's text, the *Ershiwu yan* (1605), or *The Twenty-Five Sayings*, represented a translation of a Latin version of the *Enchiridion* of Epictetus.[5]

The Kangxi emperor and the Jesuits

The apogee of Jesuit success represented the symbiosis between emperor and missionary. Born in 1654, the Kangxi emperor (reign 1661–1722) was the ruler who enjoyed the longest rule in Chinese history. Emerging from the shadow of his minority and the tutelage of a regency council after 1665, the youthful emperor took a liking to the westerners in his service. Possessing a highly intelligent and inquisitive mind, the young emperor was attracted to the knowledge and persons of the leading Jesuit courtiers. Their knowledge of the theoretical and practical sciences was unmatched by Manchu or Chinese scholars; the ways of the West offered fresh subjects for the inquisitive ruler, who was already well versed in the languages and cultures of his Manchu and Chinese subjects. From the 1670s onwards, a small group of Jesuit courtiers would tutor Kangxi: Verbiest and the Italian Philip Grimaldi (1638–1712) in mathematics and astronomy, and the Portuguese Thomas Pereira in music. Set in Kangxi's private study, these tutorials nurtured a sense of trust and intimacy; and the emperor began to look upon his Jesuit servants as informal councilors unfettered by the rules of bureaucratic politics. Three developments in particular deepened Kangxi's confidence in his Jesuit servants and would contribute to the imperial patronage that nurtured the golden age of Christianity between 1690 and 1705. The first was the help rendered by Verbiest in quelling the major rebellion that challenged Kangxi's rule; the second referred to the Jesuits' role in the diplomacy between the Qing empire and western powers; and the third represented the medical cures provided by French Jesuits that saved Kangxi's life.

In 1673, three princes rose in rebellion against the Kangxi emperor. As Han Chinese commanders who had defected to the Manchu invaders in the 1630s, the three led the Qing conquest of China and were subsequently rewarded by grants of large feudatory holdings in south and south-western China. Fearing a reduction of their autonomy as the Qing state began to consolidate power, they revolted. This was the most serious crisis faced by the young emperor. Kangxi asked Verbiest for help. The Belgian Jesuit supervised the casting of hundreds of new cannons, weapons crucial in the pacification of the rebellion of the Three Feudatories. From his native Spanish Netherlands, a land afflicted by warfare between 1568 and 1715, Verbiest might well have learned the rudiments of military engineering in the most densely urbanized region of Europe, with its highly developed technological and artisanal culture.

A second contribution of Jesuits to Qing statecraft was in diplomacy. Kangxi used the fathers as interpreters during the Portuguese and Dutch legations to Beijing. And as Russian expansion reached the Amur River in the 1680s, threatening the northern boundary of the ancestral lands of the Manchu, the emperor again employed the Jesuits to pacify the Russians. Backed by a strong show of force, the Qing empire persuaded the Russians to a peaceful border settlement. In 1689, two Jesuits, the Portuguese Thomas Pereira and the French Jean-François Gerbillon (1654–1707) traveled with the Qing army to the fort Nerchinsk, which the Russians had built on the Amur River. Negotiating in Latin, the Jesuits helped in the successful conclusion of the Treaty of Nerchinsk, which stabilized Sino-Russian relations until 1860.

The third success scored by the Jesuits outshone even their contributions to Qing statecraft: their medical expertise saved the life of Kangxi. In November 1692 Kangxi came down with fever. The emperor had survived an attack of smallpox as a child, a disease that had killed his father, the Sunzhi emperor. There was fear the symptoms reflected a fatal attack. Keeping his illness a secret, Kangxi summoned the French Jesuits Gerbillon and Joachim Bouvet (1656–1730), and recalled the medically trained Jean de Fontaney (1643–1710) from Nanjing. Using quinine, the French Jesuits cured Kangxi's intermittent fever. Three Chinese physicians were punished with exile for prescribing nothing; the two French Jesuits were rewarded with a house in the Imperial city, and their estimation rose even higher in the eyes of the emperor.[6]

From toleration to prohibition

In 1691, news of a local persecution of Christians in Hangzhou reached the Jesuits in Beijing. Pereira and Gerbillon petitioned Songgotu, the high-ranking Manchu nobleman who led the Nerchinsk negotiations and who had befriended the two Jesuits during the long voyage. Mindful of their service during the recent diplomacy with the Russians, Kangxi overruled the objection of his Chinese mandarins and proclaimed in 1692 an edict of toleration. In this brief text, the emperor explicitly stated the loyal service rendered to his father by the late Adam Schall, and to him by the late Verbiest and by the present Jesuits at court. And since Christianity was not an evil teaching that incited rebellion, it would seem unreasonable to forbid its open exercise when subjects of the emperor could freely worship in Buddhist, Daoist, and Lamaist temples.

Hailed as "the greatest triumph of Christianity in our century" by Charles le Gobien, Superior of the Parisian Province of the Jesuits, the 1692 Edict represented in fact only a privilege conceded by the emperor to his western servants for their loyal service. Exaggerated in Jesuit propaganda, this act of imperial benevolence seemed to prefigure, to the wish-thinking of many Jesuit missionaries, the imminent conversion of Kangxi. Such was the background to the publication of a celebratory biography of Kangxi in 1696 as a sagacious ruler, a philosopher-king, by Louis Le Comte (1655–1728), a French Jesuit who had returned to France from China.

Fantasy of a Chinese Constantine notwithstanding, the Edict of 1692 inaugurated the golden years of the Catholic mission in China for more than a dozen years. Imperial favors multiplied, the number of converts grew, and more Jesuits entered the Qing empire. All these positive developments occurred while the newly arrived French Jesuits were embroiled in a bitter dispute with their Portuguese *confreres* over the establishment of an independent French Jesuit Mission, subject only to their superior in France and to Louis XIV, and not to the Jesuit Vice-Province of China that stood under Portuguese protection. After many vexations, recriminations, and petitions, and under intense political pressure, Tirso González de Santalla, General of the Society in Rome, resolved the matter in favor of the French Jesuits. This came not a moment too soon, for all Jesuits in China—Portuguese, French, Italian, German, or Belgian—faced a fierce assault from their rivals in the other missionary orders.

Without exaggeration, we can say that the Chinese Rites Controversy overturned the achievements of the Jesuit Mission and caused the decline of Christianity in China. It originated in the early 1640s, when the first mendicant friars—Spanish missionaries from the Philippines—were perplexed to witness the participation of Chinese converts at rites honoring ancestors. Questioning the Jesuit interpretation of these rites as civic and pious acts, devoid of religious content, a view shared by the overwhelming majority of Chinese converts, the friars undertook their own theological and ethnographic investigations into Chinese rites honoring ancestors and Confucius. This anxiety over rituals became a hot ecclesiastical-political issue when the Dominican Juan Bautista de Morales presented

"Seventeen Questions" in 1643 to the papacy attacking the Jesuit compromise with Chinese ritual practices. The result was the first papal decree of 1645 that prohibited the practices described by Morales. In response, the Jesuit China Mission sent Martino Martini (1614–61) to Rome to remonstrate that the friars have misrepresented their position. A second papal decree ensued in 1656 to sanction the ritual practices as set forth by Martini.

With the contest between the fathers and the friars resulting in a draw, the arrival of French clerics of the MEP tipped the balance against the Society. Espousing a strongly Gallican and anti-Jesuit position, Charles Maigrot, Doctor of the Sorbonne and Vicar Apostolic of Fujian, lent his authority against the ritual practices of the Jesuit–led congregations. From his arrival in Fujian in 1684 to the interdiction of the Chinese rites in 1693, Maigrot provoked enormous ill will and resistance, both from the Chinese Christian communities and from the Jesuits. He played a pivotal role that led to the dispatch and disastrous outcome of the papal legate Charles-Thomas Maillard de Tournon, whose visit to China (1704–7) coincided with the most heated phase in the Rites Controversy. The 1704 decree, formulated by a commission of cardinals in Rome and promulgated by Tournon in China, forbade a long list of habitual practices in the Chinese Catholic Church: the terms of *tian* and *shangdi* (two terms that occur frequently in the ancient Chinese classics) to denote God; the use of the characters *jing tian* (respect Heaven) bestowed by the emperor Kangxi to decorate churches; the participation of Christians in "sacrificial" rites honoring Confucius and ancestors; the inscription of the characters *shen wei* (seat of the spirit) on the wooden tablets bearing the name of dead ancestors. All these prohibitions, on the threat of excommunication, were reiterated by Pope Clement XIV in 1715, the year that marked the effective end of the Chinese Rites Controversy.

Before the visit of Tournon to China, emperor Kangxi had sought to compromise with the papacy through the dispatch of several Jesuits as imperial legates to Rome. During the papal legate's visit to China, Kangxi became so irritated with the persons of Tournon and Maigrot, the latter in the legate's entourage in Beijing, and with the papal pronouncements on Chinese rites, that he forbade further Christian proselytizing in China, reversing his edict of 1692. Still allowed to practice their religion, decreed Kangxi in 1707, all foreign missionaries must travel to Beijing to be certified: to remain in China, they must promise to abide by the way of Father Ricci and never leave China. The Dominicans, Augustinians, and the missionaries of the MEP left China; the Franciscans were split between obedience to the pope and emperor; and among the Jesuits, the vast majority accepted the conditions imposed by Kangxi and received imperial certification.

While Chinese were legally forbidden to practice Christianity, in reality, the suppression of Christianity depended on the zeal and attitude of local officials. In the provinces, the remaining missionaries and Christians kept a low profile, and most officials did not enforce actively the prohibition. Even in the imperial capital, where the Jesuits lived under imperial protection, Chinese Christians openly attended church service. Toleration aside, the abrogation of the Edict of 1692 would eventually lead to sharpened legislation and active suppression during the reigns of Kangxi's son and grandson—the emperors Yongzhen and Qianlong—during the course of the eighteenth century.

In these momentous times, the close relations between Kangxi and his Jesuit servants continued as before. The year after the imperial certification, 1708, also saw the beginning of the large-scale mapping supervised by Jesuit scientists that is the subject of the present volume. The project, which took almost a decade to complete, was jointly undertaken by Jesuits from the French Mission and from the Portuguese Vice-Province, who persisted in their loyal service to a benevolent emperor, hoping against hope for the promise of imperial conversion and for new glory in the history of Christian missions.

Notes

1. Figures from J. Dehergne, *Répertoire des jésuites de Chine de 1552 à 1800* (Rome/Paris, 1973) as revised by Pascale Girard, *Os Religiosos ocidentais na China na Época Moderna* (Macau, 1999), 71–73. Girard includes only the major nationalities in her revised calculation; a handful of Polish and Swiss Jesuits are not included in her list. The actual number of Jesuits working in China would be slightly higher when they and the Macaist Jesuits are included.

2. Bibliothèque Nationale de France, Manuscrits Chinois 7046.

3. *Handbook of Christianity in China. Volume One: 635–1800*, ed. Nicolas Standaert (Leiden, 2002), 616.

4. For full classical references in Ricci's text, see the critical edition by Filippon Mignini, Matteo Ricci, *Dell'amicizia* (Macerata: Quolibet, 2005).

5. *Handbook of Christianity in China*, 605.

6. Letter of P. de Fontaney to P. de la Chaize, 1703 Feb. 15. *Lettres édifiantes et curieuses écrites de missions etrangères, par quelques missionnaires de la Compagnie de Jesus*. 7. Recueil (Paris: Nicolas Le Clerc, 1707), 176–92, 222–32.

JEAN-BAPTISTE BOURGUIGNON D'ANVILLE AND THE *NOUVEL ATLAS DE LA CHINE*

Mario Cams

At the time of its first publication, the collection of maps presented in this book was the most comprehensive and detailed cartographic depiction of East Asia that Europe had ever seen. Although it was in part the merit of French cartographer Jean-Baptiste Bourguignon d'Anville (1697–1782), essentially it constituted the European incorporation of a Chinese atlas that had been produced with the assistance of European missionaries. Therefore, if we wish to explore the provenance of the *Nouvel atlas de la Chine*, we first need to briefly retrace its roots and understand how this wealth of geographical information reached Europe in the first place. Only then will we be able to fully appreciate the contribution and role of d'Anville in the reception of these maps in both Europe and China.

The Chinese atlas and its transmission to Europe

The atlas of the Qing empire (or dynasty) that served as a basis for the *Nouvel atlas de la Chine*, is known in Chinese as *Huangyu Quanlantu* (皇輿全覽圖, *Complete Map of the Imperial Territory*). The result of the converging interests of the French crown, the Jesuit order and the Kangxi emperor (1654–1722), the first version of this Chinese atlas was finished by 1718 and had taken more than a decade to complete. At the time,

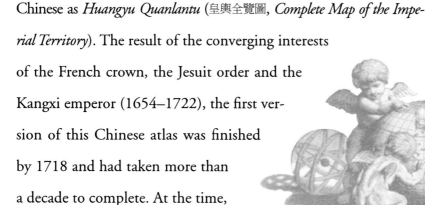

it was without doubt the largest cartographic endeavor based on exact measurements that had ever been undertaken anywhere in the world: similar projects in France and Russia were not completed until decades later. The enormous undertaking was carried out in several phases by different teams of surveyors that often operated simultaneously and consisted of two or three European missionary-mapmakers, up to four officials from different Qing institutions including a military escort, an unknown number of personal servants, and twenty to thirty horses. Working together, they travelled across the country, gathering geographical information from local officials and gazetteers, which they then verified and supplemented by combining celestial observations with methods of triangulation. Only the maps of Tibet, Eastern Turkestan and Korea—also included in the atlas—were drawn entirely on the basis of indigenous sources and surveys conducted without the assistance of European missionaries. The momentous achievement was further made possible by the personal patronage of the emperor as well as by the full cooperation of both central and local officials.[1]

During the first years of the eighteenth century, it had been the French Jesuit missionaries who convinced the emperor of the usefulness of the project and thus, in the final stages, it was the French Jesuit Pierre Jartoux (1669–1720) who led efforts to combine the regional maps and produce a large overview map of the empire, enabling the emperor to take in his vast realm in one single glance. None of the maps included in the atlas were publicly for sale in China before the twentieth century, but at least three different versions were produced for consultation in the palace: a woodblock edition of the atlas was presented to the emperor together with the overview map in 1718 and contained twenty-eight separate and detailed maps of China, Tartary (Manchuria and Mongolia), Tibet and Korea; a copperplate edition engraved by Italian secular priest Matteo Ripa (1682–1746) was finished in 1719 and consisted of seven horizontal scrolls that were further divided into a total of forty-one sheets, with new geographical information added on Tibet; and another woodblock edition was produced in 1721 as a revision of the first one, with the four Tibetan maps of 1718 replaced by seven updated and more detailed maps that also included parts of Eastern Turkestan.[2] Not long after the completion of the first woodblock edition, Jartoux managed—perhaps secretly—to send the entire atlas together with some notes and a translation of place names to his confreres in Paris, where it was entrusted to Jean-Baptiste du Halde (1674–1743), editor of the *Lettres édifiantes et curieuses*.[3] Years later, in 1725, the atlas was presented to the French king, by then possibly supplemented with other maps from China that had reached the Parisian Jesuits and that may have included sheets from other editions of the Chinese atlas as well.[4]

It took many years for du Halde to take steps to have these maps published in France as part his four volume editorial work on China, entitled *Description géographique, historique, chronologique, politique, et physique de l'empire de la Chine et de la Tartarie chinoise.*[5] Some of the French Jesuits in Paris and Beijing were not too happy with the delay. As early as 1722, Louis-François Orry, the treasurer of the Jesuit missions to China and India in Paris, wrote of his frustration to Beijing missionary Antoine Gaubil (1689–1759):

> I have not been able to see [the maps] myself. They think they must keep everything secret out of fear that [others] will deprive us of the glory of discovery, so we only communicate through our *lettres édifiantes.*[6]

But when Gaubil himself wrote about the delay to the head of the French mission in China, he showed more understanding for du Halde:

> Some complaints have been voiced here about Father du Halde: first, about how he keeps the maps for so long without having them published. [. . .] But they are wrong, and I say this in plain terms, because in 1720 Father Jartoux wrote [to ask him] not to publish these maps until further notice, due to several difficulties.[7]

According to Gaubil, there was a fear that once published, these maps could be taken back to China as gifts by other European powers, thereby undermining the French Jesuits' credibility in the eyes of the court. If these really were the motives behind postponing the publication of the atlas, it is indeed likely that the Chinese atlas was sent to Europe secretly, without the knowledge of the emperor and his court.

Had the publication of the atlas not been deferred, then First Royal Geographer and member of the *Académie des Sciences* Guillaume Delisle (1675–1726) would have been a likely choice for editing the Chinese maps. After all, the French missionaries to China had been trained by the *Académie* and entertained frequent contacts with some of its members, as well as with Joseph-Nicolas Delisle (1688–1768), the brother of Guillaume who later became an astronomer for the Russian empire in Saint-Petersburg. Guillaume himself also frequently corresponded with different missionaries to China, most notably with Czech astronomer Karel Slavíček (1678–1735), who composed the first detailed map of Beijing. But the celebrated geographer passed away in 1726, two years before an agreement was reached between du Halde and the promising young cartographer d'Anville. Whether Delisle ever got to see the atlas that was sent from China is unknown.

D'Anville's adaptations of the Chinese atlas

Jean-Baptiste Bourguignon d'Anville (1697–1782) was born at the end of the seventeenth century in Paris. He is said to have composed his first map at the age of twelve, on the basis of information that he distilled from a number of historical texts. If this is more than a legend, it would certainly characterize his later work, for d'Anville was a typical early 18th century cartographer who never left his office to conduct geographical surveys. Instead, he relied on the observational and descriptive work of others to draw his maps. Nevertheless, d'Anville appears to have had an eye for trustworthy data and made a point of excluding information that was not confirmed by other sources. He never blindly copied from earlier maps, a common practice among many of the cartographers of his time, but rather scrutinized every text he could lay his hands on in order to compare geographical information. Having published his first map at the age of fifteen and, notwithstanding his humble background as the son of a tailor, d'Anville was given the title of Royal Geographer at the age of twenty-two in recognition of his service to the crown as the geography tutor of the young king Louis XV (1710–74). At the same time, he found a patron in Louis d'Orléans (1702–52), son of the Regent. Through his connections at court, d'Anville soon began attracting the attention of other Parisian elites as well, including Claude Bertrand Taschereau de Linières (1658–1746), the Jesuit confessor of the king who would later introduce him to du Halde.[8] Consequently, the cartographer was contracted to compose maps for a number of travel accounts and compilations throughout the 1720s and early 1730s. Thus consolidating his reputation and income, d'Anville could not only afford to continue in cartography, a costly occupation back then, but also to start making choices himself with regard to the subject matter for his maps. Even so, not all his work was equally successful. While he was able to rectify earlier mistakes concerning Italy's geography, solely on the basis of literary data and later surprisingly confirmed by a detailed survey, his writings on the shape of the earth were squarely refuted by contemporary scientific measurements. However, having drawn nearly two hundred maps by the end of his life, some of them of great importance to geography as a whole, he was appointed First Royal Geographer in 1775. When he died at the age of 85, d'Anville had built a reputation that resounded all over Europe.[9]

Thus, drawing the maps of China, Tartary and Tibet for du Halde's *Description* was one of the first large assignments of d'Anville's career. In short, he was contracted to reduce and redraw the detailed maps of the Chinese provinces (fifteen maps), Tartary (twelve maps), Tibet (nine maps), and Korea (one map) which were all sent from China by the Jesuit missionaries, and to compose four new general maps of these regions. Later on, the maps of thirty-eight Chinese cities (on seven plates) and a chart of the travels of captain Beerings, obtained through indirect contacts with Russia, were also added to this list.[10] The specifics of the agreement were laid down in three documents.[11] The first contract, drawn up between du Halde and d'Anville in 1728, stipulates the cartographer's duties regarding only the maps of China and Tartary, specifies his remuneration in cash, books and maps, and gives du Halde the right to correct the printer's proofs. Intellectual rights are dealt with as well: "[I, du Halde] will be happy to oblige the said Sir [d'Anville] by referring to his work in the prospectus that I have to give to the public of my books, and in the books themselves," thus ensuring the cartographer would get the recognition he deserved. D'Anville himself, however, was responsible for the actual engravings. For this purpose, he contracted the Delahaye workshop, which he elsewhere described as "the most able [engraver] known to me".[12] The cartouches, on the other hand, were at the request of du Halde designed by a M. Humblot, who also designed the illustrations included in the *Description*. Within one year after signing the contract, d'Anville had already completed reducing and redrawing the maps of the fifteen Chinese provinces entirely on the basis of the woodblock edition of the Chinese atlas: both sets of maps coincide perfectly and leave territories beyond the provincial borders blank.

However, d'Anville appears to have had access to at least one other version of the Chinese atlas as well, since most of the detailed maps of Tartary included in du Halde's work seem to have been taken straight from the copperplate edition rather than from the woodblock one that was initially sent to Europe by the French missionaries. Not only are place names transliterations of Manchu, a language used only in the copperplate edition, but eleven of these twelve maps coincide perfectly with copperplate sheets. However, one of the detailed maps of Tartary contains data that corresponds with the first woodblock edition but differs from the copperplate edition, even though in all other respects it seems to be an exact copy of the latter.[13] Such differences in detail have led some scholars to believe that d'Anville's maps of Tartary were based on a draft version of the copperplate atlas that was produced more or less simultaneously with the first woodblock edition of the Chinese atlas.[14] There is a possibility, then, that this 'draft version' was in fact the overview map of 1718 mentioned above, since both were composed to form one large map. This means that the overview map of 1718 could have reached Paris together with the first woodblock atlas, but no definitive proof was found. Other possibilities include that copperplate-edition sheets, sent to France in the 1720s by Gaubil, were used as direct sources by d'Anville or that the copperplate edition that reached Europe in 1720 by way of Ostend was intended for du Halde.[15] On another note, the French cartographer's map of Korea is a combination of both the woodblock and the copperplate edition; Korean place names on this map are transliterations of Manchu, a language only included in the copperplate atlas, while the map's scope is nearly identical to that in both woodblock editions. The manuscript map that lies at the basis of this combination and was therefore positively identified as the original map behind d'Anville's adaptation, was sent to Paris by Gaubil in 1728 and is now preserved at the National Library of France.[16]

A second contract was signed between the two gentlemen in 1729, increasing the cartographer's remuneration in exchange for reducing the detailed maps of Tibet and parts of Eastern Turkestan, and for composing the *General Map of Tibet* (also including parts of Eastern Turkestan). Unlike his maps of Tartary, d'Anville's nine detailed maps of Tibet do not coincide perfectly with sheets from the copperplate atlas, but at first sight seem to be cut-and-paste versions, with each map consisting of two or more sheets. Yet, they also contain striking differences and cover areas that were left blank in the copperplate edition. Such discrepancies may be explained by the fact that Jean-Baptiste Régis (1663–1738), one of the original missionary-mapmakers, sent maps of Tibet that included newly acquired information from route books and measurements to du Halde in 1726.[17] Régis had further updated the Tibetan sheets of the copperplate atlas on the basis of what he was allowed to consult by the Qing court, which formed the basis for d'Anville's adaptations. Like the map of Korea, the original maps of Tibet were positively identified at the National Library of France.[18]

In a manuscript account that was recently discovered at the *Archives départementales de l'Orne*, d'Anville explicitly states that his detailed maps were very close indeed to the originals that were sent from China:

> I am glad to announce, before anything else, that the detailed maps of the provinces of China, of parts of Tartary, and even those of Tibet, all drawn to be included in the *Description de la Chine* by Reverend Father du Halde, S.J., are moderate and servile (if I may use this epithet) reductions of maps that were sent from China. It was thought necessary to retain even the style of the original design, so that this large and beautiful work could be communicated or presented to the public with more faithfulness [to the originals].[19]

Thus, given the substantial differences between different sets of d'Anville's maps, their correspondence to different editions of the Chinese atlas, and claims by d'Anville that his detailed maps were all true to their Chinese originals, there is no question that the cartographer directly based his work on different versions of the Chinese maps. Nevertheless, with these thirty-seven maps of the Chinese provinces, Tartary, Korea and Tibet completed by 1733, the reducing and redrawing of all detailed maps commissioned by du Halde had finally been accomplished.

Beyond the Chinese atlas: d'Anville's general maps

When compared to the detailed maps, the four general maps that d'Anville was commissioned to compose anew for the work of du Halde contain substantial differences, as they were not drawn entirely on the basis of maps that were sent from China. Working in the tradition of Delisle, d'Anville insisted on gathering as much extra geographical information as possible before drawing a new map. As with the detailed maps, it was du Halde who provided most of this information, since he entertained frequent contacts with the French mission in Beijing and had gathered the manuscript memoires of twenty-seven missionaries to China for his own writings, some of which contained useful geographical and astronomical data.[20] In his letters, Gaubil confirms the existence of a rich correspondence between du Halde, Régis, himself and others throughout the 1720s and early 1730s concerning the geography of regions that fell beyond the surveys involving European missionaries.[21] As mentioned above, missionaries in Beijing copied from route books and maps they were allowed to consult by the Qing court, but they also interviewed envoys from distant regions who regularly visited the capital in order to pay homage to the emperor.[22] Using all of this additional information provided by the missionaries, d'Anville was able to add important data, such as the routes that are depicted on the general maps of China and Tartary. The cartographer drew these routes separately, on the basis of translated route book excerpts and memoires that had been sent from China, only to incorporate them on his maps afterwards.[23] But he also consulted non-Jesuit sources, including a wide range of books on geography. One notable example is the *Geographia Nubiensis*, a Latin translation of an Arabic book on geography that had been published in Paris more than one hundred years earlier.[24] Other non-Jesuit sources, referred to in several of d'Anville's writings, include his correspondence with Saint-Petersburg as well as a Dutch maritime chart depicting the seas near Japan. The latter inspired him to redraw the coastline of Tartary and include Japan on the general map of this region.[25] Combining information from all of these sources, the cartographer was able to successfully complete the *General Map of China* (1730), the *General Map of Chinese Tartary* (1732), and the *General Map of Tibet* (1733).

It was then decided to make one last map that would incorporate all of these regions and cover territories as far west as the Caspian Sea. Therefore, a third and last contract was signed between du Halde and d'Anville in January 1734:

> I promise to deliver the General Map, which remains to be done, around the fifteenth of next April. If, by some accident or difficulty due to unexpected work, it should happen that this map is delayed by a fortnight, it will not annul anything that follows here below. I renounce the right or privilege of selling these maps separately for the amount of time the Father sees fit, and not to publish them separately from his printed work. The Reverend Father will not have any other person whatsoever publish these, and reserved me the right to separately publish the maps at a time he considers appropriate [. . .].[26]

This last map to be completed, the *Most General Map of China, Chinese Tartary and Tibet* referred to in this agreement, was to be the masterpiece among all maps commissioned by du Halde. Again, d'Anville could count on the Beijing missionaries for additional information. Around 1730, for example, an intercontinental debate was taking place between d'Anville and Gaubil—via the Parisian Jesuits—on the position of Astracan, a city on the western shore of the Caspian Sea.[27] Yet, even though information obtained from the French mission was without doubt indispensible for the successful completion of the *Most General Map*, d'Anville once more personally sought after other sources of data as well, as is mentioned explicitly in the foreword of the publication that is presented in this book: "Since the missionaries had some—albeit imperfect—knowledge of the lands that lie between Tibet, Tartary and the Caspian Sea, M. d'Anville has used this [knowledge] in the most general of all maps, after having compared and complemented it with what he could find elsewhere." For instance, information on the region of Bukhara, in present day Uzbekistan, was supplemented with data from the travel account of the Swedish officer Philipp Johann von Strahlenberg (1677–1747).[28] With all maps finally completed, engraved and delivered by 1 May 1734, du Halde was able to publish his work at great cost in 1735, roughly fifteen years after the original atlas had first reached Paris.

Reception and controversy

For two years after the publication of du Halde's *Description*, his confreres in Beijing waited impatiently for the four large volumes to arrive. In their eyes, the work would help their mission secure more support by showing the public how the French missionaries had worked to improve European knowledge on China. When two years later it finally did arrive, it was scrutinized by the missionaries, because word had reached them of the criticism that was voiced in Europe about the lack of justification for some of the data included in d'Anville's maps.[29] Examples of the criticism are the public debate in France on how many *li* (里) should constitute one degree of latitude and the commotion surrounding the depiction of coastlines on the *General Map of Chinese Tartary*.[30] From China, it was Joseph-Anne-Marie de Moyriac de Mailla (1669–1748), one of the original missionary-mapmakers, who took the lead in criticizing the work of both du Halde and d'Anville. With regard to the maps, his criticism was specifically aimed at the orthography of geographic names and at the newly composed general maps which, as mentioned above, were drawn after consulting different sources of data and thus contained substantial differences when compared to the original Chinese atlas. The heated discussions that ensued continued for years and ended only after d'Anville had published his *Mémoire sur la Chine*, in which he refuted much of the criticism. In providing justification for his work, d'Anville confirms du Halde's frequent correspondence with the Beijing missionaries and his use of a wide array of other sources for composing the general maps.

One year after du Halde's writings were published in Paris, a pirated edition was printed in The Hague. It did not include d'Anville's maps, however, since the publisher did not have access to the engravings that were kept in Paris.[31] Instead, his maps were re-engraved in the Netherlands, after having been copied from the original edition of du Halde's work, and published separately in the form of the 1737 atlas that is presented in this book. All of the maps commissioned by du Halde were included in this *Nouvel atlas de la Chine, de la Tartarie chinoise, et du Thibet*, with the exception of the thirty-eight maps of Chinese cities. The description of Bukhara by Strahlenberg, used by d'Anville for composing his *Most General Map*, was also added to the atlas as a form of justification, since du Halde's work did not contain detailed information on this region. At first sight, the maps that comprise the Dutch atlas appear to be exact copies of the originals, but a closer look reveals several important differences. The prints and paper of the Dutch maps are of slightly inferior quality, mountain pictograms differ, routes and other information included only in d'Anville's general map of Tartary were also added to the detailed maps of that region, and all maps of both Tartary and Tibet carry a separate cartouche, unlike the originals.

When d'Anville got to see the maps that had been copied and pirated by the Dutch publisher, he was appalled, not only by the fact that they were pirated and published separately from du Halde's *Description*, but also by the aforementioned differences in quality:

Almost all of these maps are not only terribly inferior to the original ones in terms of execution, but also very badly engraved in all respects. [. . .] the mountains on the Dutch map are of very bad taste: they are little hills, detached and randomly scattered, without being joined together in order to express the natural [landscape]; the typeface is puny and of equally bad taste. [. . .] we even find some rivers that are not depicted on the original map as they are on the Dutch copy, and if we would take pains to scrutinize it and submit all copies to a careful examination, there is no doubt that we would find many more mistakes of this sort.[32]

Notwithstanding d'Anville's strong criticism, the pirated editions of both du Halde's writings and d'Anville's maps were quite popular among the contemporary readership due their more reasonable price. Another reason for the popularity of the Dutch atlas was its larger format that made it easier to consult the maps, whereas most of the ones in du Halde's work were fold-outs. Consequently, the atlas was republished once more in Amsterdam almost fifty years later, using the same pirated engravings.[33] Meanwhile, in Paris too, it was decided to use the original engravings of d'Anville's maps once more for publishing a separate atlas in France for the first time, and to further include the thirty-eight city maps and fourteen illustrations of cultural and ethnographical interest from the work of du Halde.[34] But apart from these separate atlases, only one of the translations that appeared throughout Europe of du Halde's *Description* contained a substantial part of the cartographic material. Published by Edward Cave in London (1738–41), it included maps that were reworked and somewhat improved by John Green, an alias for Bradock Mead.[35]

Finally, it is worth mentioning that d'Anville appears later in life to have been the proud possessor of an original version of the second woodblock version of the Chinese atlas. Even though it was seen by some authors as the basis for d'Anville's maps, it had the Russian pronunciation of place names added in red ink, indicating that it was not acquired via du Halde and the Parisian Jesuits, but most likely through a Russian contact.[36] Through the patronage of the Russian court, the above mentioned Joseph-Nicolas Delisle, who headed the school for astronomy in Saint-Petersburg and frequently corresponded with d'Anville and Gaubil, must have had access to Russian embassies and trading caravans travelling to China. Therefore, it is possible that d'Anville obtained or bought the atlas with the help of Delisle, who returned to Paris in 1747. It seems negotiations on the transfer of maps from Russia to France did in fact take place later in the cartographer's life, after which he became a member of the Saint-Petersburg Academy of Sciences.[37] The atlas, like most of the pieces in d'Anville's collection, was later purchased by French diplomat and statesman Charles Gravier (1717–87), otherwise known as Count de Vergennes, and kept in a Parisian archive until it was taken to Germany during the Second World War, where it remains missing until today.

Thus, d'Anville's China maps were the product of an intercontinental exchange of geographical knowledge by an extended network of people. The French Jesuits stood at the center of this network, as it operated from Beijing, Paris and, to a lesser degree, from Saint Petersburg. While the maps were mostly based on different versions of a Chinese atlas that was produced with the assistance of European missionaries, d'Anville certainly made a substantial contribution to European geographical knowledge of continental East Asia, in particular through his newly composed general maps. With several publications and a wide circulation throughout Europe, the celebrated cartographer's maps of China, Tartary, Korea and Tibet unmistakably became an authoritative geographical work on East-Asia that influenced mapmakers until well into the nineteenth century, when strong European colonialism combined with technological advancements further improved geographical knowledge of the region.

Notes

1. The composition and size of these teams of surveyors, the personal patronage of the emperor, and the involvement of local officials are all discussed in Mario Cams, "The Early Qing Geographical Surveys (1708–1716) As a Case of Collaboration between the Jesuits and the Kangxi Court," *Sino-Western Cultural Relations Journal* 34 (2012): 1–20.

2. Walter Fuchs, *Der Jesuiten-Atlas der Kanghsi-Zeit*, Monumenta Serica Monograph Series 4, Vol. 1 (Beijing: Fu-jen University, 1943), 60. Years later, much less detailed versions of these maps were included in several published geographies.

3. *Lettres édifiantes et curieuses écrites des missions étrangères par quelques Missionaries de la Compagnie de Jesus*, 34 vols. (Paris : Le Clerc, 1702–76).

4. Antoine Gaubil, *Correspondance de Pékin 1722–1759* (Genève: Librarie Droz, 1970), 216, 302.

5. Jean-Baptiste du Halde, *Description géographique, historique, chronologique, politique, et physique de l'empire de la Chine et de la Tartarie chinoise*, 4 vols. (Paris: Le Mercier, 1735).

6. Biblithèque de l'Observatoire, B 1/10/7. This letter was also addressed to Jean-Baptiste Jacques (1688–1728), who reached China together with Gaubil.

7.   Gaubil, *Correspondance*, 216.

8.   Jean-Baptiste Bourguignon d'Anville, *Mémoire sur la Chine* (Paris: Galeries du Louvre, 1776), 8.

9.   Barbie du Bocage et Jean Denis, *Notice des ouvrages de M. D'Anville* (Paris: Fuchs, 1802).

10. *Lettre de M. d'Anville, géographe ordinaire du roi, au R.P. Castel, jésuite. Au suject des Pays de Kamtchatka et de Jeço. Et réponse du R.P. Castel* (Paris: s.l., 1737), 9.

11. All of the contracts between du Halde and d'Anville are recorded in Henri Cordier, "Du Halde et d'Anville (cartes de Chine)," *Recueil de mémoires orientaux* (Paris: Leroux, 1905), 391–400.

12. D'Anville, *Mémoire sur la Chine*, 46.

13. One example is the twin lakes that are depicted just south of 41°N on this *Fourth Detailed Map of Tartary*. In the copperplate and the second woodblock edition, this geographical feature is depicted just south of 43°N. This clearly indicates that d'Anville used different versions of the Chinese atlas for his adaptations.

14. Fuchs, *Jesuiten-Atlas*, 1:27.

15. The Bibliothèque nationale de France (BnF) conserves original copperplate sheets of Tartary. BnF, Cartes et Plans, Ge DD 2987 (7296 B-7307 B). See also Gaubil, *Correspondance*, 205–6, 302. For the Ostend possibility, see Ad Dudink, *Chinese books and documents (pre-1900) in the Royal Library of Belgium at Brussels* (Brussels: Archives et Bibliotèques de Belgique, 2006), 91–92. In these cases, the discrepancies on the *Fourth Detailed Map of Tartary* cannot be explained.

16. BnF, Cartes et plans, Ge DD 2987 (7325 B).

17. Gaubil, *Correspondance*, 187; and d'Anville, *Mémoire sur la Chine*, 14–15.

18. BnF, Cartes et plans, Ge DD 2987 (7348 B) and Ge DD 2987 (7349 B-7350 B).

19. Archives départementales de l'Orne, SHAO 252J224 (not consulted personally). On 10 January 2012, Lucile Haguet published photographs of the manuscript letter on the website of the *projet d'Anville*: http://danville.hypotheses.org/1271

20. Travel accounts by Jean-François Gerbillon (1654–1707) of his journeys into Tartary, for example, were used for the *General Map of Chinese Tartary*, as is mentioned in several of d'Anville's writings and in the preface of the *Description*.

21. Note that some of his Parisian confreres, such as Etienne Souciet (1671–1744), were also actively involved in this intercontinental cartographic exchange.

22. Gaubil, *Correspondance*, 117, 120, 187, 205, 207, 217.

23. As the manuscript maps of some of these routes clearly show. BnF, Cartes et Plans, Ge D 10589–10590.

24. BnF, Cartes et Plans, Ge D 10591. Compare with Gabriele Sionita & Joannes Hesronita, (trans. and ed.), *Geographia nubiensis: id est accuratissima totius orbis in septem climata divisi descriptio, continens praesertim exactam vniuersae Asiae, & Africae, rerumq[ue] in ijs hactenus incognitarum explicationem* (Paris: Hieronymi Blagaert, 1619), 213–14.

25. D'Anville, *Mémoire sur la Chine*, 6; and *Lettre de M. d'Anville, . . . au R.P. Castel, jésuite*, 11.

26. Cordier, "Du Halde et d'Anville," 395–96.

27. Gaubil, *Correspondance*, 258, 278–79.

28. This travel account was added to the publication that is presented in this book. See infra.

29. Gaubil, *Correspondance*, 458, 470–71.

30. Isabelle Landry-Deron, *La preuve par la Chine* (Paris: Éditions EHESS, 2002),146–47; and *Lettre de M. d'Anville, . . . au R.P. Castel, jésuite*. The latter was written as a response to this criticism.

31. Jean-Baptiste du Halde, *Description géographique* [. . .], 4 vols. (The Hague: Henri Scheurleer, 1736).

32. Jean-Baptiste Bourguignon d'Anville, "Réponse de M. d'Anville," *Mémoires pour l'Histoire des Sciences et des Beaux-Arts: Avril 1738* (Paris: Chaubert, 1738), 768–73.

33. *Nouvel atlas de la Chine, de la Tartarie chinoise et du Thibet* (Amsterdam: Barthelemy Vlam, 1785).

34. Jean-Baptiste Grosier, ed., *Altas général de la Chine; pour servir à la Description générale de cet Empire* (Paris: Moutard, 1785). Another but similar edition of this atlas exists, but cannot be dated exactly : *Atlas général de la Chine, de la Tartarie chinoise, et du Thibet. Pour servir aux différentes Descriptions et Histoires de cet Empire* (Paris: Dezauche, 1790[?]).

35. For more information regarding Bradock Mead's improvements of d'Anville's maps, see Theodore Foss, "The Editing of an Atlas of China: A Comparison of the Work of J.-B. d'Anville and the Improvements of John Green on the Jesuit/K'ang-hsi Atlas," in *Imago et mensura mundi: Atti del IX Congresso di storia della cartographia* (Rome: Istituto della Enciclopedia Italiana, 1985), 361–76.

36. Henri Cordier, *Bibliotheca Sinica*, Vol. 1 (Taipei: Ch'eng Wen, 1966), 184.

37. Georges Dulac, *Science et politique: les réseaux du dr. António Ribeiro Sanches (1699–1783), Cahiers du monde russe* 43/2 (Paris: Éditions de l'E.H.E.S.S., 2002), 265.

CARTOGRAPHY DURING THE TIMES OF THE KANGXI EMPEROR

The Age and the Background

Han Qi[1]

At the time of emperor Kangxi, of the Qing dynasty, the substantial cartographic surveys accomplished across the country of China marked an extraordinary event in the history of world geography and cartography. Based on the information collected from Chinese and Western literature and archives, I will concisely discuss in this article the origin, the process of cartographic surveys during the Kangxi reign, and the functions of the Jesuits and of the Chinese in that development. I will discuss, as well, the influence of the collective atlas *Huangyu Quanlantu* (康熙黃輿全览图, *Complete Map of the Kangxi Reign*).

I. Background of the cartography surveys and mapping in Kangxi's reign

Affected by Yang Guangxian's anti-Christianity movement, Kangxi began in his early childhood to acquire knowledge about the West. The Belgian Jesuit missionary Ferdinand Verbiest (南怀仁 1623–88), not only taught the emperor extensive knowledge of mathematics and astronomy but also worked with other missionaries, Lodovico Buglio (利类思, 1606–82) and Gabriel de Magalhães (安文思,1610–77), in a collaborative writing *Xifang Yaoji* (西方要纪, *Concise Introduction to the West*, 1669), which aimed at introducing the emperor to Western geographical knowledge. Following the map made by Matteo Ricci (利玛窦, 1552–1610) *Kunyu Wanguo Quantu* (坤舆万国全图, *Universal Map of Ten Thousand Countries*), Verbiest had compiled and drawn the *Kunyu Quantu* (坤舆全图, *Universal Map*, 1674), which helped Kangxi broaden his outlook on world geography.

After Kangxi controlled the *sanfan* (三藩, Three Feudatories) and retook Taiwan, he decreed in 1686 a revision of the *Da Qing Yitongzhi* (大清一统志, *Comprehensive Gazetteer of the Qing*). In his decree, given to Le-de-hong (勒德洪), the chief of *Da Qing Yitongzhi*, he said:

> Although the territory was vast, covering tens of thousands of *li* (里), the event motivated me to think of the whole country. [. . .] Now I specially appoint you as the chief official to lead officers of compilation to work diligently, aiming to gather extensive information and make the style [of the book] precise and refined. Thus the strategic positions of mountains and rivers, customs and people can be easily identified, and the maps of the territories can be drawn. Even though I have 10,000 matters to attend to, I will read all the reports in person.[2]

Because of its practical importance for military operations, for politics, for the inspection and harnessing of rivers, Kangxi expressed great enthusiasm for cartography and paid great heed to cartographic surveys and the charting of maps.

Many of the Catholic missionaries were talented and competent in various fields of science. They gained Kangxi's confidence and were entrusted by him with the task of cartographic surveys. On 14 November 1685, the Belgian Jesuit Antoine Thomas (1644–1709) shortly after his arrival in Beijing wrote a letter to Europe in which he mentioned that Emperor Kangxi requested that a map be drawn of the Tartar region.[3] In 1678 Verbiest wrote a letter to Europe, appealing for more Jesuits to be sent to China to preach the Catholic faith. In response to Verbiest's open letter, King Louis XIV responded positively. Under the guidance of the French Royal Academy of Sciences, the Society of Jesus in France sent off Jesuits as "King's Mathematicians" to China. Five of them, namely, Jean de Fontaney (洪若, 1643–1710), Louis-Daniel Le Comte (李明, 1655–1728), Claude de Visdelou (刘应, 1656–1737), Joachim Bouvet (白晋, 1656–1730) and Jean François Gerbillon (张诚, 1654–1707), arrived in Ningbo in 1687. Through Verbiest's mediation, the Ministry of Rites submitted the following to the emperor for decision: "Of Hong Ruo's [Jean de Fontaney] party of five, it is not yet known if they include experts in calendar studies. The group will be brought to Beijing, pending assignments; and those who are not called upon may stay if they wish." With the emperor's consent, the Zhejiang (浙江) provincial governor was thus informed. Then, the five missionaries came to Beijing. The Jesuits had brought with them "two celestial globes, two stands, two microscopic devices, three twofold microscopic devices, two star telescopes, an instrument measuring stars, three copper rings of time-measurement, an instrument measuring the sky, five astronomical pendulums, six caskets of astronomical classical books, five Western geographic maps, a small chest of magnets, totaling 30 caskets of large, medium and small sizes."[4] Among the listed items were some gifts intended for the emperor, which included European maps, and scientific instruments for cartography and astronomy such as armillary spheres, microscopes, telescopes, and pendulums (for astronomical observations).

In Kangxi's 27th year, on the 21st day of the second month (March 22, 1688), the five French Jesuits, accompanied by the Portuguese Jesuit Tomás Pereira (徐日升, 1645–1708) were brought to see the emperor at the Palace of Heavenly Purity. In the end, only Bouvet and Gerbillon were selected to remain in the imperial court in Beijing. Beginning in 1689, Kangxi, under the guidance of the two missionaries, studied the *Elemens de Géometrie* written by I.-G. Pardies[5] (几何原本, *Jihe Yuanben*), which contained examples relating to cartographic surveys.[6]

During excursions, Emperor Kangxi liked to bring along the missionaries and their retinues, of whom he could inquire whenever needed. In the 1690s Kangxi made an inspection of the western part of the country. He brought along survey equipment to measure the height of the Pole Star (latitudes). Over time information and experience accumulated and laid a solid foundation for later cartographic surveys. Gerbillon sometimes accompanied Kangxi on his travels. During those expeditions, he explained to the emperor the geography of Europe,[7] very probably with the help of maps from Europe, gifts presented to the emperor earlier.[8] Kangxi made three expeditions to the western territory, the northeast and the south of the Yangtze River (长江, *Changjiang*). During the journeys, Kangxi ordered his associates to measure the latitudes and longitudes. In 1696, he inspected *Kalun* (喀伦) himself. He instructed his Crown Prince to measure the distance between the *Kalun* areas and Beijing with a rope and to use instruments to measure the height of Pole Star at *Kalun*.[9] This method of measurement was acquired from the Jesuits. Such ongoing surveys formed the basis for national cartographic surveys in China, a herald of the future.

II. Standardization of cartographic surveys and the measuring system

To launch large-scale geodetic surveys, the formulation of a unified measurement system is of prime importance. In 1702, Kangxi visited Dezhou (德州) during his Southern inspection. His third son

Prince Yinzhi received orders to measure the longitudes in order to determine the *li* (里) system, a yardstick of measuring distance. Minister Li Guangdi (李光地), who was involved in this task, recorded:

In the 10th month of Renzi [Wu] year [1702], His Majesty arrived at Dezhou during his Southern inspection. [. . .] As calendar experts described, one degree in the sky, [is] equivalent to 250 *li* on ground level. Although I have not surveyed precisely, I feel that the distance should be 250 *li*. At present I have asked *San-a-ge* [三阿哥, third child] to carefully measure the distance from Beijing. *San-a-ge*'s mathematical skills are extremely refined. Now at Dezhou, albeit a little inclined to the East, Gou-gu method [勾股, i.e. the Pythagorean theorem] is used to measure, making use of pegs-and-chunks to note the distance. Imprecise measurements will not happen any longer. Upon return to Beijing on the 21ˢᵗ, the emperor said to [my] master: "*San-a-ge* has made the measurement, which means: one degree in the sky is exactly 200 *li* on ground level." My master said: "This is so because the system used was of eight *cun* [寸– *inch*] of Zhou dynasty's *chi* [尺– *foot*], resulting that 250 *li* equals one degree. His Majesty said: Absolutely. Through this trip I have profited a lot and learned some calculation methods."[10]

Prince Yinzhi, a gifted and intelligent person, was good at mathematics and astronomy. Kangxi asked him while he was still a child to learn from the Jesuits. Yinzhi was highly praised by the Jesuits, and was involved in the cartographic survey. Li Guangdi apparently had a fresh memory of this matter. In his *Lixiang Benyao* (历象本要, *Concise Introduction of Calendrical Science*), Li mentioned this event again:

In the winter of Renwu [1702], the emperor rode in the imperial carriage to make an inspection of the South. He ordered the prince to bring the *Xiyang chouren* [西洋筹人, mathematician from the West ocean] on the trip. They departed from the south of Beijing city for Dezhou, a distance of more than 700 *li*. The survey and observations were conducted precisely and lasted for several weeks or a month. Precise data about the stars and earth were obtained. The conclusion was that the distance on ground level of 200 *li* equals one degree difference of the height of Pole Star. The older sources claimed 250 *li*, probably too loose an estimate. Now, the ruler used is one made by the Ministry of Works so that the ancient one *chi* equals eight *cun*, but how this came about is still unknown. I was in the retinue of the emperor and learned this.[11]

By cross-referencing Western literature, it becomes clear that the term *"Xiyang chouren"* actually referred to the Belgian Jesuit Antoine Thomas.[12] Kangxi sent his third son Yinzhi and Thomas to some places near Beijing to measure their latitudes and longitudes. The task was to estimate the actual distance along the meridian for the longitude from Bazhou (霸州) to the Jiao River (交河), and to establish the correspondence between one degree in the sky along that longitude and the distance measured on the ground along the meridian line. Prince Yinzhi, the organizer of the survey and one of its surveyors, played an important role in this mission. Under Yinzhi's leadership, the survey measurement undertaken by Thomas and others was very precise. The findings corrected the mistakes of China's ancient measuring scale. Henceforth, a new rule in measurement of length was levied. Based on the yardstick, one degree in the sky equals 200 *li* on ground level. And the ruler of the Ministry of Works was adopted as a standard ruler with 18 *zhang* (丈) as one *sheng* (绳), and 10 *sheng* (180 *zhang* or 1,800 *chi*) equals one *li*. Also, the distance 200 *li* equaling one degree in longitude was formalized, and this was an innovative and pioneering act at the time, thanks to the influence of Thomas and others.

Concerning the cartographic survey in 1702, the emperor himself also recorded this case. In Kangxi's 41st year, on the 24th day of the 10th month (December 12), the emperor instructed the grand minister Zhang Yushu (张玉书) and Li Guangdi, provincial governor of Zhili (直隶), who were in his retinue, saying:

Use survey instruments to measure the far and near distances, this is a fixed standard, absolutely no discrepancy in measurement. Should there be any mistakes, it would be due to misuse of the method, and not due to inaccuracy in calculation. By using this method to calculate the areas and calculate the farmlands, the result can be attained at once. However, one must be very careful and vigilant in the techniques so that the survey and testing can be precise and accurate. On the whole, the method used is mostly geometrical triangulation. Although the name *sanjiaoxing* [三角形, triangle] did not exist before, the mathematical method must always have it as its basis. For instance, the method of Gou-gu [Pythagorean theorem] is derived from triangle, and this method was passed down from ancient times. However it was not recorded in books. Therefore people do not know its origin.[13]

Note that here he mentioned the use of geometrical triangulation.

In Kangxi's 50th year (1711), he inspected the embankments of Tongzhou (通州). He was accompanied by seven princes. In the second month, he took a boat from Heshaotun (和韶屯) to inspect the river. At the scene, a demonstration on how to use the instruments to measure the topography was carried out. Kangxi instructed the princes, ministers and others: "Use this to measure the sky and the earth, and to predict the eclipses of the sun and the moon. Such things are easy to calculate."[14]

In the fifth month of the same year, grand ministers and others were instructed:

> Both the degree of the sky and the distance on the ground coincide with each other. If the ruler of Zhou Dynasty is used, one degree in the sky equals 250 *li* on ground. However, if measured by the ruler of today, one degree in the sky equals 200 *li* on ground. Since ancient times, cartographers did not follow the degrees in the sky to calculate the geographic distance, far or near, therefore there were many discrepancies and mistakes. I formerly appointed some good artists to draw the mountains, rivers and topography in the northeast region, and based on the degrees in the sky to project and calculate, and then paint the details into their maps and drawings.[15]

Therefore, around 1702, the standardization of the measurement system was established. During the period of map-surveying (1708–17) in the country, the standard was followed in the measurement of the northeast and Korean borderlands. After having measured the latitudes and longitudes of the places near Beijing, the capital, Kangxi inspected the Northeast and the South. He frequently ordered the accompanying missionaries to determine the latitudes and longitudes. The unification of standards laid the foundation for a full development of cartographic surveys in China.

III. The origin and process of the cartographic survey

The cartographic surveying in Kangxi's times began in 1708 and ended in 1717, and thus lasted for a decade. The map *Huangyu Quanlantu* (皇輿全览图, *Complete Map of the Kangxi Reign*) was finally completed. Now, the origin and process of the cartographic survey will be briefly discussed in this section.

In 1705, Antoine Thomas, Joachim Bouvet, Jean-Baptiste Régis (雷孝思, 1664–1738), and Dominique Parrenin (巴多明, 1665–1741) took part in the cartographic surveying of the surrounding areas and rivers in Beijing. Afterwards, a nationwide large-scale cartographic survey was launched because Kangxi listened to the advice of Parrenin.[16] The cartographic survey began on 4 July 1708, and was done under the guidance of the Jesuit missionaries Jean-Baptiste Régis, Pierre Jartoux (杜德美,

1669–1720), J.M.A. de Moyriac de Mailla (冯秉正, 1669–1748), Pierre-Vincent de Tartre (汤尚贤, 1669–1724), Romain Hinderer (德玛诺, 1668–1744), Joachim Bouvet, João Francisco Cardoso (麦大成, 1677–1723), Ehrenbert Xaver Fridelli (费隐, 1673–1743), and the French Augustinian missionary Guillaume Fabre Bonjour (山遥瞻, 1669/1670–1714). In 1708, Bouvet, Régis, Jartoux surveyed the Great Wall. In 1709, Régis, Jartoux and Fridelli surveyed Liaodong (辽东) – Jilin (吉林), Liaoning (辽宁) – and Mongolian areas, and then surveyed Zhili (直隶). In 1710, the Heilongjiang (黑龙江) area was surveyed, and later Shandong (山东), Shanxi (山西), Shaanxi (陕西), Jiangnan (江南), Zhejiang (浙江), Henan (河南), Jiangxi (江西), Guangxi (广西), Guangdong (广东), Huguang (湖广), Fujian (福建) and Taiwan (台湾), as well as the Southwest and part of the Northwest area. For Tibet (西藏), lamas, such as Chu-er-qin (楚儿沁) who studied mathematics at the Imperial Board of Astronomy, and Sheng-zhu (胜住) from Lifanyuan (理藩院, the Court of Colonial Affairs) were assigned to go on the survey expeditions.[17]

In connection with the map-surveying, Kangxi made use of many experts versed in mathematics from across the country (such as Mei Juecheng-梅毂成, He Guozong-何国宗, Ming Antu-明安图 etc.), to compile the *Lüli Yuanyuan* (律历渊源, *Source of the Pitch-Pipes and Calendar*), including *the Shuli Jingyun* (数理精蕴, *Essential Principles of Mathematics*), *Qinruo Lishu* (钦若历书, *Imperial Commissioned Calendrical Sciences*), *Lülü zhengyi* (律吕正义, *Exact Meaning of the Pitch-Pipes*). Mathematicians and astronomers gathered at the Bureau of Mathematics (算学馆, Suanxueguan), the Studio for the Cultivation of Youth (蒙养斋, Mengyangzhai) inside the Imperial villa Changchunyuan (畅春园), and were guided by the missionaries. Jesuits Bouvet, Parrenin, Jartoux, and Jean Françoise Foucquet (傅圣泽, 1665–1741) taught subjects related to mathematics and astronomy.[18] Some of the mathematicians who worked at the Bureau of Mathematics also participated in the map-surveying; for example, He Guozong's brother, He Guodong, "served at the imperial court because of his skill in calendar-making." In Kangxi's 53rd year (1714), he was ordered "to travel to different provinces south of Yangtze, and measure the height of the Pole Star and the shadow of the sun. In Kangxi's 58th year, the map was completed."[19]

In Kangxi's 51st year (1712), some persons "proficient in drawing" were sent to survey and map the mountains and rivers of the Northeast. The geographers had to follow the estimated degrees of the sky, and then draw the maps with details. On the seventh day of the 53rd year of Kangxi (February 20, 1714), Prince Yinzhi and others presented a memorial to the emperor:

In the past, when Guo Shoujing [郭守敬, of the Yuan dynasty] was compiling the *Shoushi* calendar [授时历], many were dispatched to various provinces to observe the shadows of the sun. Therefore the results were accurate. Now, to revise the calendar books, except in Changchunyuan and the observatory, no daily observations are needed in each province. However, only in the seven provinces of Guangdong, Yunnan, Sichuan, Shaanxi, Henan, Jiangnan and Zhejiang, where there are big differences in *li* [里差, literally difference of *li*], it is necessary to dispatch someone to measure the height of the Pole Star and the sun's shadows in order to gather concrete data to understand the differences in *li* between the East, the West, the South and the North, and the radius of the sun on the sky. The imperial order was handed down, saying: Let He Guodong [何国栋] go to Guangdong, Suozhu [索柱] to Yunnan, Bai Yingtang (白映棠) to Sichuan, Gong'e [贡额] to Shaanxi, Nahai [那海] to Henan, Li Ying [李英] to Jiangnan and Zhaohai [照海] to Zhejiang.[20]

The imperial court obviously attributed great importance to map-surveying. Kangxi dealt with the matter in person. He assigned the officers of the Imperial Board of Astronomy, of the Hall of Military Glory (武英殿, *Wuyingdian*), and provincial officials to be in charge of the surveying. The parties were escorted by military personnel. Completed maps were submitted to the imperial court by local governors. In 1716, the map-surveying was completed. Finally, the Jesuits Régis and Jartoux completed the assembling of the multiple maps. In 1718, Emperor Kangxi's atlas *Huangyu Quanlantu* was completed.

The map-surveying during Kangxi's reign, mainly national large-scale geometrical triangulation surveys and the latitude and longitude measurements, was very important. At that time, observations of the lunar eclipses and the immersions and emersions of Jupiter were used to determine longitudes, based on the tables of the French astronomer Giovanni Domenico Cassini and others. Ascertaining the latitudes was done mainly by measuring the height of the sun at noon and the height of the Pole Star. The Jesuit Karl Slavicek (严嘉乐, 1678–1735) also introduced a method to determine the latitudes. Many new instruments were used in the surveys. More than 600 sites were measured to determine the latitudes and the longitudes. This was the world's largest cartographic undertaking up until then.[21]

About the same time, under the guidance of the astronomers of the Royal Academy of Sciences, map-surveying was also conducted in France.[22] The map-surveying of the missionaries naturally was influenced by the Royal Academy of Sciences, since the work was mostly done by the French Jesuits who had close contacts with the Royal Academy. They had mastered new map-surveying methods and used the famous astronomer Cassini's tables on Jupiter. By observing the immersions and emersions of Jupiter, they could ascertain the longitudes, making the observations more precise. In Kangxi's 49th year (1710), Régis and Jartoux worked in the Northeast between the latitudes of 41 and 47 degrees, to determine the distance along the meridian line corresponding to each degree of meridian line. The findings from the surveys showed that the greater the latitude, the larger the distance along each degree of the meridian line. Therefore, it was believed the length of the meridians was certainly unequal.[23] In the early eighteenth century, there was a debate about the shape of the earth between Newton and Cassini. Newton's theory was confirmed by the data and findings of China's extensive cartographic surveys.[24]

IV. *Huangyu Quanlantu* and Jean-Baptiste Bourgignon d'Anville's *Nouvel Atlas de la Chine*

On 12th day of the second month of Kangxi's 58th year (April 1, 1719), the emperor issued a decree to Jiang Tingxi (蒋廷锡), a minister of his cabinet: "The *Huangyu Quanlantu* has cost me more than thirty years' effort to complete." He presented the map to the ministers.[25] There are five editions of *Huangyu Quanlantu*. One copperplate edition, engraved by the Italian missionary Matteo Ripa (马国贤, 1682–1745),[26] two woodcut editions (one in 56th year of Kangxi, one in the 60th year), one color-painted edition (now preserved in the First Historical Archives of China)[27] and a later woodcut edition.[28] On the basis of those maps, after the extensive cartographic surveys, the Jesuits still continued improving the latitudes and longitudes. They sent the relevant data and maps back to France.[29] Later, the French Jesuit J.-B. du Halde (1674–1743) commissioned J.-B. Bourgignon d'Anville (1697–1782), the Royal Cartographer, to make maps and compile them into *Description géographique, historique, chronologique, politique, et physique de l'Empire de la Chine et de la Tartarie chinoise*.[30] The book was translated into many languages,[31] and had great influence in Europe.

In 1737, d'Anville's *Nouvel atlas de la Chine* was published exclusively in The Hague, Netherlands.[32] The atlas included maps of China and neighboring countries (1734), of China alone (Han areas), northern Zhili, Jiangnan, Jiangxi, Fujian, Zhejiang, Huguang (湖广), Henan, Shandong, Shanxi, Shaanxi, Sichuan, Guangdong, Guangxi, Yunnan, Guizhou (贵州), Tartar (鞑靼) (1732), Korea, Tibet etc., and maps of some parts of Northeast China, totaling 42 maps.[33] Those maps either in du Halde's book or in the *Nouvel atlas de la Chine* were the world's most precise and most authoritative China maps before the 20th century. They were widely quoted and affected Europeans' perspectives on the geography of China. Regrettably, Kangxi's atlas *Huangyu Quanlantu* was kept in the palace and its influence was not widespread in China. This limited Qing scholars' views of geography in China.

Notes

1. The author is Professor in the Institute for the History of Natural Sciences, Chinese Academy of Sciences. Professor Han Qi's essay has been translated from Mandarin Chinese into English by Annie Lam.

2. *Shengzu Shilu* (圣祖实录) (II), *Juan* 126, Kangxi 25th Year (Beijing: Zhonghua Book Company, 1985), 342–43.

3. Mme. Yves de Thomaz de Bossière, *Un Belge mandarin à la cour de Chine aux XVIIe et XVIIIe siécles: Antoine Thomas 1644–1709* (Paris, 1977), 67.

4. Qi Han and Wu Min (eds.), *Xichao Chong Zheng Ji, Xichao Ding An (Wai San Zhong)*, (《<熙朝崇正集>，<熙朝定案>(外三种)》) (Beijing: Zhonghua Book Company, 2006), 168–69.

5. Ignace-Gaston Paradies, *Élemens de Géometrie, où par une methode courte & aisée l'on peut apprendre ce qu'il faut sçavoir d'Euclide, d'Archimede, d'Apolonius, & les plus belles inventions des anciens & des nouveaux Géometre.* (Paris: Sebastien Mabre-Cramoisy, 1671).

6. Qi Han, "French Jesuits' scientific activities in China during the Kangxi reign," *Gugong Buowuyuan yuankan*, No. 2 (1998): 68–75; "The Mathematical Education and Its Social Context during the Kangxi Reign," in *Faguo Hanxue (Sinologie Française)* (VIII) (Beijing: Zhonghua Book Company, 2003), 434–48; and "The Jesuits and the Transmission of Mathematical Knowledge during the Kangxi Reign," in *Aomen shi xin bian* (*New History of Macao*) (III), (Macao Foundation, 2008), 967–86.

7. Mme. Yves de Thomaz de Bossière, *Jean-François Gerbillon, S.J. (1654–1707): Mathématicien de Louis XIV, premier superieur general de la Mission française de Chine.* (Leuven: Ferdinand Verbiest Foundation, 1994).

8. The First Historical Archives of China still preserves the maps of France, probably those presented to the imperial court during Kangxi's reign.

9. *Kangxi yuzhi wenji* (康熙御制文集, *Collected Writings of the Kangxi Emperor*) II, *Juan* 19: "From *Dushikou* to *Kalun*, the distance is 800 *li* by rope measurement. [. . .] The Crown Prince can delegate a person to measure by rope. In *Kalun* area, instruments were used to determine the height of the North Pole Star. It was five degrees higher than Beijing. Based on this data, the distance should be 1,250 *li*." In Kangxi's 36th year, on 5th day of leap month of 3rd month, the Crown Prince decreed: "I used the instruments to observe the North Pole Star, it is one degree twenty minutes lower than the capital, there are differences of 2,150 *li* between the East and West. Now, Antoine Thomas used the method to calculate, saying that the solar eclipse is 9 minutes 46 seconds, and it is clear day when the solar eclipse happens. When observed, the solar eclipse lasted for more than 9 minutes 30 seconds, but it was not dark enough to let us see the stars." *Kangxi yuzhi wenji* (*Collected Writings of the Kangxi Emperor*) II, *Juan* 24.

10. Li Guangdi, *Rongcun xu yulu* (榕村续语录), *Juan* 17, Li Qi, ed. Chen Zhuwu, (Beijing: Zhonghua Book Company), 813. *Shengzu shilu, Juan* 210, also has a similar record.

11. Li Guangdi, *Lixiang Benyao* (历象本要), woodblock edition of Qianlong reign, 44–45.

12. Antoine Thomas, who was involved in that matter, also talked about that survey event. His record could serve as a cross-reference to the Chinese. See H. Bosmans, "L'Œuvre scientifique d'Antoine Thomas de Namur, S.J. (1644–1709)," *Annales de la Société Scientifique de Bruxelles* 44 (1924): 169–208, and 46 (1926):154–81. Mme. Yves de Thomaz de Bossierre, *Un Belge mandarin à la cour de Chine aux XVIIᵉ et XVIIIᵉ siècles: Antoine Thomas 1644–1709* (Paris, 1977). The former explains in detail Antoine Thomas's survey work.

13. *Shengzu Ren Huangdi Yuzhi Wenji* (圣祖仁皇帝御制文集), Book III, *Juan* III.

14. *Shengzu Shilu* (III), *Juan* 245 (Beijing: Zhonghua Book Company), 431.

15. *Shengzu Shilu* (III), *Juan* 246 (Beijing: Zhonghua Book Company), 440–41.

16. A. Gaubil, *Correspondance de Pékin, (1722–1759)*, ed. R. Simon, (Geneva, 1970), 301.

17. The Jesuit Pierre Jartoux had taught the lamas some knowledge of mathematics.

18. Qi Han, "The Academy of the Investigations of Things and the Studio for the Cultivation of the Youth—The Scientific Contacts between China and France in the Seventeenth and Eighteenth Centuries," *Faguo hanxue (Sinologie Française)* (IV) (Beijing: Zhonghua Book Company, 1999), 302–24.

19. *Qingshi Gao* (清史稿), *Juan* 283, Book 70 (Beijing: Zhonghua Book Company, 1994), 10185.

20. *Shengzu Shilu* (III), *Juan* 261 (Beijing: Zhonghua Book Company), 571.

21. Before Kangxi's *Huangyu Quanlantu* was surveyed and drawn, some places had already conducted surveys on latitude and longitude. The Jesuits François Nöel (卫方济, 1651–1729), Antoine Thomas and Jean de Fontaney had done many astronomical observations in many places of China. Some of the findings were published. See E. Souciet, *Observations mathématiques, astronomiques, géographiques, chronologiques & physiques tirées des anciens livres chinois ou faites nouvellement aux Indes et à la Chine, par les PP. de la Compagnie de Jesus, redigées et publiées par le P. Souciet* (Paris, 1729–32).

22. Josef Konvitz, *Cartography in France 1660–1848: Science, Engineering, and Statecraft* (Chicago: University of Chicago Press, 1987), 1–31.

23. J.-B. du Halde, *Description géographique, historique, chronologique, politique et physique de l'Empire de la Chine et de la Tartarie chinoise* (Paris: P. G. Le Mercier, 1735), preface, p. XLV. On Jean-Baptiste Régis, see Shannon McCune, "Jean-Baptiste Régis, S.J., An Extraordinary Cartographer," in *Chine et Europe: Evolution et Particularités des Rapports Est-Ouest du XVIe au XXe Siècle* (Taipei, 1991), 237–48.

24. Du Shiran and others, *Zhongguo Kexue Jishu Shigao* (II) (中国科学技术史稿) (Beijing: Science Press, 1982), 213.

25. *Shengzu Shilu* (III), *Juan* 283 (Beijing: Zhonghua Book Company, 1985), 765.

26. There was also a lithograph edition. See Qi Han, "Matteo Ripa's Activities at the Imperial Court as seen from Chinese and Western Sources," in *Matteo Ripa e il Collegio dei Cinesi*, Atti del Colloquio Internazionale, Napoli, 11–12 febbraio 1997, ed. Michele Fatica and Francesco D'Arelli (Naples: Istituto Universitario Orientale, 1999), 71–82.

27. Feng Baolin, "Research on the *Huangyu quanlantu* during the Kangxi Reign," (*Gugong buowuyuan yuankan*, 1985), No.1, pp. 23–31, 35.

28. Walter Fuchs, *Der Jesuiten Atlas der Kanghsi Zeit: China und die Aussenlaender* (Peking, 1943). This map adopted the projection of French cartographer Nicolas Sanson (1600–67). See Wang Qianjin, "New research on the type

of projection in the copperplate edition of *Huangyu Quanlantu,*" *Ziran Kexueshi yanjiu* (*Study in the History of Natural Sciences*) 10/2 (1991): 186–94.

29. *Neifu yuditu*, kept in the Bibliothèque Nationale de Paris (Res. Ge. FF. 14550, a copy in a box with 9 volumes, the first volume missing), with covers in yellow silk, including a universal map, maps of Zhili (with Rehe), Shengjing, Ningguta, Wusuli Jiang, Wula (vol. 2), Jiangnan (vol 3), Jiangxi, Huguang (vol. 4), Fujian, Shandong, Shanxi, Henan (vol. 5), Shaanxi (vol. 6), Sichuan (vol. 7), Guangdong, Guangxi (vol. 8), Yunnan, Guizhou (vol. 9), with the seal of Bibliothèque du Roy, probably sent back to France by the Jesuits.

30. J.-B. du Halde, *Description géographique, historique, chronologique, politique, et physique de l'Empire de la chine et de la Tartarie chinoise, enrichie des cartes generales et particulieres de ces pays, de la carte générale & des cartes particu-lieres du Thibet, & de la Corée, & ornée d'un grand nombre de Figures & de Vignettes gravées en Taille-douce,* 4 vols. (Paris: P.G. Le Mercier, 1735). See T. N. Foss, *A Jesuit Encyclopedia for China: A Guide to Jean-Baptiste du Halde's Description* [. . .] *de la Chine (1735)* (Ph.D. diss., University of Chicago, 1979), as well as his "Reflections on a Jesuit Encyclopedia: Du Halde's Description of China (1735)," in *Appréciation par l'Europe de la tradition chinoise* (Paris: Belles Lettres, 1983), 67–77. Qi Han, *Zhongguo Kexue jishu de xichuan jiqi yingxian* (中国科学技术的西传及其影响) (Shijiazhuang: Hebei People's Publishing House, 1999). Isabelle Landry-Deron, *La preuve par la Chine: la "Description" de J.-B. Du Halde, jésuite, 1735* (Paris: Editions de l'École des Hautes Études en Sciences Sociales, 2002).

31. In 1736, a pirate copy was printed in The Hague, the Netherlands, and was quickly translated into English, German and Russian. J.-B. du Halde, *A Description of the Empire of China and Chinese-Tartary . . . ,* 2 vols. (London: Printed by T. Gardner in Bartholomez-Close, for Edward Cave, at St. John's Gate, 1738–41). The preface described the map as the great treasure of geography. J.-B. du Halde, *The General History of China. Containing a geographical, Historical Chronological, political and physical description of the Empire of China, Chinese Tartary, Corea and Thibet. Including an Exact and Particular account of their customs, manners, ceremonies, religion, arts and sciences. The whole adorn'd with curious Maps, and variety of copper-plates,* 4 vols. (London: Printed by and for John Watts at the Printing-Office in Wild-Court near Lincolns-Inn Field, 1736).

32. Jean-Baptiste Bourguignon d'Anville, *Nouvel atlas de la Chine* (The Hague, 1737). His other writings included *Mémoire de M. d'Anville, Premier Géographe du Roi, Des Académies Royale des Belles-Lettres, & des sciences. Sur la Chine* (Pékin, 1776) and *Traité des mesures itinéraires anciennes et modernes* (Paris: De l'Imprimerie Royale, 1769).

33. In du Halde's *Description géographique, historique, chronologique, politique, et physique de l'Empire de la Chine,* the *Carte générale de la Chine* in the first volume was completed in 1730. However in the *Nouvel atlas de la Chine* (1737), there was no year of production. The *Nouvel atlas de la Chine's* maps of countries neighboring China had some differences with the maps in du Halde's book (vol. 4). Other maps in du Halde's book (vol.1, including all provincial maps) were same as those in the *Nouvel atlas de la Chine.*

REPRODUCTION OF THE ORIGINAL TITLE PAGE AND TRANSLATION OF THE FOREWORD

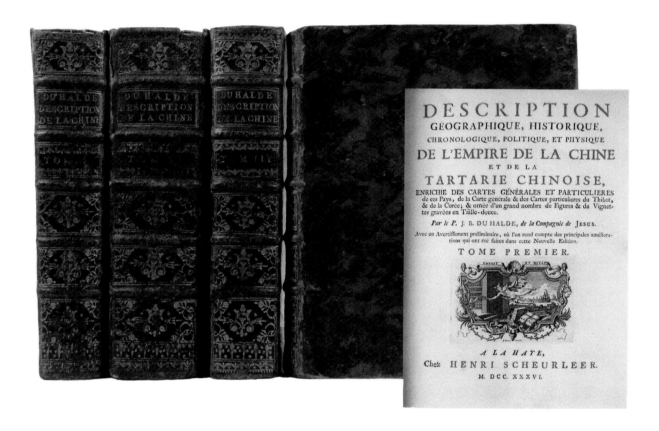

DESCRIPTION
GÉOGRAPHIQUE, HISTORIQUE,
CHRONOLOGIQUE, POLITIQUE, ET PHYSIQUE
DE L'EMPIRE DE LA CHINE
ET DE LA
TARTARIE CHINOISE,
ENRICHIE DES CARTES GÉNÉRALES ET PARTICULIERES
de ces Pays, de la Carte générale & des Cartes particulieres du Thibet,
& de la Corée; & ornée d'un grand nombre de Figures & de Vignet-
tes gravées en Taille-douce.

Par le P. J. B. DU HALDE, *de la Compagnie de* JESUS.

Avec un Avertissement préliminaire, où l'on rend compte des principales améliora-
tions qui ont été faites dans cette Nouvelle Edition.

TOME PREMIER.

A LA HAYE,
Chez HENRI SCHEURLEER.
M. DCC. XXXVI.

DESCRIPTION

GEOGRAPHIQUE

HISTORIQUE, CHRONOLOGIQUE,

POLITIQUE, ET PHYSIQUE

DE L'EMPIRE DE LA CHINE

ET

DE LA TARTARIE CHINOISE,

ENRICHIE DES CARTES GENERALES ET PARTICULIERES
de ces Pays, de la Carte générale & des Cartes particulieres du Thibet, & de
la Corée, & ornée d'un grand nombre de Figures & de Vignettes gravées
en Taille-douce.

Par le P. J. B. DU HALDE, de la Compagnie de JESUS.

TOME QUATRIE'ME.

A PARIS,

Chez P. G. LE MERCIER, Imprimeur-Libraire, rue Saint Jacques,
au Livre d'Or.

M. DCC. XXXV.

AVEC APPROBATION ET PRIVILEGE DU ROY.

NEW ATLAS OF CHINA, CHINESE TARTARY AND TIBET:[1]

Which includes The general and more detailed maps of those
countries as well as the map of the Kingdom of Korea;

*The maps were with the greatest possible accuracy surveyed for
the most part on location by Jesuit Missionaries to China or by
Tatars from the Mathematics Tribunal, by order of Emperor
Kang Xi, They were then all reviewed by the same Fathers.*

*Each map was prepared for publication by M. d'Anville,
official geographer to His Most Christian Majesty.*

*It is preceded by a description of Bukharia written by a
Swedish officer who lived for some time in that land.[2]*

In The Hague,
at Henri Scheurleer.
MCCCXXXVII

Foreword

Having considered it highly desirable to assemble in one body and as a fifth volume all maps pertinent to the *Description de l'Empire de la Chine & de la Tartarie Chinoise* published by Father du Halde, we believe we need to explain the reasons behind our decision. The determining factor is the format of our publication. Obviously, maps of such size, which would have to be folded in a folio publication of the book, and even some maps in this atlas, could not fit into a quarto format without great damage due to folding. This would have also disfigured the volumes by the sheer space taken up between the pages and the thickness it would have imposed on the volumes.

Our purpose has been to please the public: separating maps from the description allows those who wish to ignore the latter to have separate access to the former, in whole or in part. Regarding the ordering of the parts, we have followed what seems most natural. It is true that Korea, as well as the trip of Captain Bering, seem as if they should be placed after the detailed maps of Tibet. Yet, we believe we can assign them another position because the kingdom, bordering on Eastern Tartary on the continental side, is represented on the general map of Chinese Tartary.

Here it would be appropriate to say a word about the significant differences between our maps and those of the Paris edition, but a sufficiently detailed explanation is found in our Preface to volume one of the changes made to a number of maps, which provides a basis for judging the others. However, in order to satisfy our readers who have bought the atlas separately, and to explain when and by whom the maps were drawn, we now provide a brief summary of Father du Halde's original preface.

For the most part the surveying method used was Triangles combined with Eclipses observed in places geographically distant from one other. Those who understand the precision of the two methods, particularly when they are combined and used to support each other, as is the case here, will not doubt the accuracy of the maps.

What follows highlights the time needed to bring to completion this great undertaking, the most extensive of its kind ever achieved, done according to best practice.

The Emperor Kang Xi put the Jesuit missionaries in charge of drawing up the maps of all provinces of China, as well as of Tartary that is subject to him. Fathers Bouvet, Régis and Jartoux undertook work on a map on 4 July 1708 to determine exactly the location of the Great Wall. The map they brought back to Beijing was longer than fifteen feet [*pieds*].

In 1709, Fathers Bouvet, Régis and Fridelli made a map that included the province of Liaodong,[4] the ancient land of the Manchus, the northern limits of Korea, the lands of the Yupik,[5] the settlements of the Kechintase[6] and all the districts of the Mongols from the 45th degree of northern latitude to the 40th.

Those three fathers began on 10 December of the same year [to map] the Beizhili province, and concluded their work on 29 June 1710. On 22 July of the following year, the same fathers received the order to make a map of the new settlements established by the Emperor on the river Amur.[7] It was completed on 14 December 1710 and included mainly the territories of Qiqihar,[8] Mergen and the Amur river. In the year of 1711, Fathers Régis and Cardoso undertook the mapping of the province of Shandong, while Fathers Jardoux, Fridelli and Bonjour, who traveled to the land of Hami,[9] measured almost all the lands of the Khalka. This work was divided up in 1712. Fathers Cardoso and de Tartre were given the provinces of Shanxi, Shaanxi, Jiangxi, Guangdong and Guangxi. The maps they made of the two first provinces each measured ten square feet.

The provinces of Henan and Jiangnan, of Zhejiang and Fujian were given to Fathers de Mailla and Henderer, while Fathers Fridelli and Bonjour did the provinces of Sichuan and Yunnan. But one of the Fathers died [Bonjour], and the other fell sick. Father Régis completed the province of Yunam in 1715, and was later joined by Father Fridelli who by that time had recovered his strength. Together they surveyed the provinces of Guizhou and Huguang.[10] The whole project was completed in 1716 when the missionaries gathered in Beijing. Under the supervision of Father Jartoux, they worked to unify all the provinces into a general map, which was finally presented to the Emperor in 1718.

Tibet was not surveyed by the missionaries, and a different surveying method was employed. Therefore we had to refer to detailed reports made by the Tatars from the Tribunal of Mathematics sent by the Emperor to measure the land. They were given instructions and directions by the Jesuits. The Jesuits were not allowed to enter Korea, and therefore they could not survey it. Although this might seem a problem, it does not mean the result is imperfect. On the contrary, if any map is correct, this is the one, since it was originally surveyed by Korean geographers, under the orders of the king, and the original map is preserved in his palace. The map given here is based on this original. We understand the missionaries did not discover any significant differences between their own observations at the northern borders of the kingdom and the limits marked on the map. Otherwise they would have mentioned it. This circumstance alone validates the accuracy of the map.

Once the maps were coordinated into a single project, Fr. Du Halde presented them to His Most Christian Majesty just as they were received from the missionaries. The maps are preserved in the Royal Library. Before being handed to the engravers, they were given to M. d'Anville, official geographer of His Majesty, who after reviewing them, established the larger maps. For the maps of Tartary he used the one made earlier by Father Gerbillon by comparing it with specific maps, and in order to fill the space, he added Japan and other islands further north. In the general map of Tibet, maps provided its basis but knowledge of the land's boundaries with Industan was also taken into consideration. Finally, the missionaries limited knowledge about countries in the Tibet, Tartary and the Caspian Sea regions meant M. d'Anville had to collect and compare knowledge gathered from elsewhere to accurately compile the most general map.

And that is our summary of Father du Halde's preface. Those who have read the preface can ignore this foreword as it will tell them nothing new. It does serve however to help those who are more interested in the maps of this vast empire and less in the description of China.

But among the other things that M. d'Anville added to the general map, as we have just described it, is the land of Bukhara or Bukharia, which is mentioned only is passing by Father du Halde on page 64 of volume four. We have added a small report of this part of Tartary that has never to this time been printed. It was conveyed to us by a Swedish Officer, who was in fact its author. This is a new merit that our edition holds compared to the one from Paris, and we believe the public will be grateful for it.

[Editor's note: Although the account by the "Swedish officer" is interesting, it is not pertinent to the maps and their making, and therefore we decided not to include it.]

Notes

1. Translation and notes of the original French text is by Filip Nobel, except when otherwise indicated. For all Chinese names, the translator has used the modern pinyin transcription.

2. Emperor Kang Xi 康熙 was the fourth Emperor of the Qing dynasty and ruled the Chinese Empire from 1661 to 1722. The geographic name, rendered as Boucharie in French, appears as Bucharia in books printed in English from the seventeenth century on. The translator has opted for the "Bukharia" spelling which is the closest to the original Turkic pronunciations of the city of Bukhara (pronounced Bokhara in Persian/Tajik).

3. In an effort to simplify and unify all persons and geographic names in accord with contemporary usage and the most commonly accepted spelling, the translator used Bering (even though the French original uses Beerings).

4. Liaodong, 辽东, covers the south-east of Manchuria, or what is now China's Northeast region.

5. The original French says Yupitase, which most likely refers to the Yupik, a Siberian native nation, also present in today's Alaska.

6. The name of the people living on the Dondon and on the Amur below Dondon

7. The French original uses the name of Saghalien-Oula, which refers to the Amur River in its original Manchu form.

8. Qiqihar is the pinyin version of 齐齐哈尔, Cicigar in Manchu, its original name.

9. Hami is a city in today's Xinjiang, which also had the name of Kumul, قۇمۇل in Uyghur and also appears under the name of *Camull* (to be mentioned later in the Atlas) on European maps from the sixteenth century. The Chinese name is Kunmo 昆莫.

10. The Province of Huguang (湖广) was divided under the Qing dynasty as today's provinces of Hubei (湖北) and Hunan (湖南).

LIST AND ORDER
OF THE MAPS.

1. The most general map of all, including China, Tartary and Tibet   74

2. General map of China   76

3. The Province of Beizhili 北直隶   80

4. The Province of Jiangnan 江南   82

5. The Province of Jiangxi 江西   84

6. The Province of Fujian 福建   86

7. The Province of Zhejiang 浙江   88

8. The Province of Huguang 湖广   90

9. The Province of Henan 河南   92

10. The Province of Shandong 山东   94

11. The Province of Shanxi 山西   96

12. The Province of Shaanxi 陕西   98

13. The Province of Sichuan 四川   100

14. The Province of of Guangdong 广东   102

15. The Province of of Guangxi 广西   104

16. The Province of of Yunnan 云南   106

17. The Province of of Guizhou 贵州   108

18. General map of Chinese Tartary   110

19. First detailed page [of Chinese Tartary]   114

20. Second detailed page [of Chinese Tartary]   116

21. Third detailed page [of Chinese Tartary]   118

22. Fourth detailed page [of Chinese Tartary]   120

23. Fifth detailed page [of Chinese Tartary]   122

24. Sixth detailed page [of Chinese Tartary]   124

25. Seventh detailed page [of Chinese Tartary]   126

26. Eighth detailed page [of Chinese Tartary]   128

27. Ninth detailed page [of Chinese Tartary]   130

28. Tenth detailed page [of Chinese Tartary]   132

29. Eleventh detailed page [of Chinese Tartary]   134

30. Twelfth detailed page [of Chinese Tartary]   136

31. The Kingdom of Korea   138

32. General Map of Tibet   140

33. First detailed page [of Tibet]   142

34. Second detailed page [of Tibet]   144

35. Third detailed page [of Tibet]   146

36. Fourth detailed page [of Tibet]   148

37. Fifth detailed page [of Tibet]   150

38. Sixth detailed page [of Tibet]   152

39. Seventh detailed page [of Tibet]   154

40. Eighth detailed page [of Tibet]   156

41. Ninth detailed page [of Tibet]   158

42. Captain Bering's trip   160

FACSIMILE OF THE MAPS

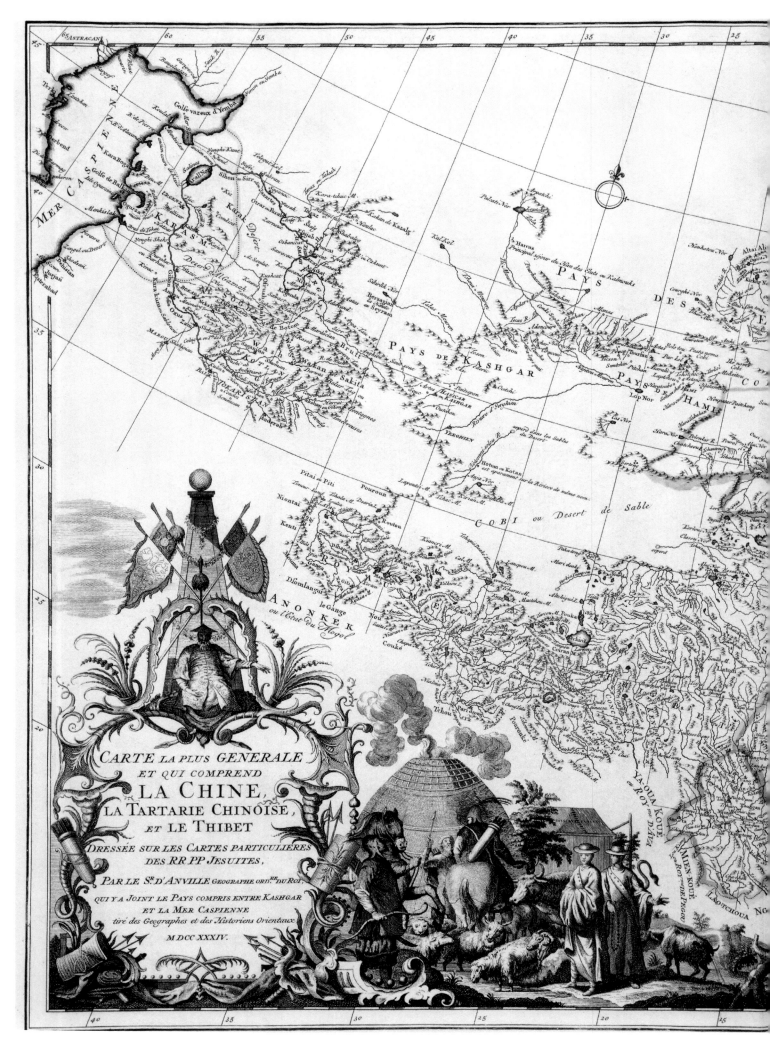

MAP 1.   The most general map of all, including China, Tartary and Tibet

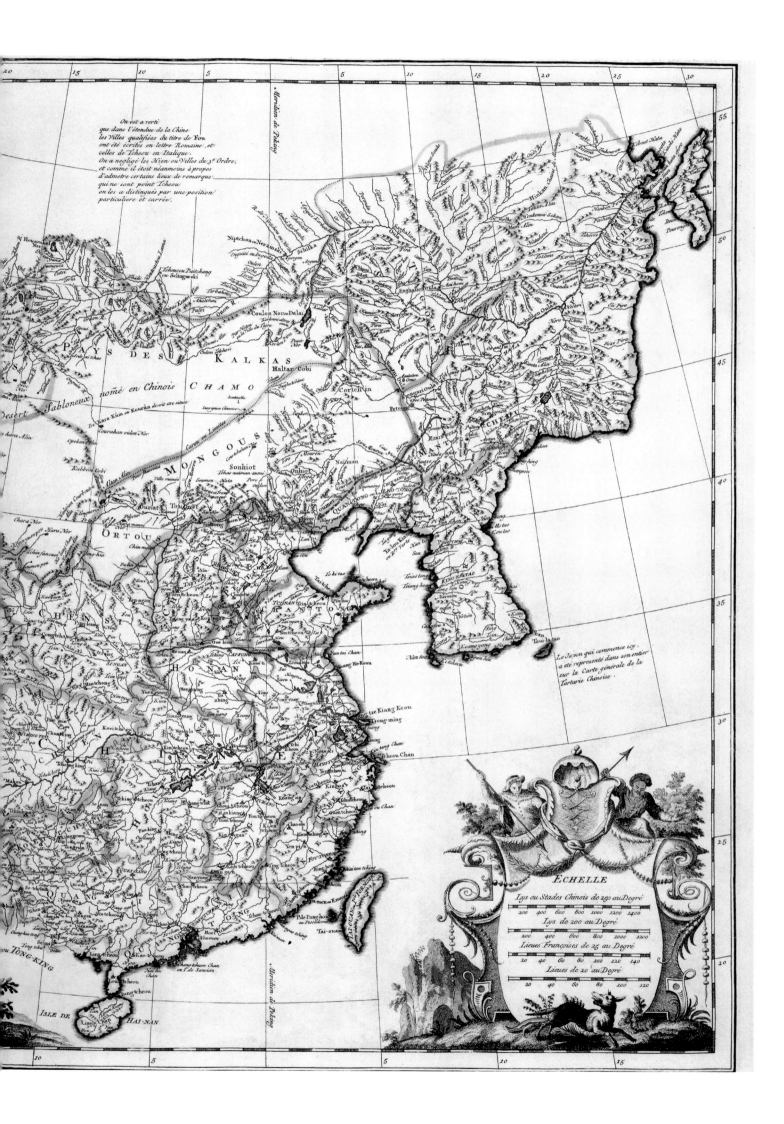

On est averti
que dans l'étendue de la Chine
les Villes qualifiées du titre de Fou
ont été écrites en lettre Romaine, et
celles de Tcheou en Italique.
On a negligé les Hien ou Villes du 3e Ordre,
et comme il étoit néanmoins à propos
d'admettre certains lieux de remarque
qui ne sont point Tcheou
on les a distingués par une position
particuliere et carrée.

PAYS DES KALKAS

nomé en Chinois CHAMO

Desert Sabloneux

MONGOUS

Sonhiot

ORTOUS

CHENSI

HONAN

CHINE

HOQUANG

TCHEKIANG

CHANTONG

KIANG-NAN

SE-TCHUEN

QUEICHEOU

HOUQUANG

KOEITCHEOU

QUANG-SI

QUANG-TONG

TONG-KING

ISLE DE HAI-NAN

TAI-OUAN ou FORMOSE

KIN-CHEOU

PE-TCHE-LI

LEAO-TONG

QUANTONG

CORÉE

KING-KI-TAO

Le Japon qui commence icy
a été représenté dans son entier
sur la Carte générale de la
Tartarie Chinoise.

ÉCHELLE

Lys ou Stades Chinois de 250 au Degré
200 400 600 800 1000 1200 1400

Lys de 200 au Degré
200 400 600 800 1000 1200

Lieues Françoises de 25 au Degré
20 40 60 80 100 120 140

Lieues de 20 au Degré
20 40 60 80 100 120

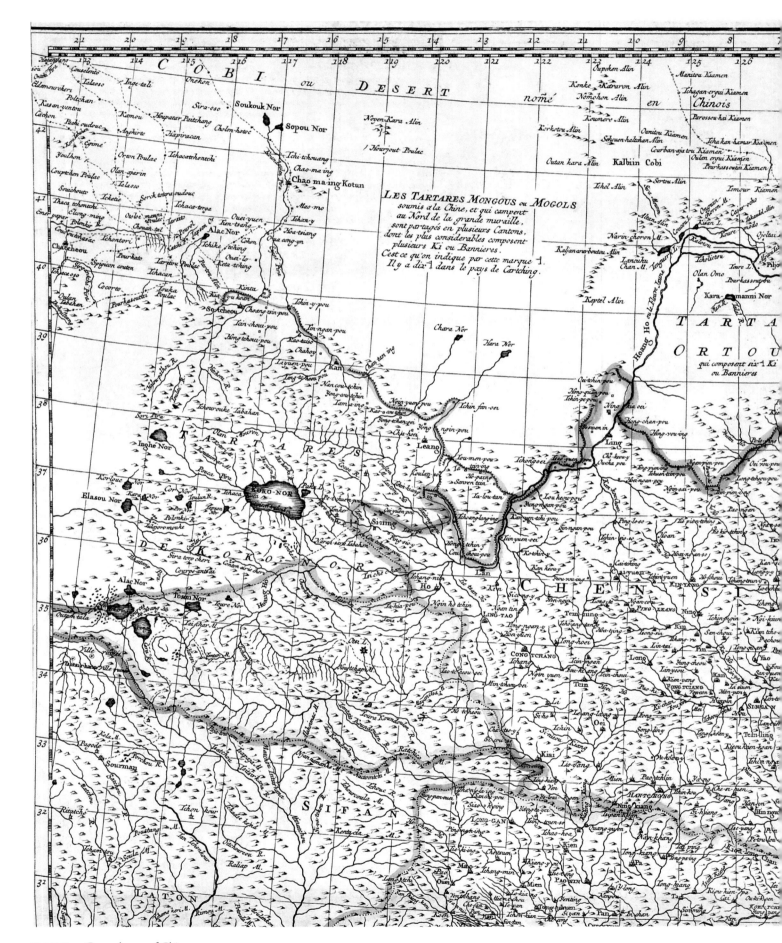

MAP 2.   General map of China
(JOINS AT PAGE 68–69 AT BOTTOM)

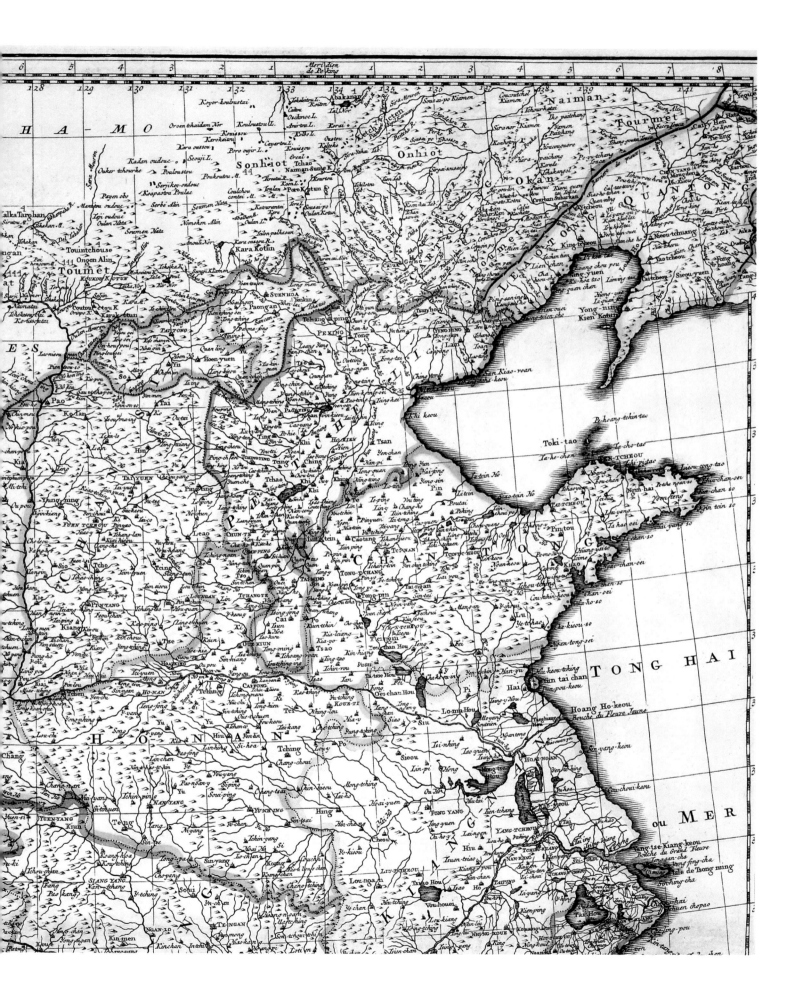

MAP 2.   General map of China
(JOINS AT PAGE 66–67 AT TOP)

CARTE GENERALE DE LA CHINE
DRESSÉE SUR LES CARTES PARTICULIERES
QUE L'EMPEREUR CANG-HI A FAIT LEVER SUR LES LIEUX
PAR LES R.R.P.P.JESUITES MISSIOÑAIRES DANS CET EMPIRE
PAR LE Sr.d'ANVILLE GEOGRAPHE ORDre. DU ROI.

Lys ou Stades Chinois, dont 250 font un Degré.
50 100   200   300   400   500   600   700   800   900   1000

Lieues communes de France, à 25 au Degré.
5   10   20   30   40   50   60   70   80   90   100

Lieues Marines, à 20 au Degré.
5   10   20   30   40   50   60   70   80

MER DU MIDI

NAN HAI ou

L'ORIENT

FORMOSE

HAI-NAN

Tropique du Cancer

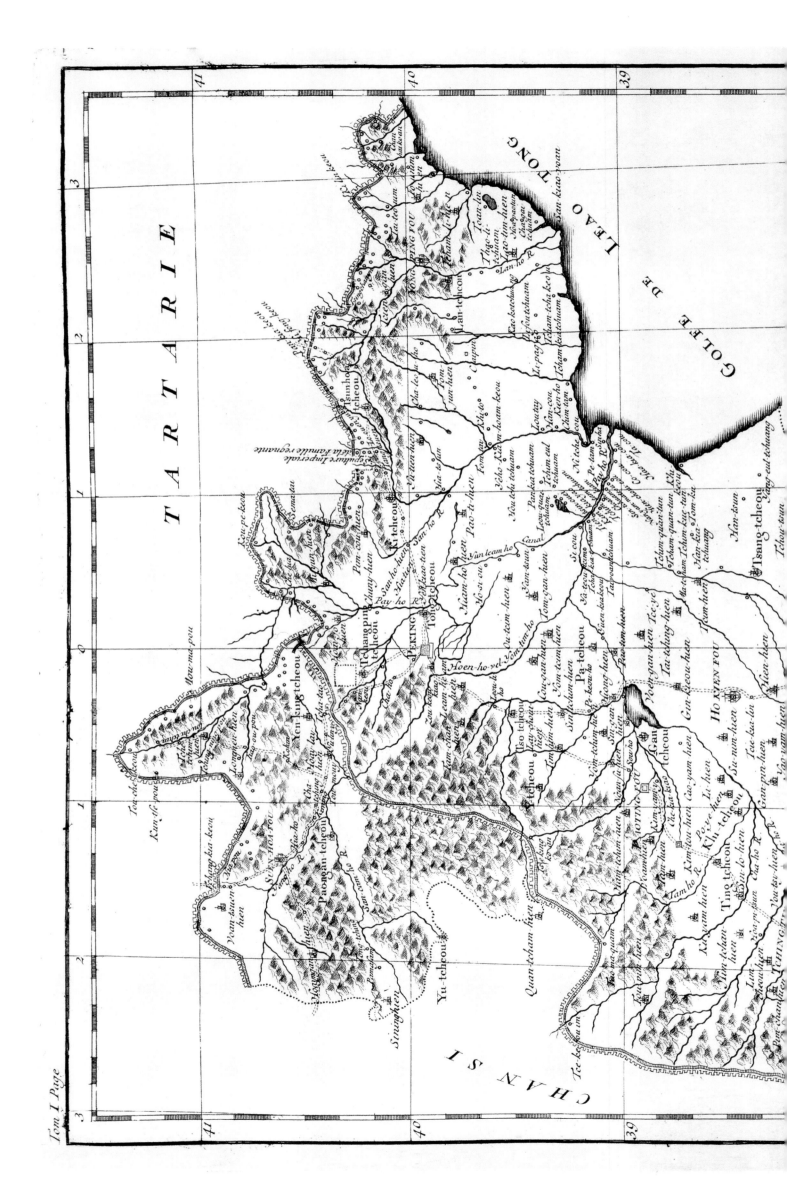

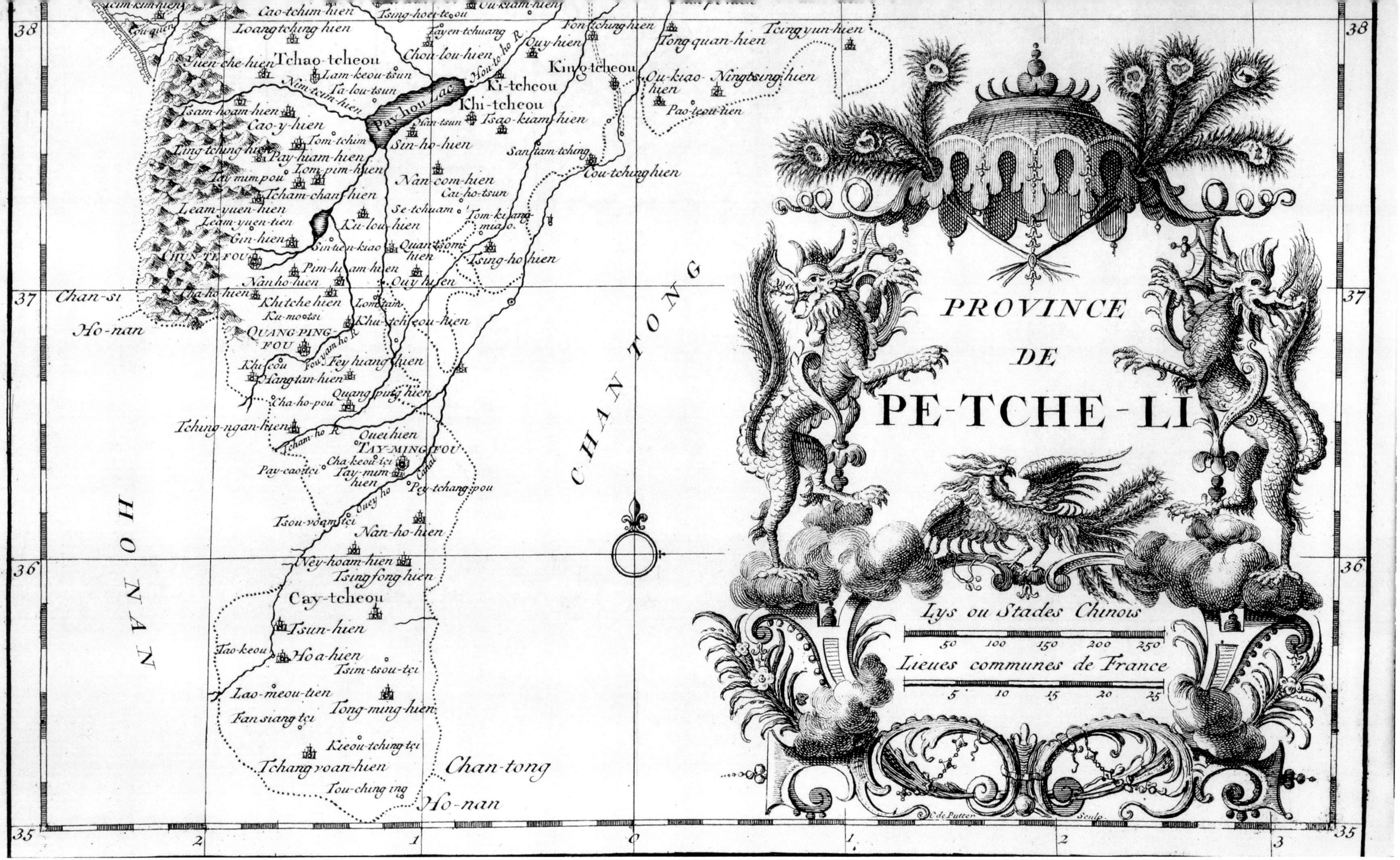

MAP 3. The Province of Beizhili 北直隶

PROVINCE DE PE-TCHE-LI

Lys ou Stades Chinois

Lieues communes de France

50 100 150 200 250

5 10 15 20 25

CHAN TONG

HO NAN

Chan-tong

Ho-nan

Chan-si

Ho-nan

Tchao-tcheou

King-tcheou

Ki-tcheou

Chi-tcheou

Quang ping fou

Cay-tcheou

Tsun-hien

TAY-MING FOU

Tsong-yuen-hien

Tong-quan-hien

Ningtsung-hien

Pao- long-hien

CHAN - TONG

Hoang-ho-keou

Hoang-ho

Hai-tcheou

Kao - yeou-hou

N A N

H o

MAP 4.   The Province of Jiangnan 江南

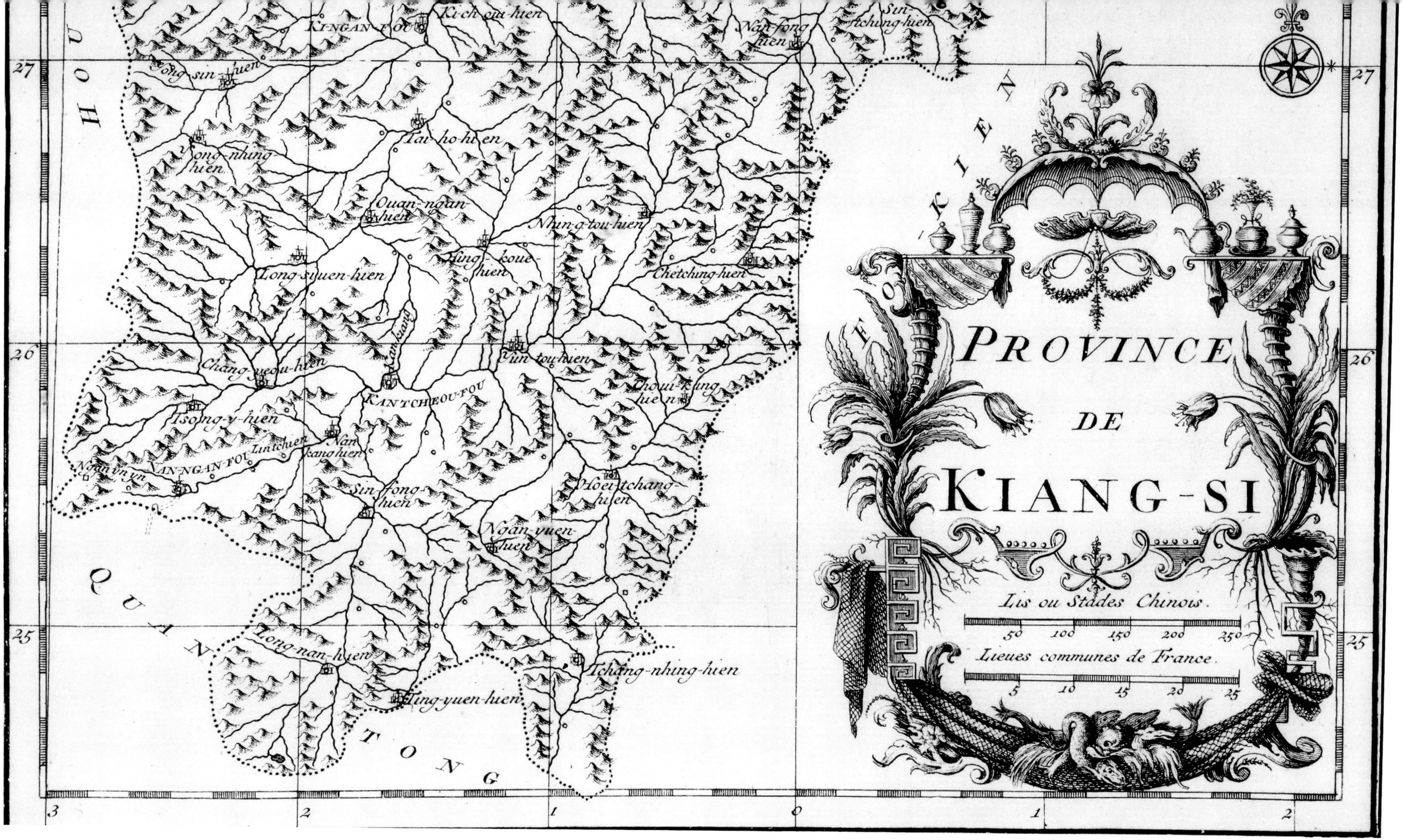

MAP 5. The Province of Jiangxi 江西

PROVINCE

DE

KIANG-SI

Lis ou Stades Chinois.

Lieues communes de France.

FO-KIEN

HOU-QUAN

TONG

QUAN-TONG

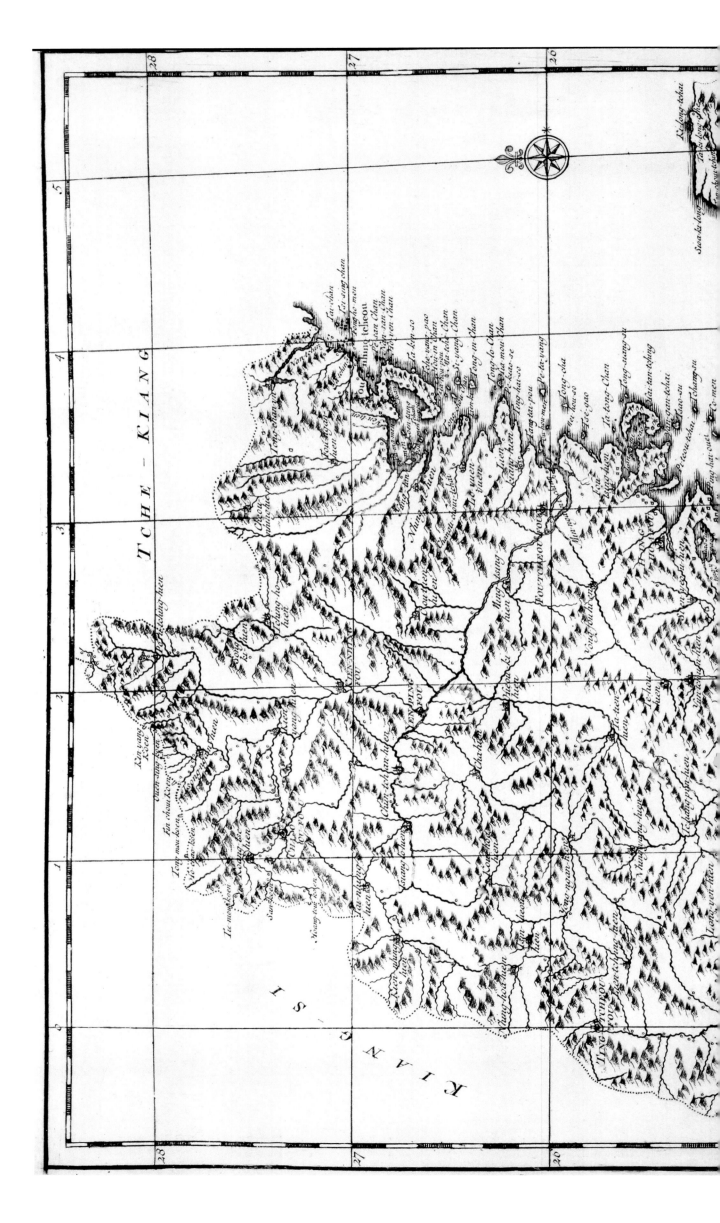

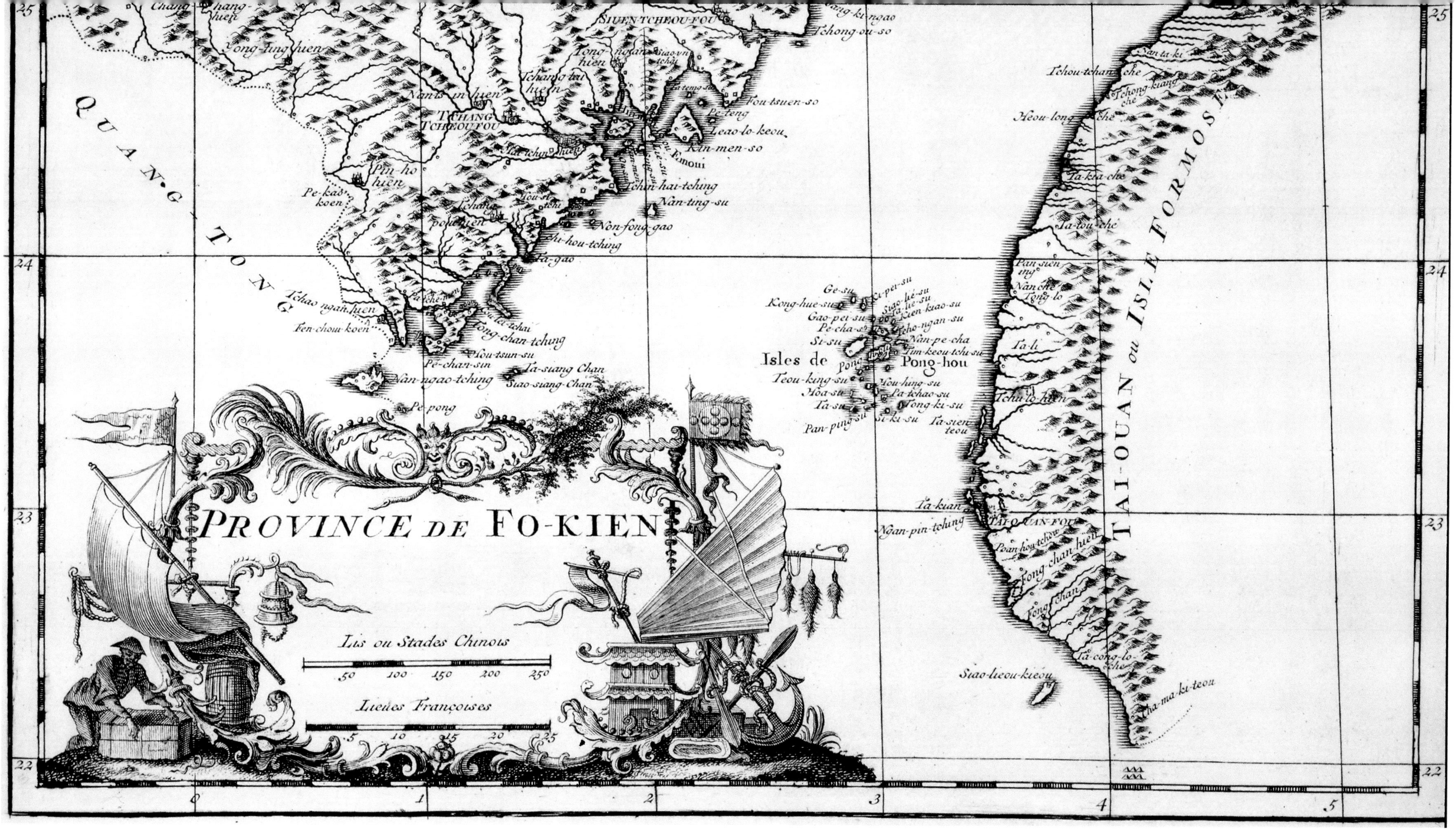

QUANG-TONG

PROVINCE DE FO-KIEN

TAI-OUAN ou ISLE FORMOSE

Isles de Pong-hou

Pong-hou

SIUEN-TCHEOU-FOU

Emoui

TCHANG-TCHEOU-FOU

Lis ou Stadias Chinois
50   100   150   200   250

Lieües Françoises
5   10   15   20   25

MAP 6.   The Province of Fujian 福建

PROVINCE DE TCHE KIANG

ORIENT

KIANG-NAN

Ngan ki-tcheou

Tai-hou

Fai-hou

Tchou-chan Isle

Tchang yu-hien

NING-PO-FOU

CHAO-HING FOU

HANG-TCHEOU

KIA-HING FOU

HOU TCHEOU FOU

YEN-TCHEOU-FOU

KIN-HOA-FOU

MAP 7. The Province of Zhejiang 浙江

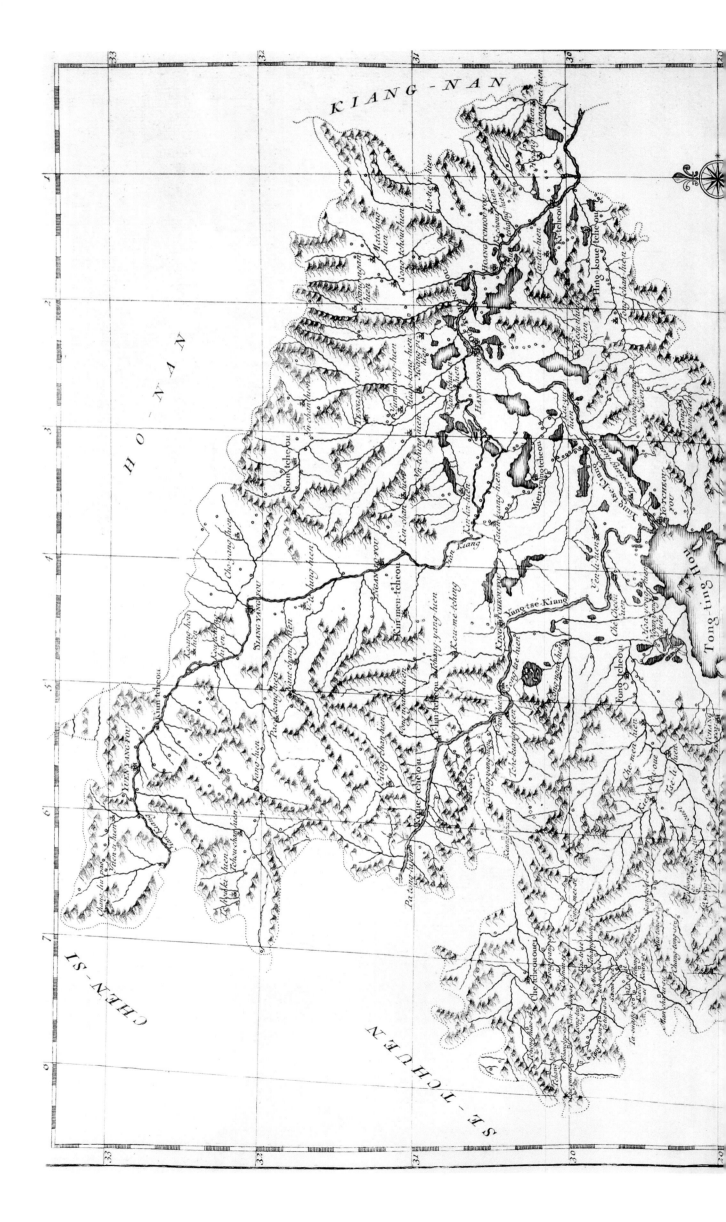

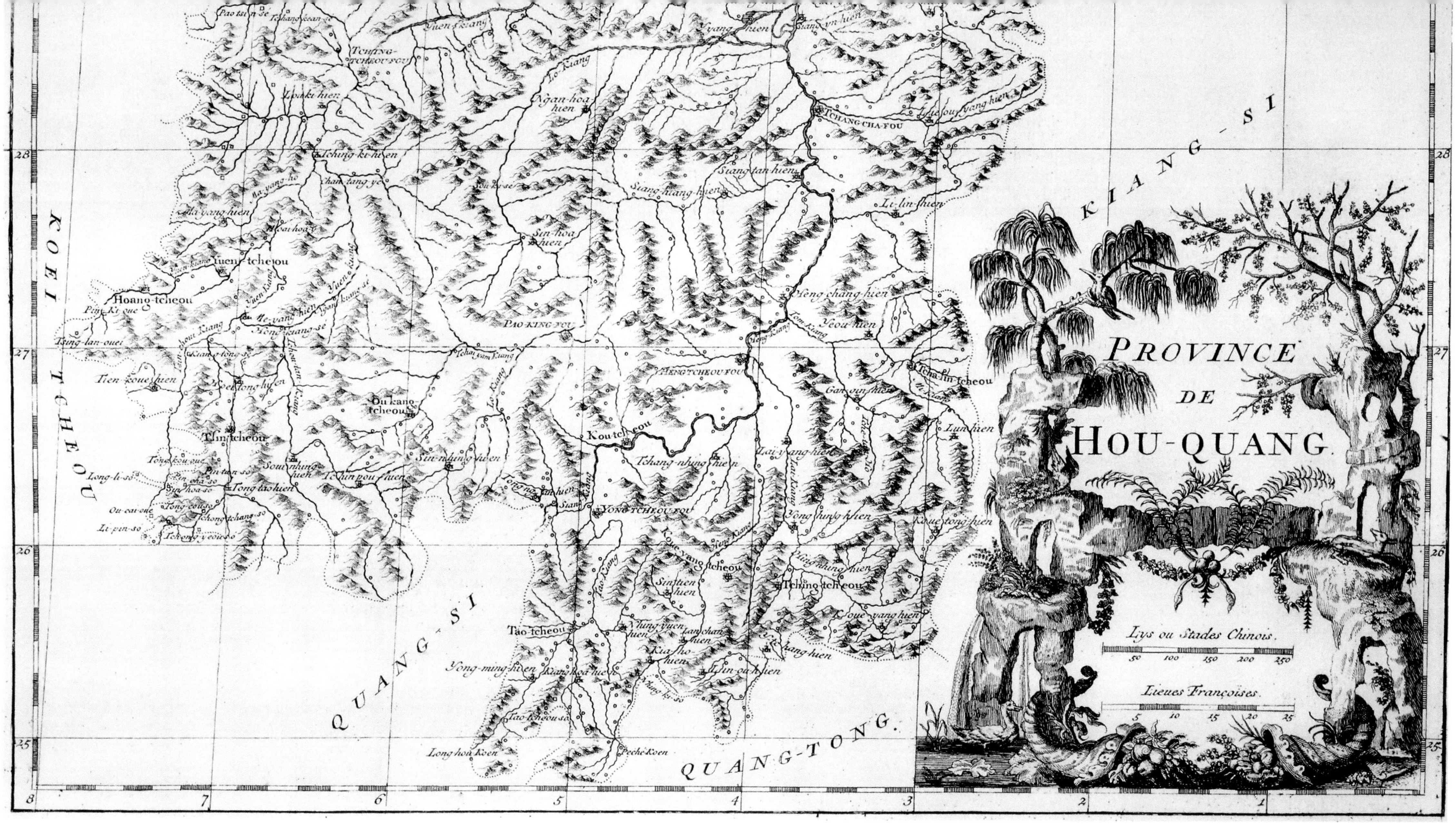

MAP 8. The Province of Huguang 湖广

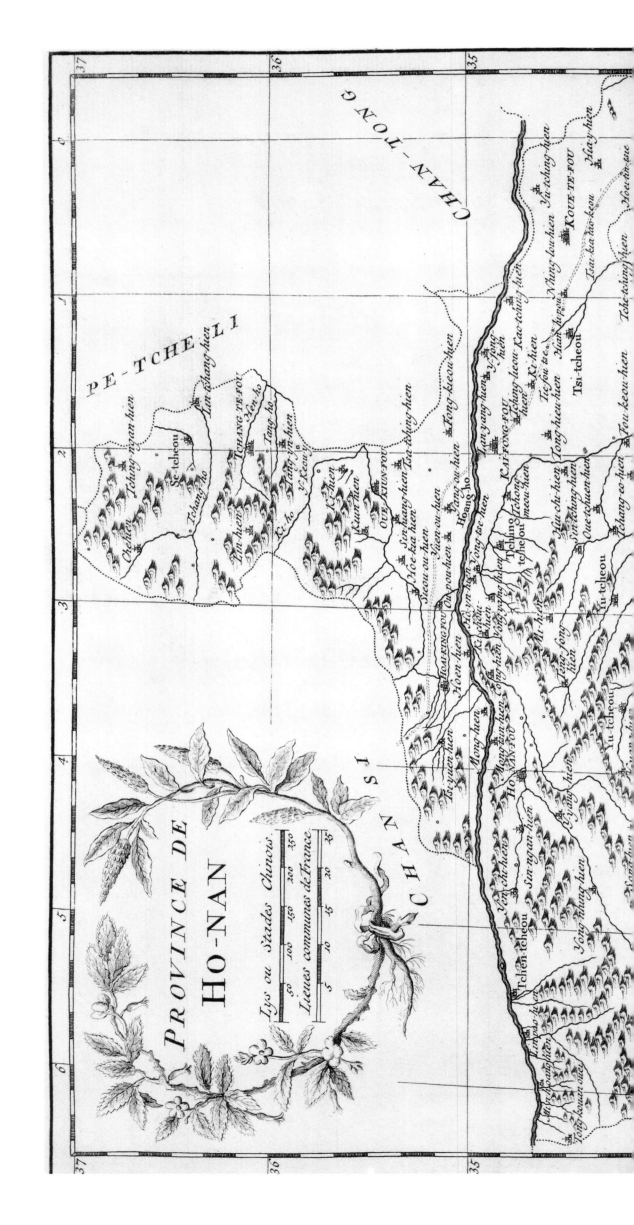

PE - TCHE LI

PROVINCE DE
HO-NAN

Lys ou Stades Chinois.

Lieues communes de France.

CHAN - TONG

CHANSI

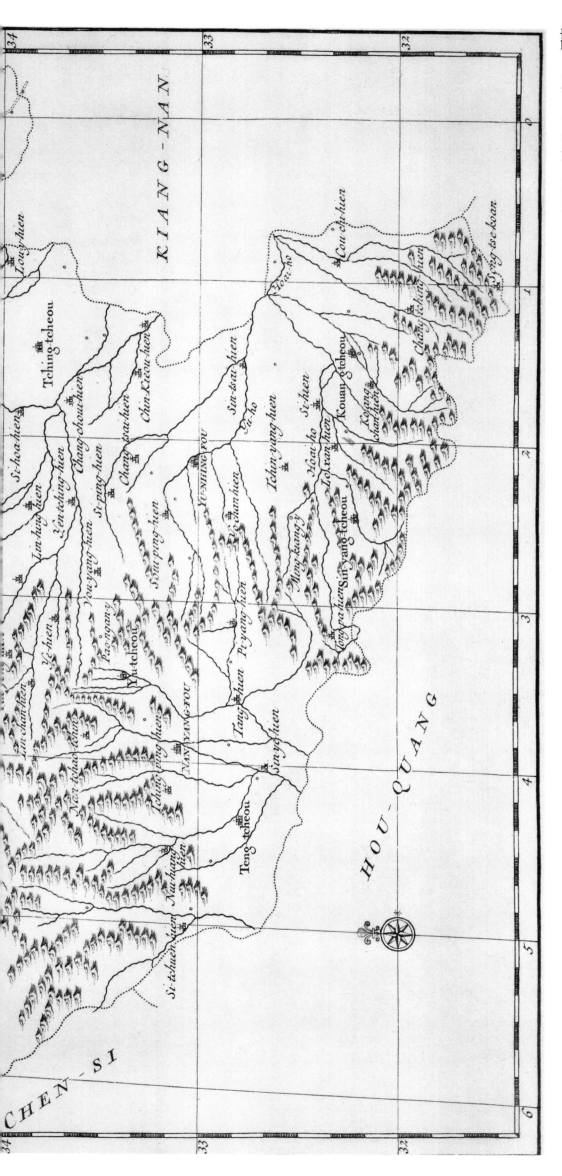

MAP 9. The Province of Henan 河南

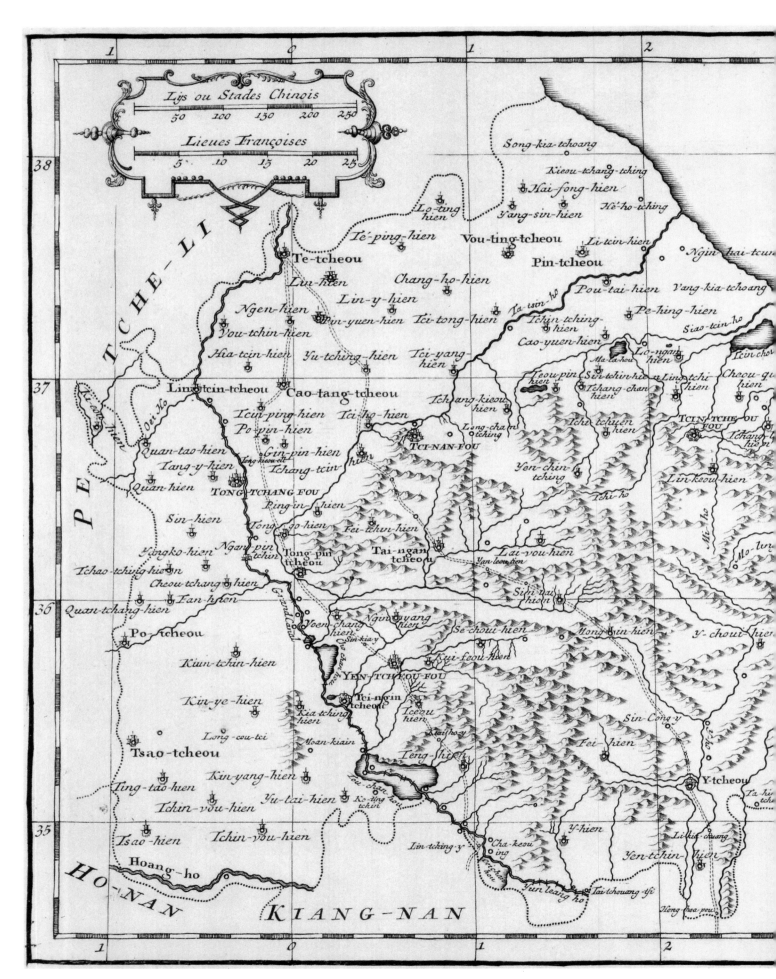

MAP 10. The Province of Shandong 山东

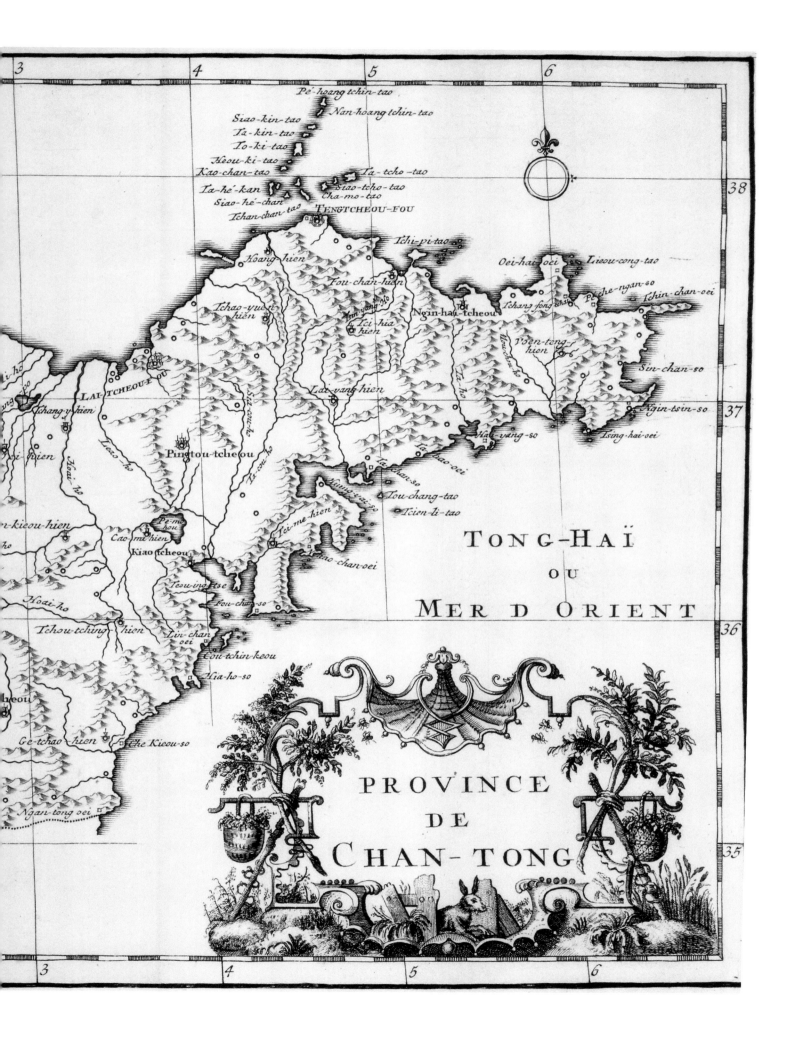

3   4   5   6

Pé-hoang tchin-tao

Siao-kin-tao   *Nan-hoang tchin-tao*

Ta-kin-tao

To-ki-tao

Heou-ki-tao

Kao-chan-tao   *Ta-tcho-tao*

Ta-hé-kan   *Siao-tcho-tao*

Siao-hé-chan   *Cha-mo-tao*

Tchan-chan-tao   TENGTCHEOU-FOU

38

Tchi-pi-tao

Oei-hai oei   *Lieou-cong-tao*

Hoang-hien

Fou-chan-hien

Tchang-song-tchao   *Pe-che-ngan-so*   *Tchin-chan-oei*

Tchao-yuen hien

Tsin-yang so

Tci-hia hien   *Ngin-hai-tcheou*   *Foen-teng-hien*

Sin-chan-so

ho   LAI TCHEOU-FOU

Tchang-y-hien   *Lai-yang hien*   *Ngin-tsin-so*   37

Tci hien   *Keou ho*   *Liao ho*   *Hai-yang-so*   *Tsing-hai-oei*

Pingtou-tcheou   *Ta-cou-ho*

Ta-tcho-oei

Si-cou-ho   *Ta-chan-so*

Pe-ma hou   *Niang-tai-so*   *Tou-chang-tao*

n-kieou-hien   *Cao-me hien*   *Tci-me hien*   *Tcion-li-tao*

ho   *Kiao tcheou*

TONG-HAÏ

Teou-ing-tse   *Niao-chan-oei*

Hoai-ho   *Fou-chan-so*   OU

Tchou-tching-hien   *Lin-chan-oei*   36

Cou-tchin-keou   MER D ORIENT

Hia-ho-so

heou   *Ge-tchao hien*   *Che Kieou-so*

Ngan-tong oei

PROVINCE

DE

CHAN-TONG

35

3   4   5   6

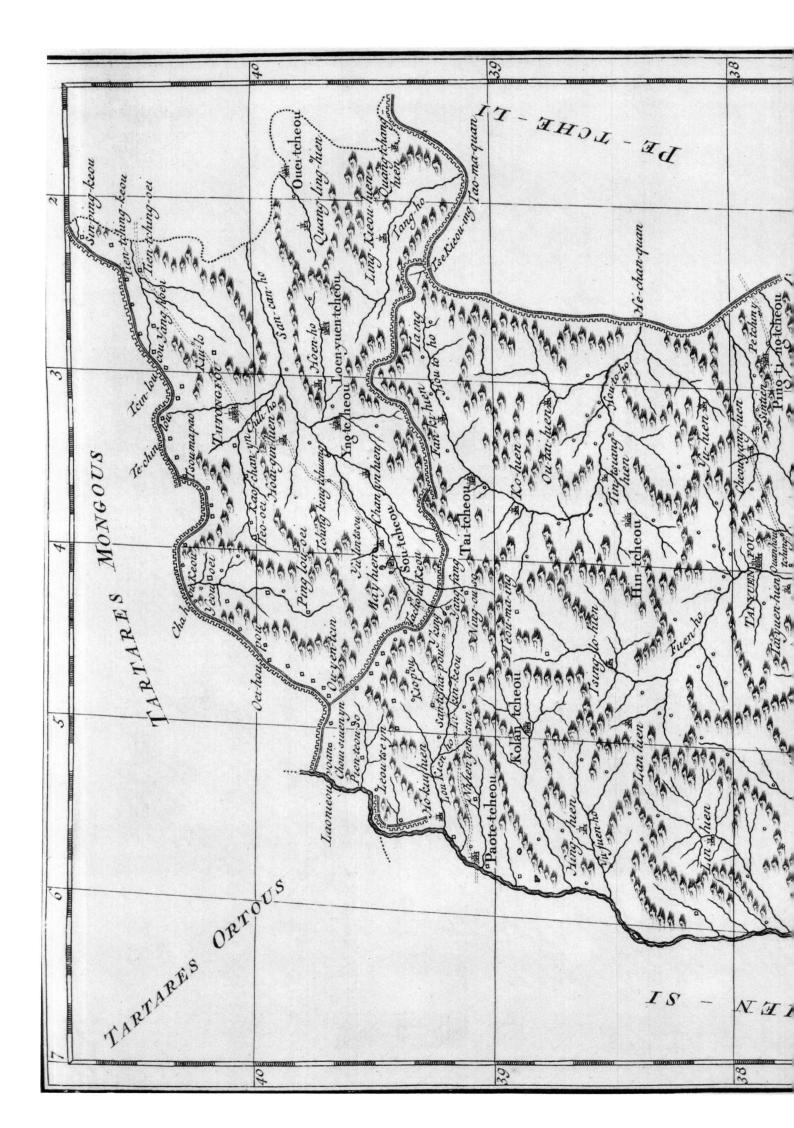

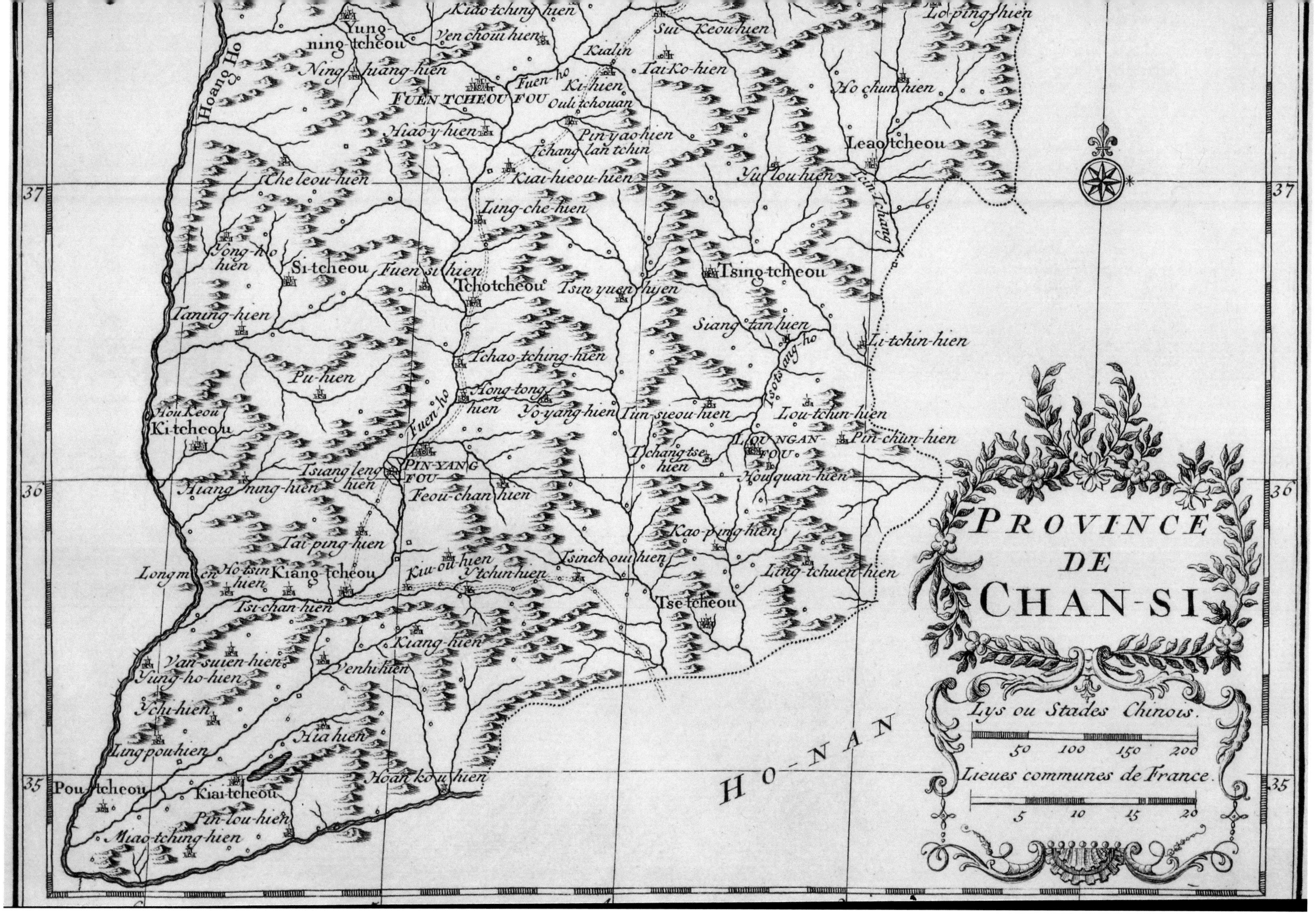

PROVINCE DE CHAN-SI

Lys ou Stades Chinois.
50   100   150   200

Lieues communes de France.
5   10   15   20

HONAN

Hoang-Ho

MAP 11.   The Province of Shanxi 山西

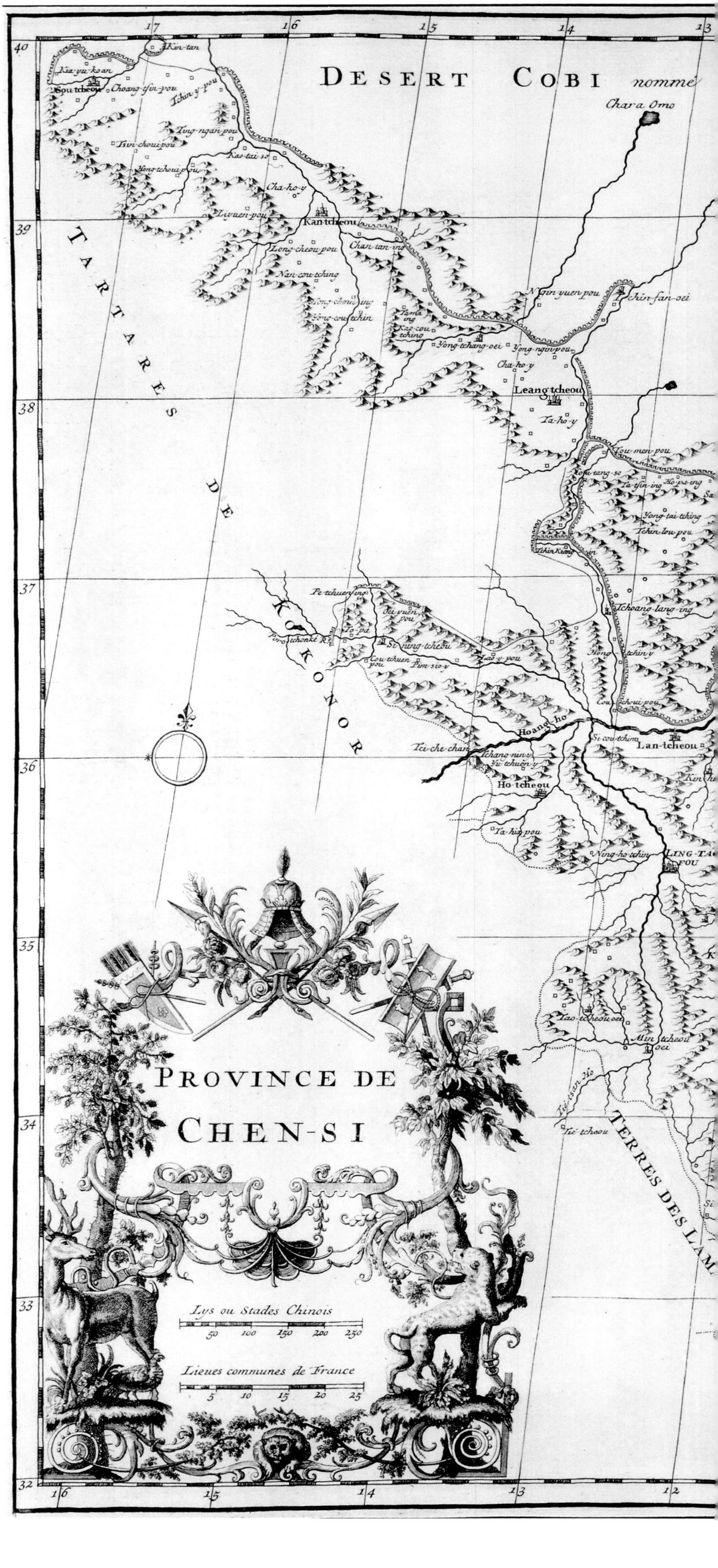
DESERT COBI nommé
Chara Omo
TARTARES DE KOKONOR
Kan-tcheou
Leang-tcheou
Hoang-ho
Lan-tcheou
Ho-tcheou
LING-TAO FOU
TERRES DES LAM
PROVINCE DE CHEN-SI
Lys ou Stades Chinois
50 100 150 200 250
Lieues communes de France
5 10 15 20 25

MAP 12. The Province of Shaanxi 陕西

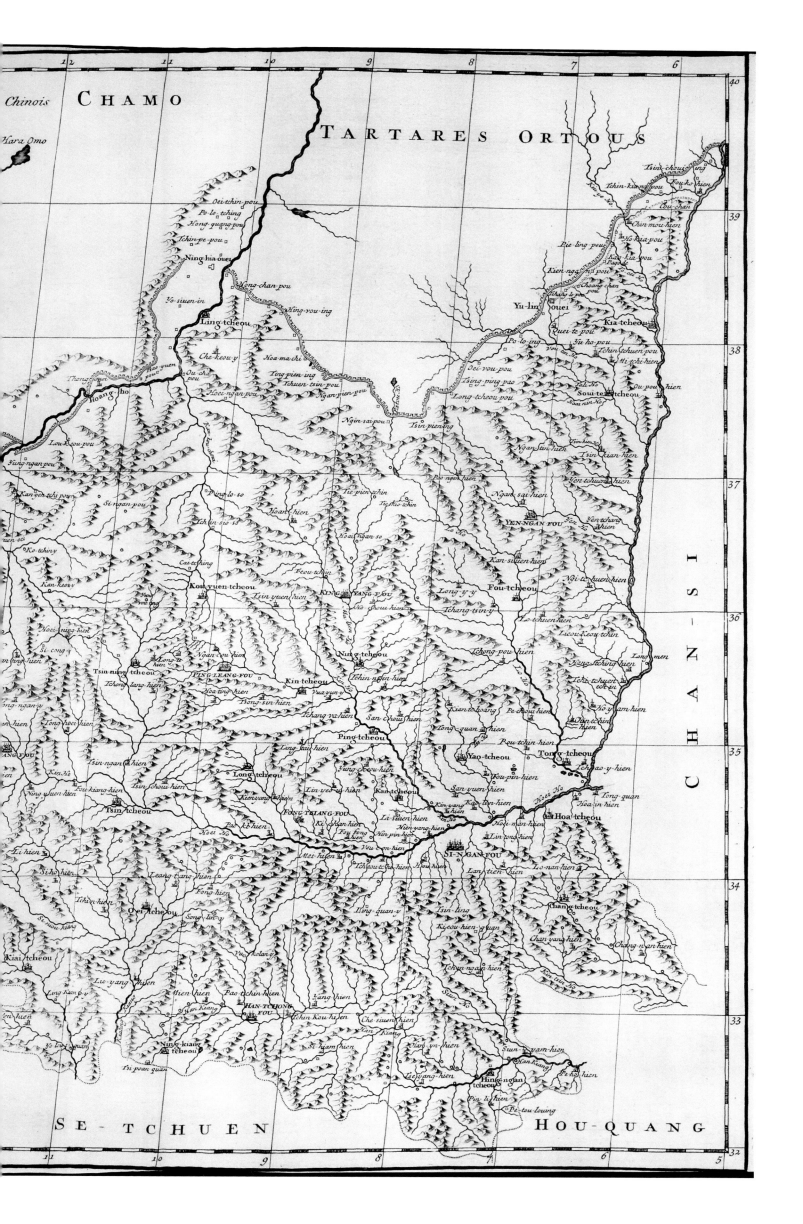

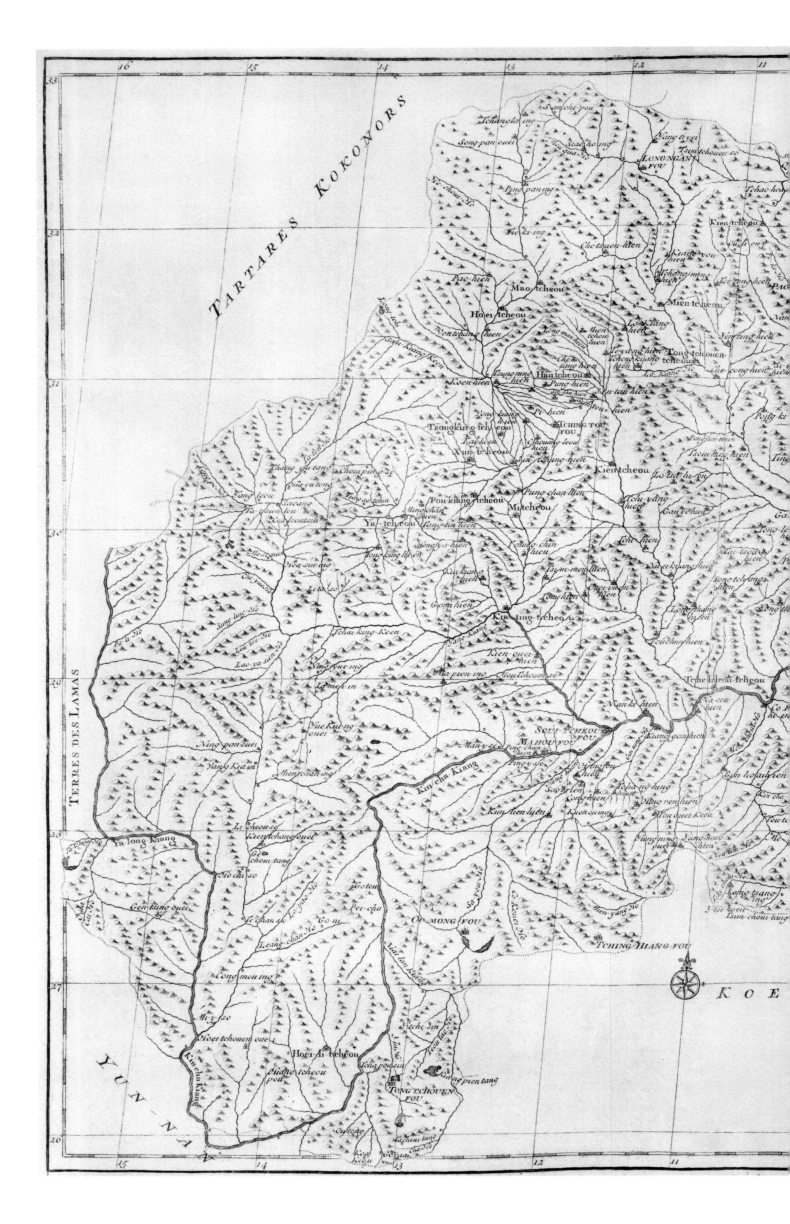

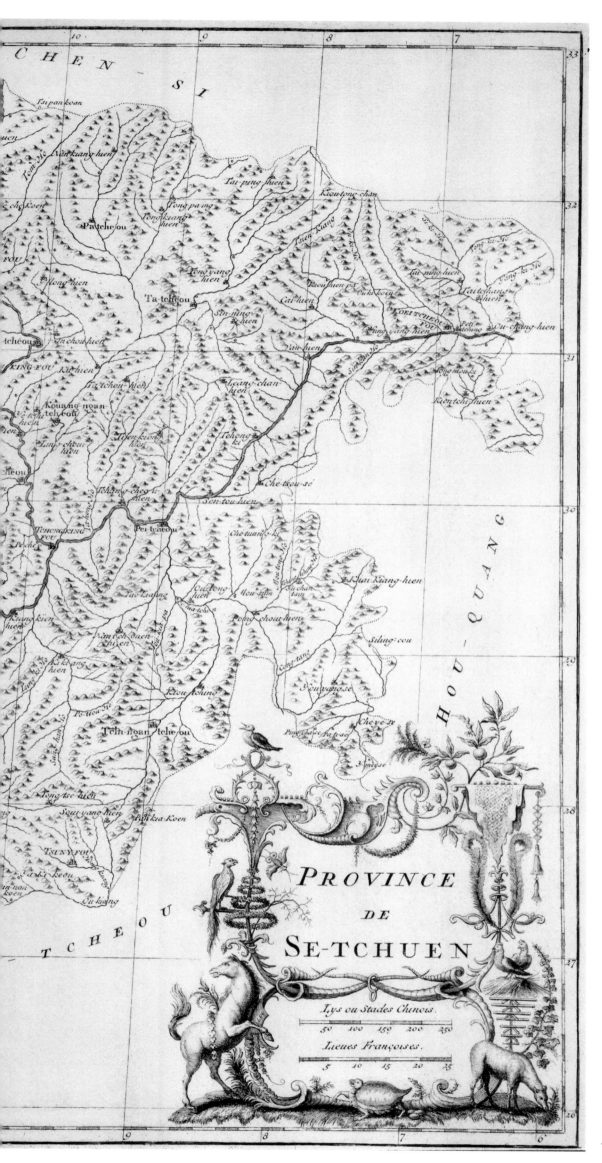

CHEN SI

Tsi pan koan

Nan kuang hien

Tai ping hien

Tong pa ing

Kiou tong chan

Pa tcheou

Tong kiang hien

Tong yang hien

Tsien Liang

Tai ning hien

Tong ki he

Tong ki he

Hong hien

Ta tcheou

Sin ning hien

Tcheou hien

Rcou hien po

Ouki koen

Cai hien

KOEI TCHEOU FOU

Tai tchang hien

Peti tchong

Ou chang hien

Tcheou hien

Incheu hien

Yan hien

Ping yang hien

Sin chui hou

KING FOU

Kiu hien

Tseu tcheou hien

Leang chan hien

Ouo mou ki

Kouang noan tch cou

Kien tchi hien

Tsien kiong hien

Tcheng ki

Lang chou hien

Tchang tcheou hien

Che tsou se

Sen tou hien

Tchong king fou

Pei tcheou

Che tuang ki

Ou tong hien

Hou sin

Siu chan tsun

Kiai Kiang hien

Kiang kien

Tao liang

Pong chou hien

Silung cou

Nan tch ouen hien

Cong tang

Tchi kiang hien

Tong yang se

Riou tchong

Che ye se

Ps tcou

Tch noan tcheou

Ping chang se fa tse

Tmeuse

Tong tse hien

Sou yang hien

Pat kia koen

TSIN Y FOU

La ki keou

in naa koen

Ou kiang

T C H E O U

HOU-QUANG

PROVINCE
DE
SE-TCHUEN

Lys ou Stades Chinois.
50 100 150 200 250

Lieues Françoises.
5 10 15 20 25

MAP 13.
The Province of Sichuan 四川

MAP 14.
The Province of
Guangdong 广东

Map labels:

Lys ou Stades Chinois.

50 100 150 200 250

Lieües communes de France.

5 10 15 20 25

QUANG SI

HOU...

Cu kien hien
Fong tchuen hien
Te king tcheou
Si ning hien
Fong men so
Tong ngan hien
Laoting tcheou
Le king so
Sin hing
Tai p...
Lishe chan hien
Sung y hien
Ting tchun hien
Ngen ping hien
Ngouing
Kao tcheou fou
Kin tcheou
Kien Kiang
Lien Kiang
Lie tcheou fou
Hoa tcheou
Yang kiang hien
Tai lang s...
Ngan nan kiang
Chefi chang hien
Hien yo hien
Choam yu so
Siao lin Chan
Hoa tcheou
NGAN-NAN ou TONG KING
Seu kie hien
Cu tchuen hien
Fang ki Chan
Long men so
Sin men kiang
Tchi ho vai ha
N A N
Tan choui Kiang
LEI TCHEOU FOU
Nan hai hiu
Su lie
Sieuen hien
Chin li hien
QIONG TCHEOU FOU
Feou Kieou Chan
ISLE
Linkao hien
Ting ngan hien
Ouen tchang hien
Tchen tcheou
Tcin lan so
Tchang hoa hien
Hoei tong hien
Limoui Kiang
TCHI CHAN
Hoei hien
Kan ngen hien
LI MOU CHAN
Ouan tcheou
Ling choui hien
Teng kao
Tsiao tcheou
DE HAI-NAN

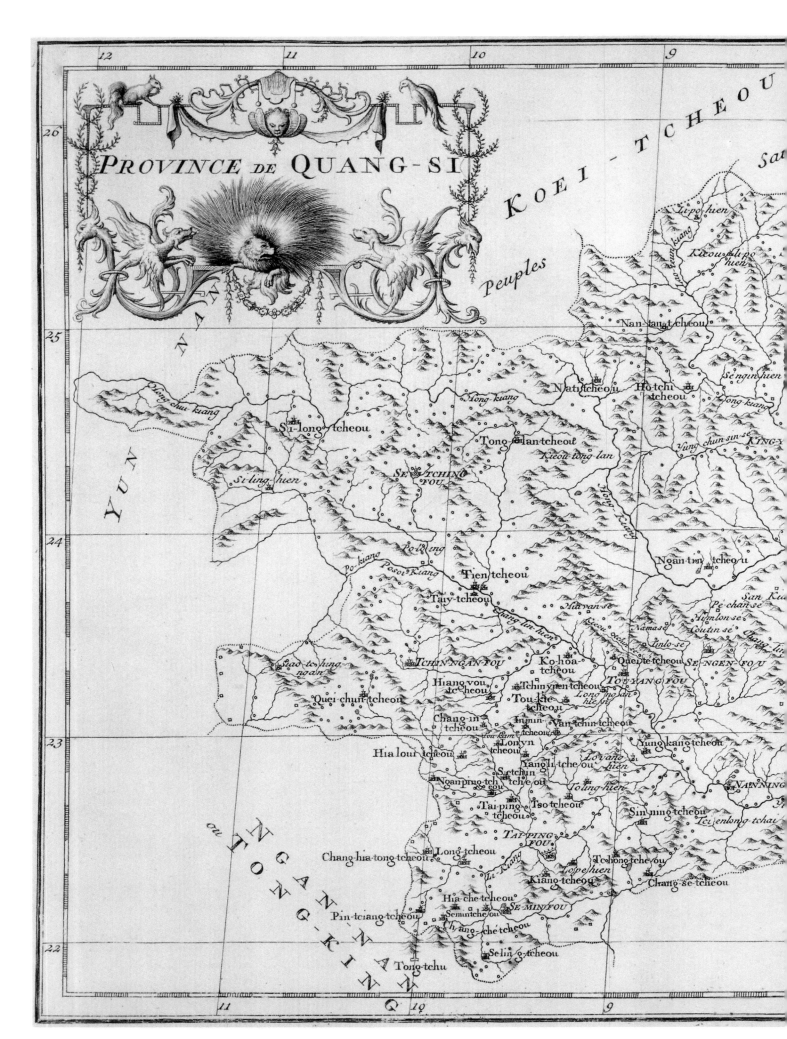

PROVINCE DE QUANG-SI

KOEI - TCHEOU

Peuples

YUN - NAN

NGAN - TONG - KING ou

MAP 15. The Province of Guangxi 广西

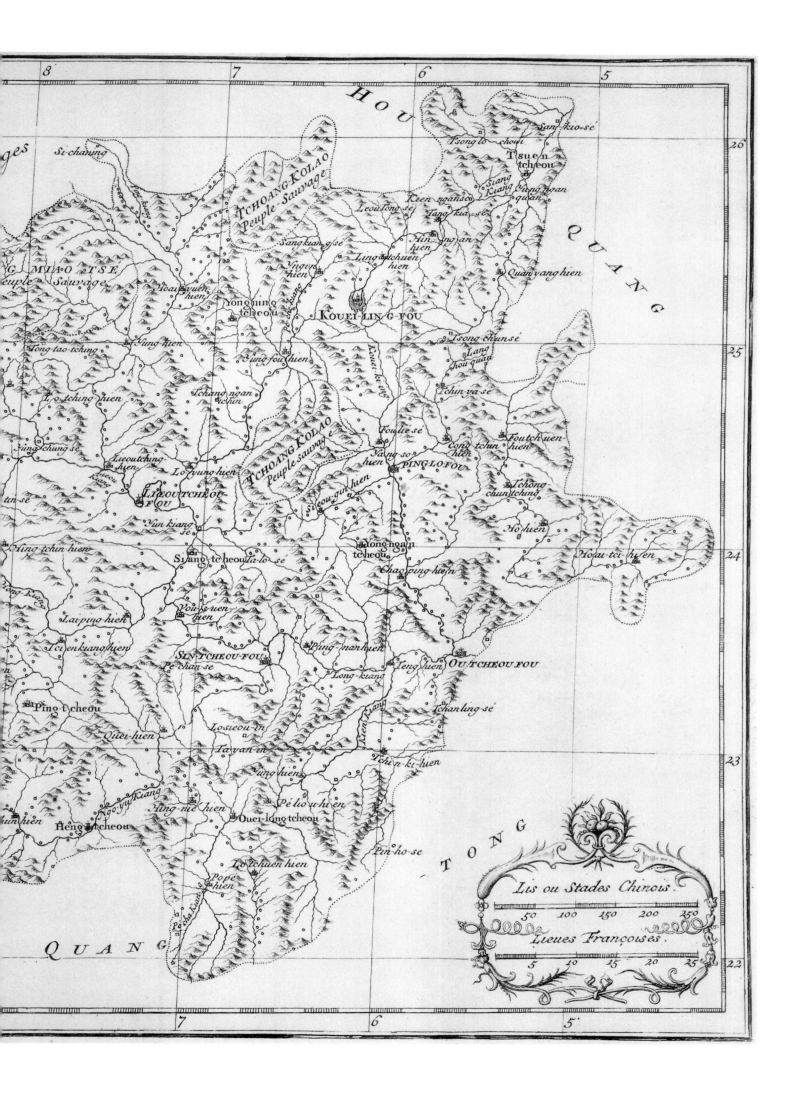

H O U

Q U A N G

Si-chaning

26

TCHOANG KOLAO
Peuple Sauvage

Tsong lo chou

San kio sé

Tsuen
tcheou

Kien ngansé

Siang
Kiang

Chung ngan
quan

G MIAO TSÉ
euple Sauvage

Leou Tong sé

Sang kiang sé

Yang kia sé

Hoai yuen
hien

Yngiu
hien

Ling tchuen
hien

Hin ng an
hien

Yong ning
tcheou

Kouei ho kiang

KOUEI-LING-FOU

Quan yang hien

Tong tao tching

Jung hien

Jung fou hien

Tsong chun sé

25

Kouei ki ing

Lang
hou quan

Tchang ngan
tchin

Lo tching hien

Tchin ya sé

Jung chung sé

TCHOANG KOLAO
Peuple sauvage

Foulie sé

Cong tchin
hien

Fou tch uen
hien

Lieoutching
hien

Lo jyung hien

Yang so
hien

PING LO FOU

Lieou
Kiang

LIEOUTCHEOU-
FOU

Sieou qui hien

Tchong
chun tching

Yun kiang
sé

Ho hien

Ping tchin hien

Siang tcheou Ta-lo sé

Yong ngan
tcheou

Hoai tci hien

24

Long Kiang

Chao ping hien

Lai ping hien

Voü ts uen
hien

Tci en kiang hien

Ping nan hien

Teng hien

OU TCHEOU FOU

SIN TCHEOU-FOU

Long kiang

Pe chan sé

Tchan ling sé

Ping tcheou

Kien Kiang

Ouei hien

Losieou in

Ta yan in

Tchin ki hien

23

Yung hien

Ngo yu Kiang

Hing niè hien

Pé lio u hi en

un hien

Heng tcheou

Ouei long tcheou

Lo tchuen hien

Pope
hien

Pin ho sé

T O N G

Pé chan

Q U A N G

Lis ou Stades Chinois.

50   100   150   200   250

Lieues Françoises.

5   10   15   20   25

22

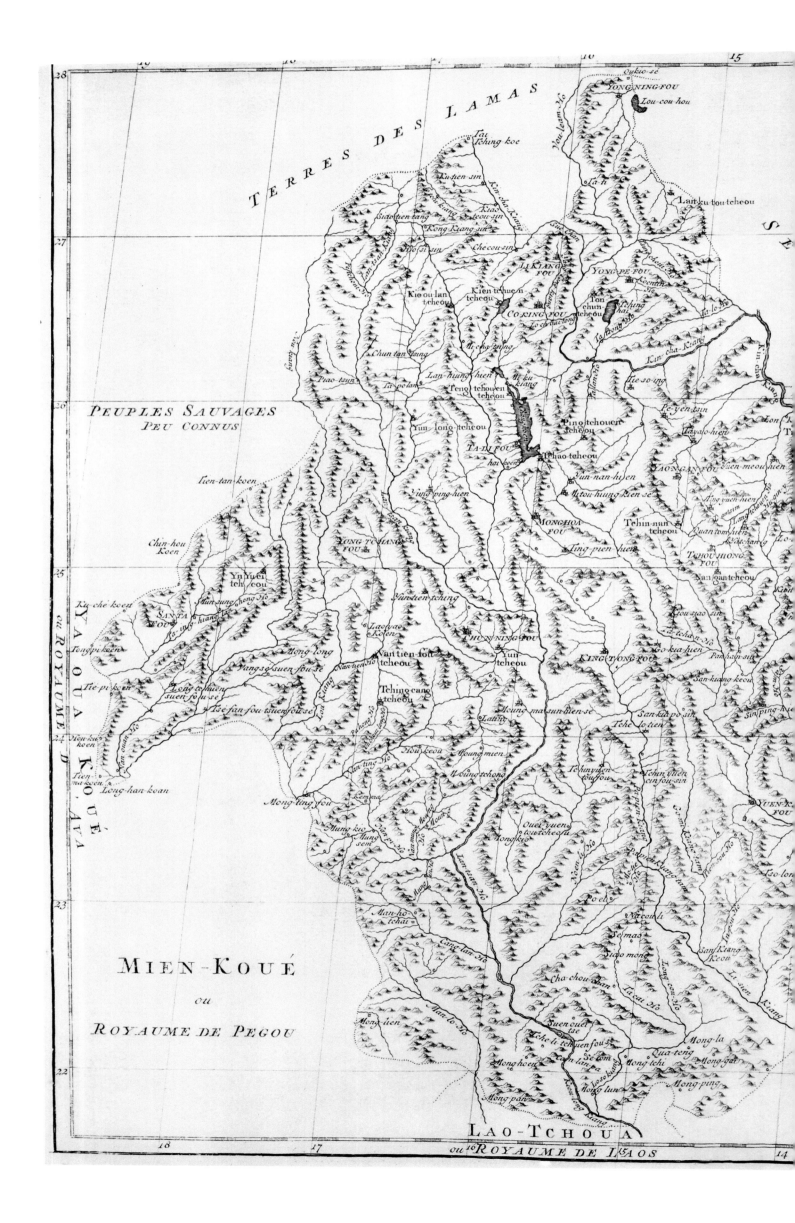

TERRES DES LAMAS

Oukio-sé

YONG-NING-FOU

Lou-cou-hou

27

Ta Tching koe

Lu-hien-sin

Kiao kiang si

Kiao-Kiang

Siao tien tang

Kong-Kiang-sin

Che-cou-sin

Ho si sun

LI KIANG FOU

YONG-PE-FOU

Kie ou lan tcheou

Kien tchuen tcheou

CO-KING FOU

Ton chun tcheou

Tchai

Lo che ou long

Mi cha ning

Chun tan tsing

Lan-hiung hien

Mi ku kiang

Teng tchouen tcheou

Piao-tsun

Ta-po lan

26

PEUPLES SAUVAGES
PEU CONNUS

Yun long-tcheou

Pino tchouen tcheou

Pe-yen tsun

TA-LI FOU
hai koen

Tchao tcheou

Yun-nan-hien

Hayalo-hien

TAON-GAN FOU

Yuen-meou hien

Tien-tan-koen

Ying ying-hien

Mtou-hiung kien se

Ang yuen hien

Tchin-nan tcheou

Quan tom hien

Chun-hou Koen

YONG TCHANG FOU

MONGHOA FOU

Ting-pien hien

TCHOU HIONG FOU

25

Yn-Yuei tch cou

Nan gan tcheou

Ku che koen

Yun tien-tching

Mun sung chong Jo

Kiou qiao sin

SAN-TA FOU

Laoqiao Koen

Go-kia hien

Pan hien sin

Tong pi koen

Mong-long

Van tien fou tcheou

CHUN-NING-FOU

Yun tcheou

KING-TONG FOU

Sin ping hie

Tie-pi koen

Yangs o suen fou se

Nan tuen lo

San-kiang keou

Long te hien suen fo u se

Tching cang tcheou

Moung ma sun hien-se

San kia po sin

24

Hen ku koen

Tse fan fou tsuen fou se

La tu

Houkeou

Moung mien

Tchn yuen tou fou

Tchn yuen cin fou sun

Tien mu koen

Wong tchong

YUEN FOU

Long-han-koan

Mong-ting fou

Kemena

Mung kie

Ouei yuen wa tcheou fu

Mung sem

Mongkio

23

Man-ho tchai

Nacou li

Cang lan Jo

Sé mao

Siao mong

SanKiang Keou

MIEN-KOUÉ

Cha chou chan

ou

ROYAUME DE PEGOU

Mong tien

Suen ouei tse

Mong-la

Qua teng

Tche li tchuen fou s

Mong-tchi

Mong gai

Se tom lan pa

Mong tchi

Mong hoen

Can lan pa

Mong ping

22

LAO-TCHOUA

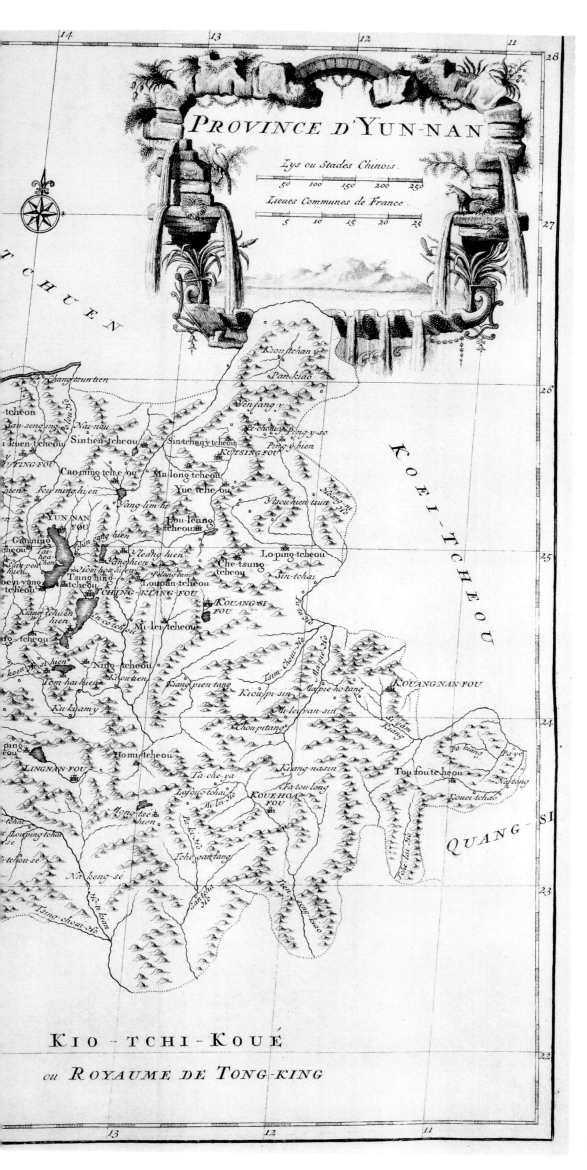

PROVINCE D'YUN-NAN

Lys ou Stades Chinois.
50   100   150   200   250

Lieues Communes de France.
5   10   15   20   25

T C H U E N

KOEI-TCHEOU

QUANG-SI

Kioutchany
Pan-kiao
Yen-fang-y
Pe-chouei Ping-y-so
Sin-tchany tcheou
KUTSING-FOU Ping-y-hien
Cao-ming-tcheou Ma-long-tcheou
Fou-ming-hien Yue-tcheou
Wang-lim-hi Hoang-Ho
Yisou-hien tsun
YUNNAN FOU Lou-leang tcheou
Gan-ning Lo-ping-tcheou
Ngan cang hien Che-tsung tcheou
Ueang-hien Sin-tchai
Tai-hoa-hien Yang-hien
Hoei-hoa-hien Pelong-tan
Tsing-hing tcheou Loupan-tcheou
TCHING-KIANG-FOU KOUANG-SI FOU
Kiang tchuen hien Mi-lei-tcheou
Gin-co-tcho-hi
Ta-pie-Ho
Ning-tcheou Tsin-chout-Ho Ma-pie-ho-tang
Tom-hai-hien Kiou-tien Kioupi-sin
Ku-kuam-y Kiang-pien-tang Mi-lei-pan-sin KOUANG-NAN-FOU
Choupitang Si-yam-Kiang
Po-kiang Pa-ye
Ho-mi-tcheou Pa-tou-long
LINGNAN-FOU Ta-che-ya Kiang-nasin Tou-fou-tcheou Na-tong
Lofong-tchai Ta-tou-long Couei-tchao
Mong-tse-hien KOUEHOA FOU
Pa-ki-Ho
Tche-gan-tang
Na-keng-se
Cantchia-Ho Pien-seng-kao
Ki-ti-kien
Tsung-chout-Ho

KIO - TCHI - KOUÉ

ou ROYAUME DE TONG-KING

MAP 16.
The Province of Yunnan 云南

PROVINCE DE KOEI-TCHEOU

SE-TC

Yong-ning-tcheou

Tche-cheou-sin
Siao-pou-sin
Ni-se-koen
Tsing-cheou-tang
Tchin-nan-Koen

Y-tsi-Ho
Ou-kiang-tching Ou

Po-tsie-hien
Si-fong-sa

Ho-ti-sin
He-tchang-sin
Isi-li-koen
Tai-ning-tcheou
Kien-si-tcheou
Siou-sso
Ouen-tai-tcheou

Ou-meng-tsing-Ho
Co-le-yang-ting
Lou-quang-sin
Pay-si-se
Yang-song-se
Pa-yang-s

Kio-suei-sin
Se-pou-sin
Tien-seng-kao
Teou-hoei-Ho
Yu-tchi-s-sin
Siou-ouen-hien
Ho-tsoui-se
Cou-long-s

Bung-chau-Ho
OUEL-NING-FOU
Cai-tchong-sin
Yeou-sin
Ping-yuen-tche-fou
KOEI-YANG-FOU
Koei-hien

Kiai-li-sin
Ho-tchai-sin
Pa-oua-sin
Tsing-tchin-hien
Tcho-lean-se

Oua-tcha-Ho
Y-tsie-sin
Chui-tchong-sin
Pe-leou-Ho
San-cha-Ho
Tsing-gae
Kyty-hien

Mou-tong-ho
Ho-tsou-Ho
Gan-Yping-hien

He-hoa-sin
Teng-nan-sin
Quoangchuen-tcheou
Ping-fa-se
Tai

Si-pou-se
NGAN-CHUEN-FOU
Quei-fan-se
YUN-NAN
Pe-tsie-sin
Tching-ning-tcheou
Ti-el-siao
Tang-fan-tcheou
Ping-fa-sing

Yong-ning-tcheou
Va-long-se
Tchin-fan-se

Re-jao-sin
Ké-men-Ho

Pan-ki-ang-ing
Ku-yang-se
Ta-hoa-se
Lien-Kiang
Leng-cha-tchai
Pinguhe

Tchuang-kiang-y
Gan-tsian-hien
Ning-cou-se
Makiang-se
Roen-keouing
Nan-ping-se

Pou-ngan-tcheou
Po-gan-hien
Yuen-sou
Cangou-se
Ouet-yuen-se
Tsou-pô-tchai

Ye-se-congy
Gan-csu
Kiang-se

Ping-o-y-so
Sin-tching
SENG-MIAO-SE
Peuple non soumis

Chui-lai-Ho
Chui-si-Ho
Mou-che-tou-tchai
Leou-keou-Ho
tout est Montagne

Cha-ing
Ma-pien-tong
Ngan-tang-tchia

Hoang-tsao-pa
He- pie-Ho

QU

HUEN

Kong tou Ho

Yen ho sé

Ou tchuen hien

Ma tou se   Saen tong ing

Nan tsen Hien kie keou

In kiang hien

Ou Kiang

Long teou ing

Tsin tchoui kiang

Tai ping ing

Yang se Ho   SE-NAN-FOU Mei ta ing

Long tsuen hien   Pan che ing

Tchin ta ing

Mi tan hien   Ti ki sé

TONG-GIN-FOU

Yu king se   CHE-TSIEN-FOU

Kiang keou sin Tchi sé

Nuou tchang Ho

Ouang tao sé

Cai tsou Ho Se tcheou Ho

Yu king hien   TCHI-YUEN-FOU SE-TCHEOU-FOU

sao tang se   Pien kiao se

u gan hien   Che ping hien   In tchoui sé

Tai mung Ho

Quoang ping tcheou   Kiou hien

G YUEN   Tcho gan kiang Cai men se   Kao sé tchai Nang tong

FOU   Tsin ping hien

Yang tao se   Tsing che ta kiag

a ha   Mie ti fang kiai   Kou sé

heou

Ping ting chan sé tout est Montagne Leang tchoui sé

Geou yang sé

Long si sé   Pa tcheou sé Sin hoa sé

SENG-MIAO-SE

TOU-YUEN   Peuple non soumis   Ou kia kiang

FOU

Ou kia se

g san se   Peng kiang Yong tsong hien

San kie tchai

Si chan ing   Ki ma tchai chan

Lan tsou sé

u chan tcheou

no hoa sé

ANG SI

HOU-QUANG

Lis ou Stades Chinois

50   100   150   200

Lieues Francoises

5   10   15   20

MAP 17.
The Province of Guizhou 贵州

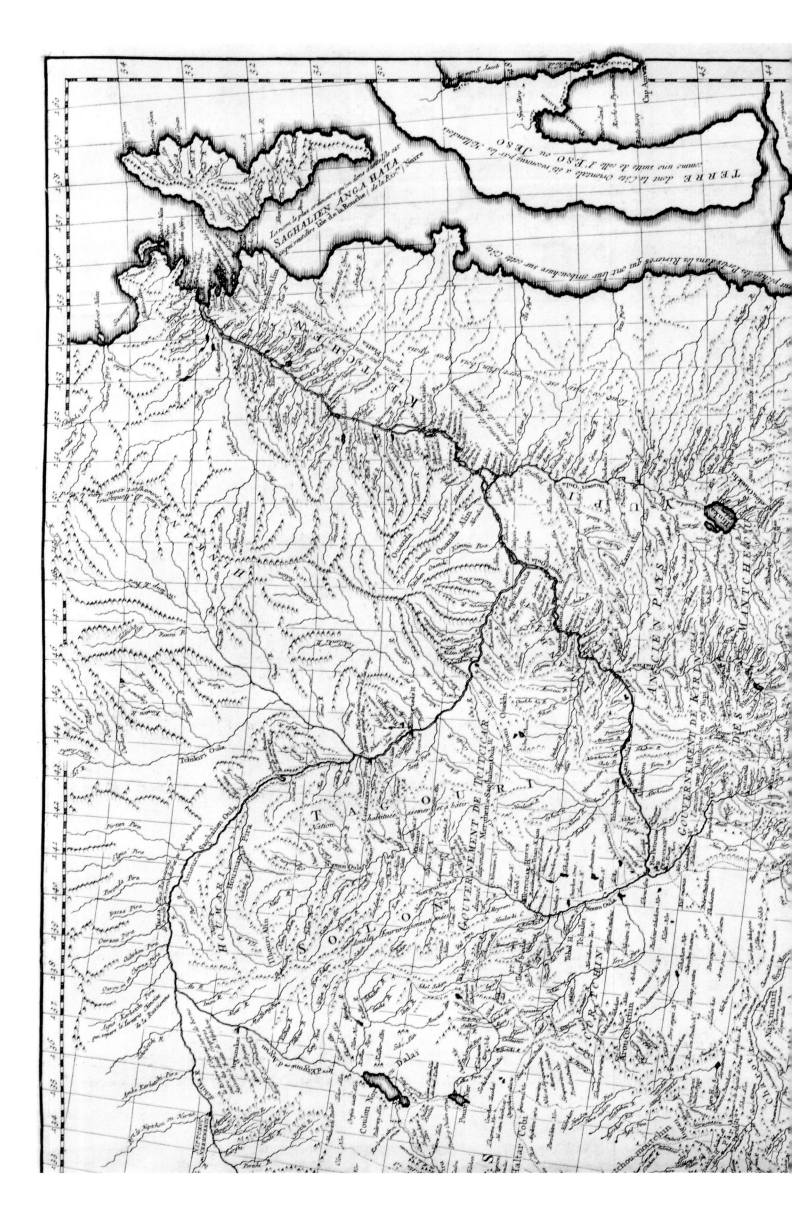

MAP 18.   General map of Chinese Tartary
(JOINS AT PAGE 114–115 AT TOP)

EDSO-GASIMA
ou ISLE DE JEDSO

TESSOI

YESSO

SIMODSE

TOTOMI
MICAWO

NONGO SINKINAI

TSISIMA TANGO

IDSUMO

AKI

KAOLI KOUE ou ROYAUME DE CORÉE
nommé aussi TCHAO SIEN ou ROYAUME DE SOLGO
et par les Mandchous SOL HOKOUROUN

KIANG YUEN

LEAO TONG

HOANG HAI ou MER JAUNE

Quelpaert Isle

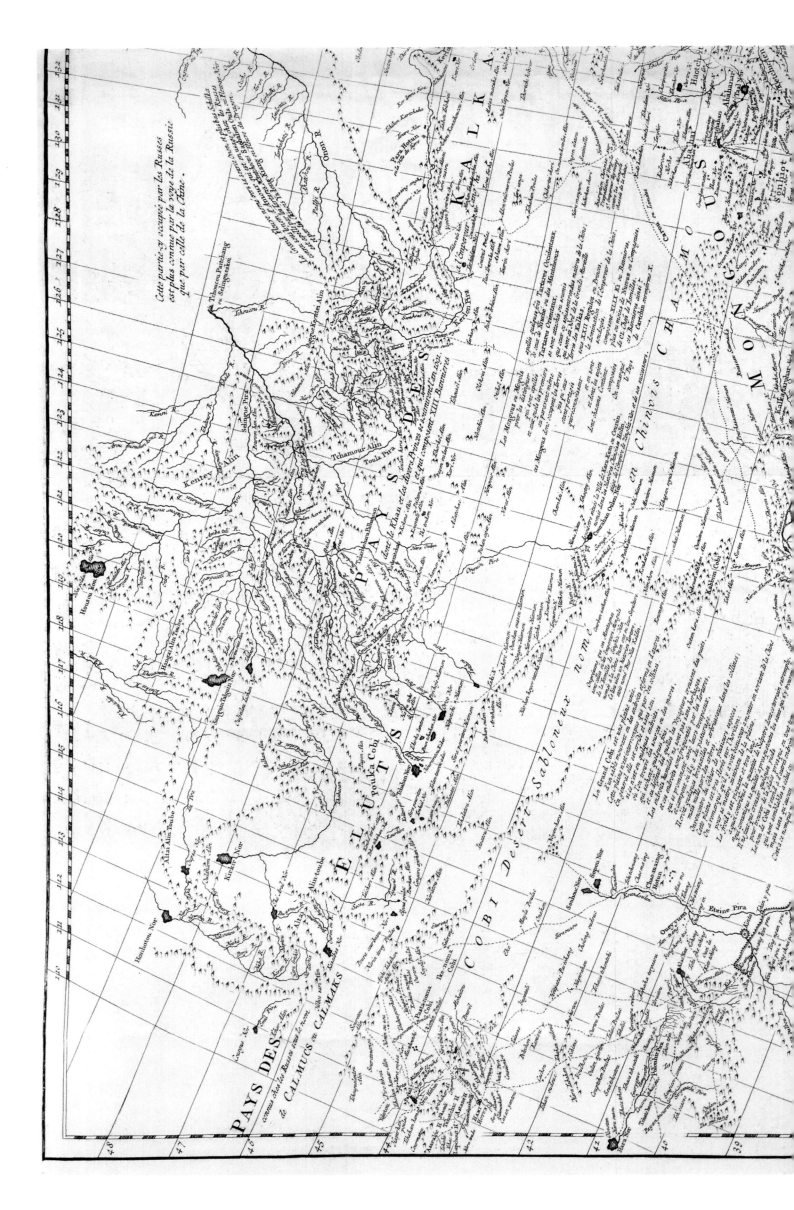

CARTE GENERALE DE LA TARTARIE CHINOISE

DRESSEE SUR LES CARTES PARTICULIERES
FAITES SUR LES LIEUX PAR LES RR PP JESUITES
ET SUR LES MEMOIRES PARTICULIERS DU P GERBILLON
PAR LE S.r D'ANVILLE GEOGRAPHE ORD.re DU ROI
MARS MDCCXXXII.

EXPLICATION

de quelques Dénominations générales répandues dans cette Tartarie.

Oula . . . . . Fleuve ou Grande Rivière
Pira . . . . . Rivière
Omo . . . . . Lac ou Etang
Sekin . . . . Source de Rivière
Mouren . . . Rivière
Nor . . . . . Lac ou Etang
Poulac . . . . Fontaine ou Source
Afin . . . . . Montagne
Hata . . . . . Roche
Tabahan . . . Montagne élevée en pointe de Montaigne

Dans la Langue des Tartares Orientaux ou Mantchoux.

Dans la Langue des Tartares Occidentaux ou Mongols.

Hotun . . . . et par abreviation H. Ville.
Cajan . . . . Village
Paitehan . . . Lieu fermé ou qui aune Enceinte
Hiamen . . . Poste sur une Route fréquentée

(Explanatory notes follow regarding denominations in the region.)

PAYS D'ORTOUS

Scale bars:
Lys ou Stades Chinois à 200 par Degré
Werstes ou Stades Russes à ...
Lieues Marines à 20 au Degré
Lieues communes de France à 25 au Degré

MAP 18. General map of Chinese Tartary
(JOINS AT PAGE 112–113 AT BOTTOM)

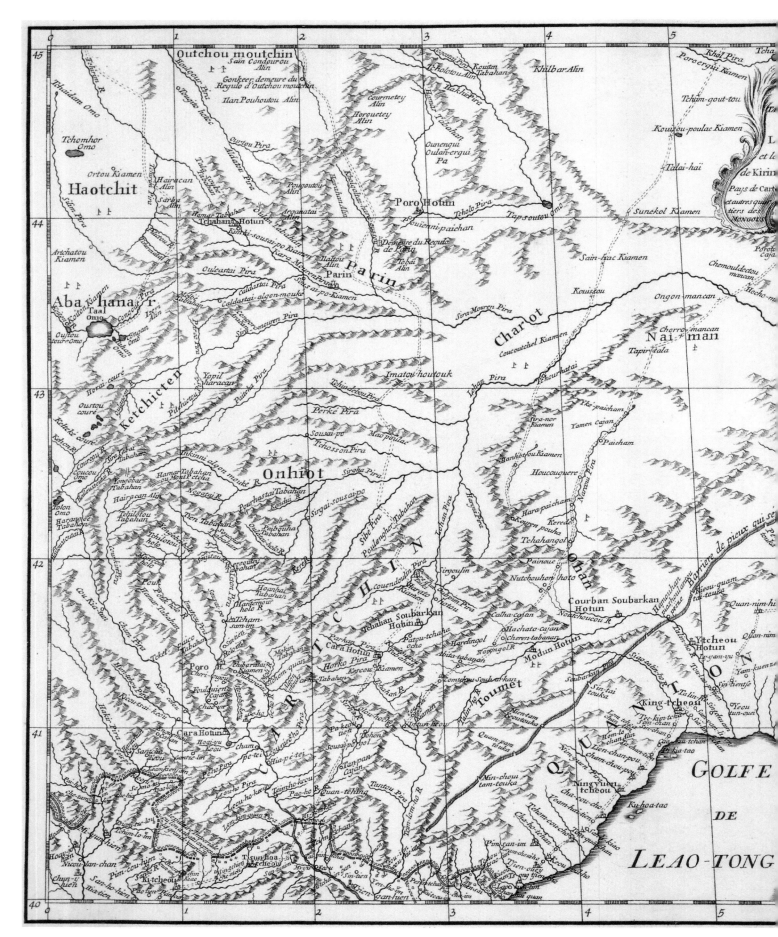

MAP 19.　First detailed page [of Chinese Tartary]

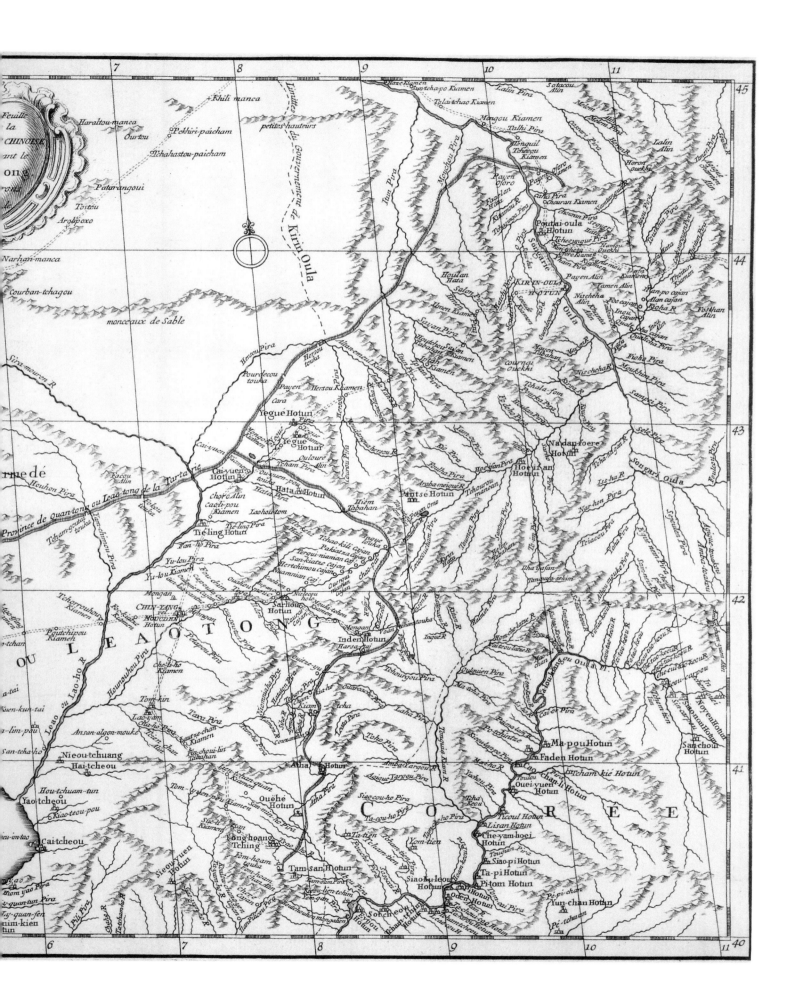

Top border (left to right): 7   8   9   10   11

Right border (top to bottom): 45   44   43   42   41   40

Bottom border (left to right): 6   7   8   9   10   11 40

Feuille la
CHINOISE
ant le
ong

Haraltou-manca
Khili manca
Pekhiri-paicham
Ourtou
Tchahastou-paicham

Hazi Kiamen
Puntchapo Kiamen
Tchai chao Kiamen
Lalin Pira
Sotacou Alin

Mongou Kiamen
Talhi Pira

Patarangoui
Tortou
Aroh-oxo

Tienquil
Tcheeou Kiamen

Narhan-manca

Payen Ojoro
Payge Ki amen
cana Pira
Chouran Kiamen

Courban-tchagou

monceaux de Sable

petites hauteurs

Houlan Hata
Salem Pira
Umen Kiamen

KIRIN-OULA
HOTUN

Poutai-oula
Hotun
Tchesungui Pira
Nantou Ouekhi

Sira-mouren R

Hetou Pira
Pourdecou touka
Hersou touka

Payen
Cara
Hersou Kiamen

Soyan Pira
Houdcheu Soton
Tahatanl Kiamen
Igoh Kiamen

Oula
Payen Alin

Daisa Kiamen
Thotun Kiamen

Inou Cajan
Soha R

arme dé

Yegue Hotun
Pira

Tchala-tom
Pira
Koro Pira

Nan-po cajan
Quala cajan
Voskhan Alin

Houhon Pira
Facou Alin
Cai-yuen

Cai-yuen
Hotun

Mongou Kiamen
Ouloure Alin
Tcham Pira
Yegue Hotun

Yamce Pira
Bio Pira

Nischeha R
Moukhin Pira

Province de Quantong ou Leao tong de la Tartarie
Tcham-goum touka
Yen chimen Pira

choz Alin
Caeli-pou Kiamen
Hata Hotun

Hiem Tabahan
Laohoietom

Pantse Hotun

Nadan-foere
Hotun
Hoei-fan Pira
Hoei-fan Hotun

Iss-ha R
Songari Oula

Tie-ling Pira
Tie-ling Hotun

Holi
Touka

Tchao-kili Cajan
Pakiatsa Cajan
San-kiatse Cajan
Hertchimou Cajan
Niamnian Caj

Chuo-vut

Ingue
Hetho Tabahan

Triacou Pira
Toha Pira

Pan ho Pira
Yu-lou Pira
Yu-lou Kiamen

Fou chim

Ourhou Iki

Mongan
CHIN-YANG vel MOUCDEN Hotun

Sarhou Hotun

Yan chimtouka
Mongan

Iha Tasan

Tcherrouhouy Kiamen
Po-kiaje Kiamen

Pgutchipou Kiameh

Che-tcho Kiamen

Indem Hotun
Harsa Caj

Tchourgou Pira
Ouinien Pira

OU LEAOTONG

Hounouhou Pira
Tom-kin
Traxi Pira

Indem R

Ma tcha Pira

Ya-lou-kang ou Oula R
Cot ok Pira

Tchan-tai
Kuen-kun-tai

Lao-yam Cha-ho
Tien chan

Shta R
Tchara Pira
Tcham kiache
Tcha

Laha Pira
Toho Pira

Ma-pou Hotun
Faden Hotun

San-chou
Hotun

-lim-pou
San-tcha-ho

Ansan-algon-mouke

Kaut-ze-chan Kiamen

Atha Hotun

Amba Yargou
Amba Yargou Pira

Cao Chan-li Hotun
Ouei-yuen Hotun

Istcham kie Hotun

Nieou-tchuang
Hai-tcheou
Hou-tchuam-tun

Ouehe Hotun
San-min-ho Pira

Siao-cou-ho Pira
COREE
Ta-cou-ho Pira

Ticoul Hotun
Lisan Hotun
Che-yam-hoei Hotin

Yao-tcheou
Kiao-teou-pou

Fong-hoang Tching

Ta-tien
Yom-tien

Siao-pi Hotun
Touguan Pira

Cai-tcheou

Pom-hoam touka

Tam-san Hotun

Siao-ku-leou Hotun
Ta-pi Hotun
Pi-tom Hotun

ao Pira
hom yao Pira
-quan-tun Pira
ai-quan-sen
nim-kien

Sieou-yuen Hotun

Oden Hotun
Yun-chan Hotun
pe-pi-chan
pe-tcham

Sohcheou Hotun

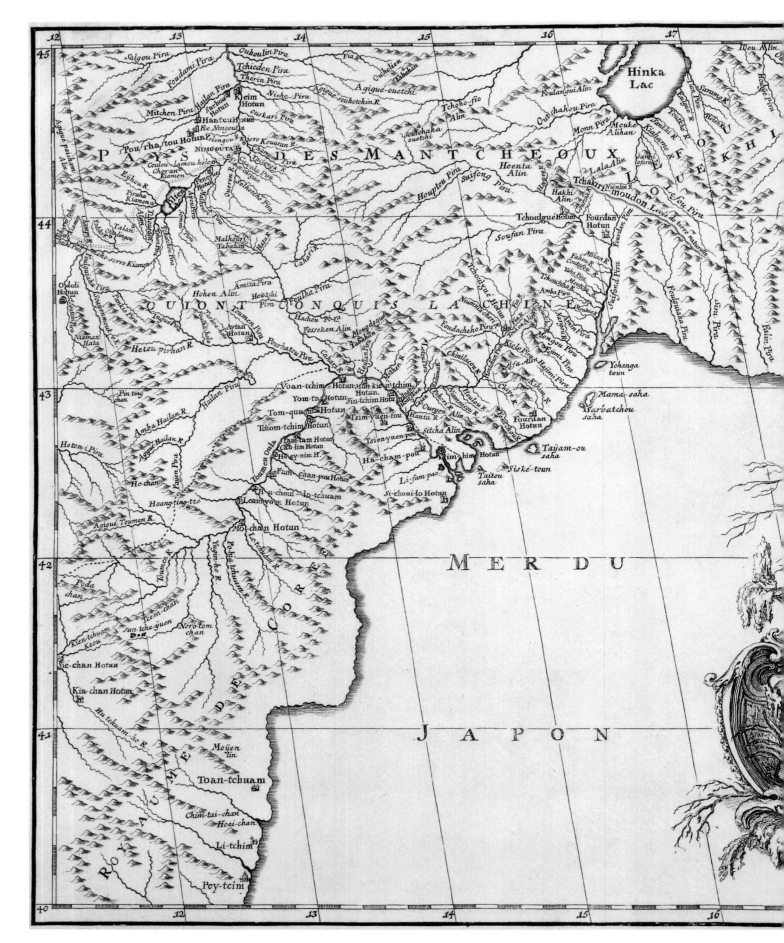

MAP 20. Second detailed page [of Chinese Tartary]

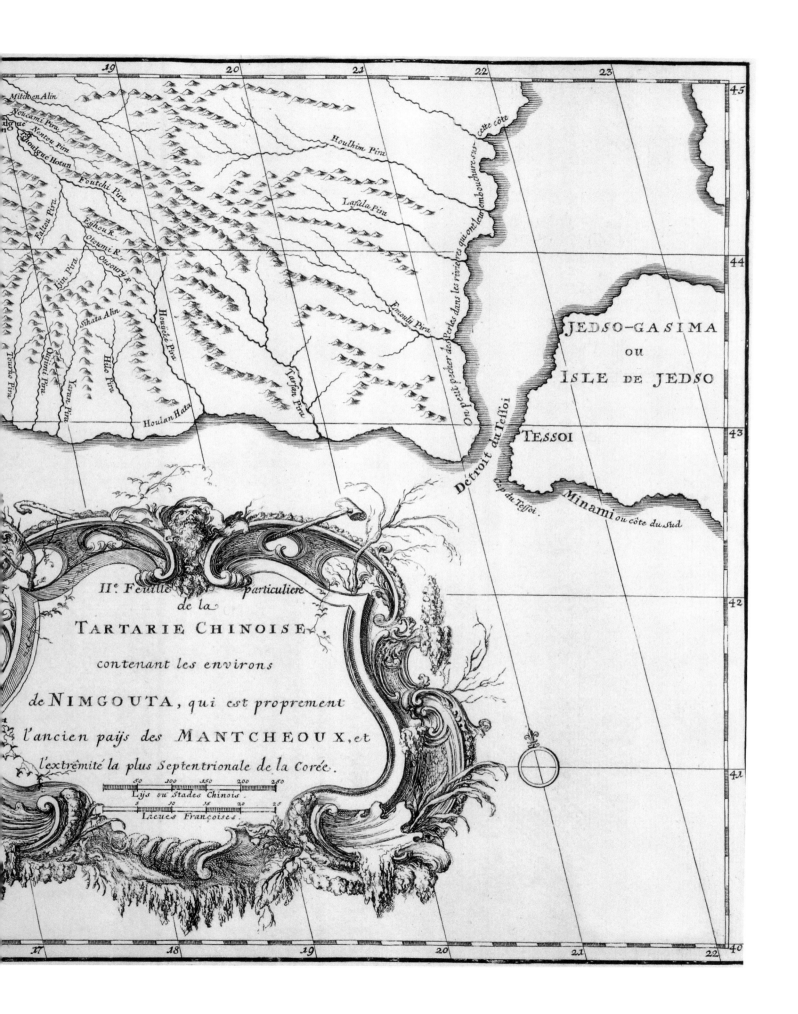

JEDSO-GASIMA
ou
ISLE DE JEDSO

TESSOI

Minami ou côte du Sud

Détroit du Tessoi

Mitch en Alin
Noucami Pira
Nentou Pira
Houlgue Hotun
Foutchi Pira
Falou Pira
Eghou R.
Oloumi R.
Ousouri R.
Ljin Pira
Sihata Alin
Houiché Pira
Oujini Pira
Yaxan Pira
Hilo Pira
Touatho Pira
Houlan Hata
Taefan Pira
Emouly Pira
Lafala Pira
Houlhim Pira
Où l'on peut pêcher des Perles dans les rivieres qui ont leur embouchure sur cette côte

II.e Feuille   particuliere
de la
TARTARIE CHINOISE,
contenant les environs
de NIMGOUTA, qui est proprement
l'ancien païs des MANTCHEOUX, et
l'extrêmité la plus Septentrionale de la Corée.

50   100   150   200   250
Lys ou Stades Chinois.
5   10   15   20   25
Lieues Françoises.

Grid coordinates (top): 11   10   9   8   7

45

Chamkai Alin

Hana Hata

Ici devoit être située la Ville de Kara-Kum ou Couran nommée dans les Histoires Chinoises HOLIN, Siège de l'Empire de Zinghiz-Han et de ses successeurs.

Tchetchey Alin

Courahan-oulen Omo

C O B I   D e s e r t   s a b l o n n e u x

Ouljintou Kiamen

Kouthin Kiamen

Pombatou Kiamen

Kodoli Kiamen

44

Soougi Kiamen

Tchaptchial Kiamen

Kiaha Kiamen

Oski Kiamen

Courban-saikan Alin

Kedercou Kiamen

Palhassun Kiamen

Postes établies hors de la grande muraille

Manitou Kiamen

III.e feuille particuliere de la

TARTARIE CHINOISE,

Oupeken Alin

Konké Kararon Alin

Tchagan-ergui Kiamen

contenant les quartiers occupés par

Nomohon Alin

les MONGOUS au Nord de la Gr. Muraille

43

Perossouhai Kiamen

et le Païs D'ORTOUS, environné

Koumere Alin

de la Riviere HOANG-HO

Horhotou Alin

Sekouen-haltchan Alin

Vounitou Kiamen

Tchahan-hamar Kiamen

Outan-kara Alin

Courban-agatou Kiamen

Oulan-ergui Kiamen

Pourhassoutai Kiamen

Kabbün-Coby

42

Temour Kiamen

T   A   R   T

Tsitsirhan Kiamen

Tchel Alin

Serten Alin

Carou ou Limites entre les

Kalka-targhur Aspa

Siretou Alin

Aibhan Kiamen

Onghin-chorong Alin

Cajar hocho

Tahandel Alin

Mkomingan

Tchahan Tchilaetou Tchahan tsolo Kiamen

Kisan Omo

Kouré-modo

Paichanteu Poulae

Allan R.

Colcou omo

Kalotou Omo

Ojoltai Omo

Ouraf

Tsiran tolohoei

Poutanton Alin

41

Narin choron omo

Kalotou, bras du Hoang-ho

Mokoc hocho

Haitou Tabahan

Piloatai

Pa Hong-

Halqan-courboutou Alin

Haritena R.

Torgouri omo

Lanchu-chan Alin

Tcholictou, bras du Hoang-ho

Ninghia

Mok hocho

Toure omo intou

Kouen oudeue

Piloatai Hotun

Sarji caran

Hamar paichan

Route de l'Empereur en allant a Ninghia

Tchique-Pira

Olan Omo

Pourhassoutai

Naimalai Omo

Tchekessoutai omo

Heptel Alin

Kara-manni omo

T   A   R   T   A   R   E   S   O   R   T   O   U

Olan R.

Telai Pira

Icy tout est sable et brossailles

Hoang-ho

40

Grid coordinates (bottom): 11   10   9   8   7   6

MAP 21.   Third detailed page [of Chinese Tartary]

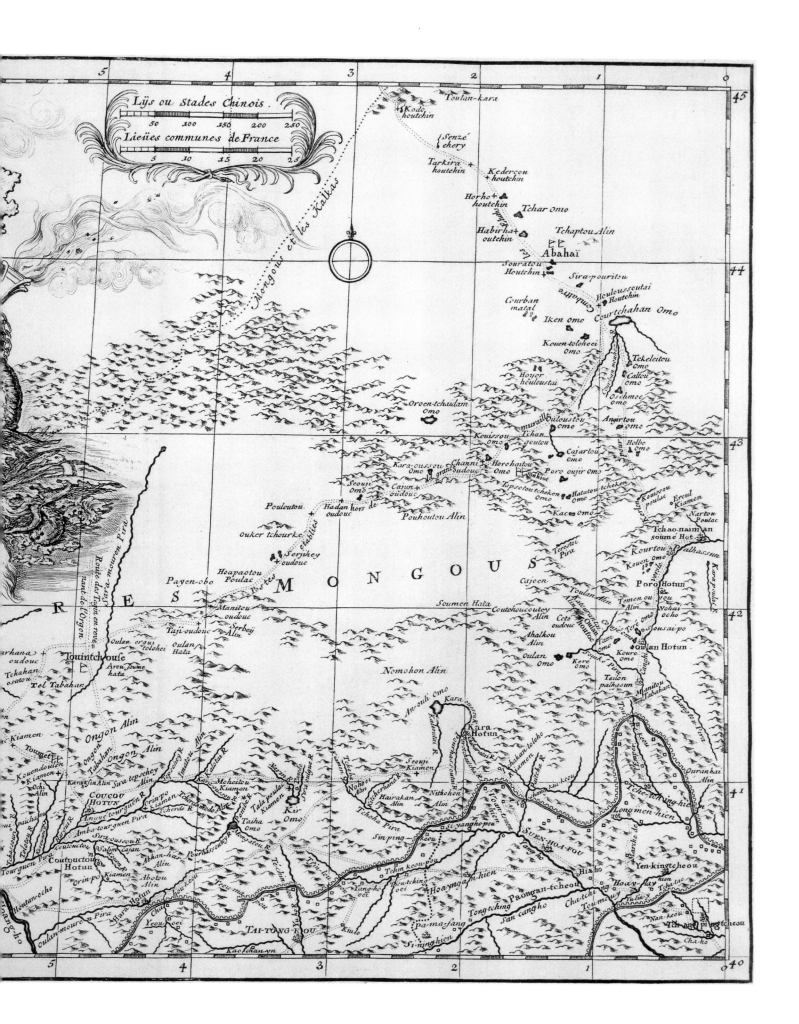

Lijs ou Stades Chinois.

Lieües communes de France

Toulan-kara

Kodo houtchin

Senzé chery

Tarkira houtchin

Kedercou houtchin

Horho houtchin

Tchar omo

Habirhat outchin

Tchaptou Alin

Abahaï

Souratou Houtchin

Sira-pouritou

Courban matal

Houloussoutai Houtchin

Iken omo

Courtchahan Omo

Kouen-tolohoei omo

Tekeleitou omo

Calfou omo

Oschmei omo

Hoyer heuloustai

Angartou omo

Oulouslou omo

murail Tchan goutou

Kouissou omo

Cajartou omo

Holbe omo

Oroen-tchaudam omo

Kara-ouscou omo

Channi grand oudouc

Horohaitou omo

Poro oujir omo

Ercul Kiamen

Seouji omo

Cajun oudouc

Huhie

Tapsotoutcheken omo

Matatou tcheken omo

Kouissou poulac

Narton poulac

Pouloutou

Hadan hors de oudouc

Pouhoutou Alin

Kac omo

Tchao-naiman soume Hot.

ouker tchourke

Serjihey oudouc

Payen-obo

Hoapaotou Poulac

Postes

MONGOUS

Soumen Hata

Teteotoi Pira

Toulan Alin

Cajoen

Kouen omo

Kourtou Palhassun

Poro Hotun

Kara poulac K.

Manitou oudouc

Serbey Alin

Coutchoucoutey Alin

Cote oudouc Houttoe

Temen ou you Alin

Nohai ocho

Sousai po

Taji-oudouc

Oulan Hata

Ahalkou Alin

Oulan Houtun

Koure omo

Oulan Hotun

Oulan ergui tolohei

Arou joume hata

Touintchouse

Oulan Omo

Kere omo

Tailon palhassun

Manitou Tabahan

arhana oudouc

Tchahan osatou

Tel Tabahan

Route des Tajin en revenant de l'Orgon

Nomohon Alin

An-ouli omo

Kara

Kara Hotun

Ongon Alin

Ongon Tabahan

Ongon Alin

Seouji Kiamen

Nithohon Alin

Chang-ta Tira

Ouranhai Alin

Kiamen

Toumett

Kouendoulen Kiamen

Kara-sin Alin

Sira tepochey Alin

Coutchoukoutey R.

Imatou Alin

Tehtonaimoun

Nohoi Alin

Hairakan Alin

Ahakan-toloho

Kiamen

Tche-tching-hie

Long-men-hien

Ochi Alin

COUCOU HOTUN

Orin po Kiamen

Tchiatamodo

Telapoulac Kiamen

Tchoha Pira

Si-yanghopou

SUEN-HOA-FOU

Amba-tourguen Pira

Taiha omo

Kir omo

Sinping

kcou

Yen-kingtcheou

Sira oussour R.

Salun cajun

Kir omo

Tehin keou pou

Hiaho

Houy-lay hien tao

Coutouctou Hotun

Abotou Alin

Pourhassoutey

Teng-atou R.

Techin

Pen-tching oei

Hoayngan hien

Paomgan-tcheou

Cha-tchi

Tcha-tao

Orin po Kiamen

Abkan-har Alin

Houkeou

Yang-ho oei

Tong-tching

San-cang-ho

Toumous

Nan-keou

Tch

Ping-tcheou

Ongou R.

Hara Hotun

Cha

Char tao

Kiulo

Pa-ma-fang

Cha-ho

Ouang-mouren Pira

Yeou oei

TAI-TONG-FOU

Si-ning hien

Kao-chan-yn

45

Tchouguelentou Alin   Soroto-anga   Sourtou Alin   Tchaca pourhaso   Aji Tabahan Aji Alin   Haratou Alin

Honin-oso   Kecheou noutey Poulac   Ouron Poulac

Hara-oso   Mingan Poulac   Sevolij Alin

Porotchoui   Cor

N O M I N   C O B I   D E S E R T

Chaca-hamar   Ourgoustai Poulac

Opto-kiltekai   Alac-tchoutchi   Nomin Poulac

44

Tchahan-hamar Alin   Parcoul Omo   Koukelon rivvean

Artchahar Alin   Eloukè Poulac   Sira toloho et Alin

Cossirtou ouela   Tourcoul Omo

Tchacteli   Coteudres Poulac   Tagourie

Tchalamaha Alin

Tohotchi Hotun   Tezenpouric Alin   Alpia

Astanè Hotun

Soumen harho Hotun

43   Laptchout Hotun   HAMIL HOTUN   Hatamtam   Cousolento   Pourkelto

Sira-ouleussou   Yagetali   Ontchi Pira   Tala-oso

Edemour chery   Ouipon haratou Alin

Poltchon   Houpatart Saikan Alin

Kazan yentou   Kaniou   Houpatar Paitchang

Cachon   Tchao oudouc   Hapircan

Tchohon oudouc   Anghirto

C O B I   D E S E R T   nommé

Kara Tabahan   Echemè   Tchaca-tchontchi

Youlhon

Oulan-ajerin

Talac Poulac

Couptchen Poulac   Tekelic

Souichonto   Serek-toura oudouc   Tchaca-tergaso

41   Olosotai   Tchaca tchontchio   Otolec-manni Poulac

Hara-oso   Tchaca-tohoi   Emer-yapar   El-cong-ming   Chouangtal   Pourol Alac Omo

Poulonour Pira

Tchetcheou Hotun   Quatcheou   Coucou-tchaesao   Taritou Poulac   Keta-tching

Tam Pira   Hapta-hai

Pouro-tchontchi   Pourhai

Paijanmoureno   Sirhalij Pira   Sipgicon-couten   Tas-poulsason   Tchahan Paicham Partou Alin   Ejney Pira

MAP 22.   Fourth detailed page [of Chinese Tartary]

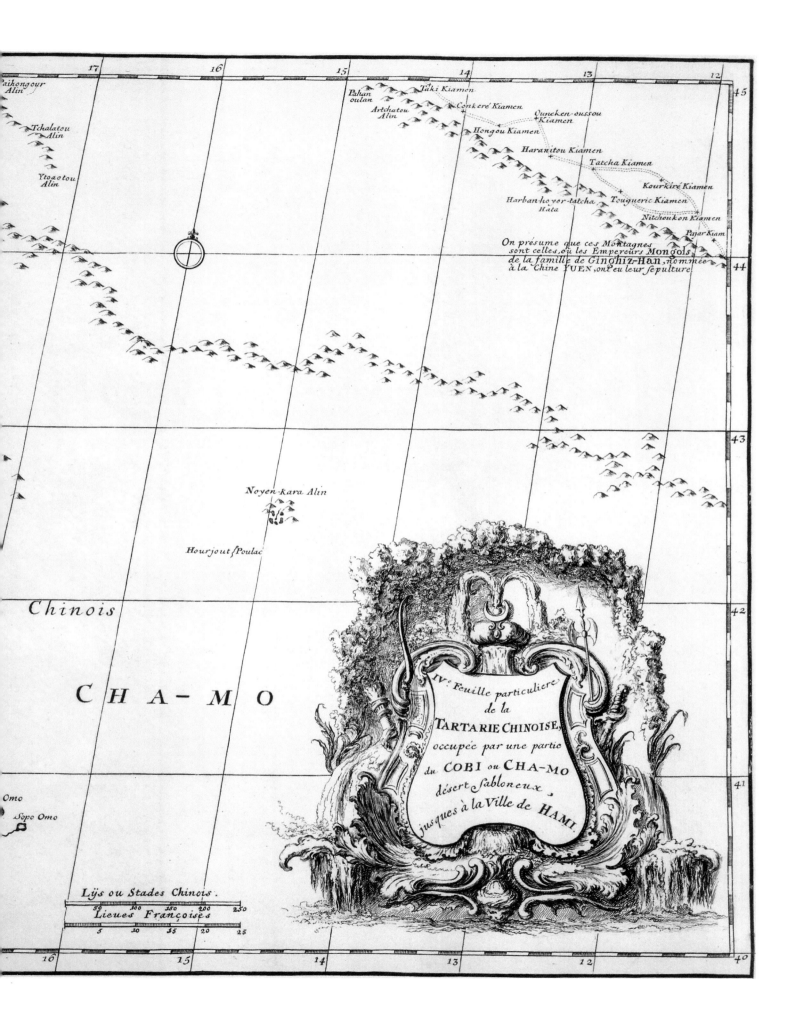

aihongour
Alin

17　　　　　　16　　　　　　15　　　　　　14　　　　　　13　　　　　　12

Tchalatou
Alin

Pahan
oulan

Tüki Kiamen

Artchatou
Alin

Conkeré Kiamen

Ouneken-oussou
Kiamen

Hongou Kiamen

Ytoaotou
Alin

Haranitou Kiamen

Tatcha Kiamen

Kourkiré Kiamen

Harban-ho yor-tatcha
Hata

Touigueric Kiamen

Nitchoukon Kiamen

Pajar Kiam

On présume que ces Montagnes
sont celles, où les Empereurs Mongols
de la famille de Ginghiz-Han, nommée
à la Chine YUEN, ont eu leur sépulture.

45

44

43

Noyen-Kara Alin

Hourjout ſPoulac

Chinois

42

CHA-MO

Omo

Sopo Omo

IVᵉ Feuille particuliere
de la
TARTARIE CHINOISE,
occupée par une partie
du COBI ou CHA-MO
désert ſabloneux,
jusques à la Ville de HAMI.

41

Liis ou Stades Chinois.

50　　100　　150　　200　　250

Lieues Françoises.

5　　10　　15　　20　　25

16　　　　　　15　　　　　　14　　　　　　13　　　　　　12

40

MAP 23. Fifth detailed page [of Chinese Tartary]

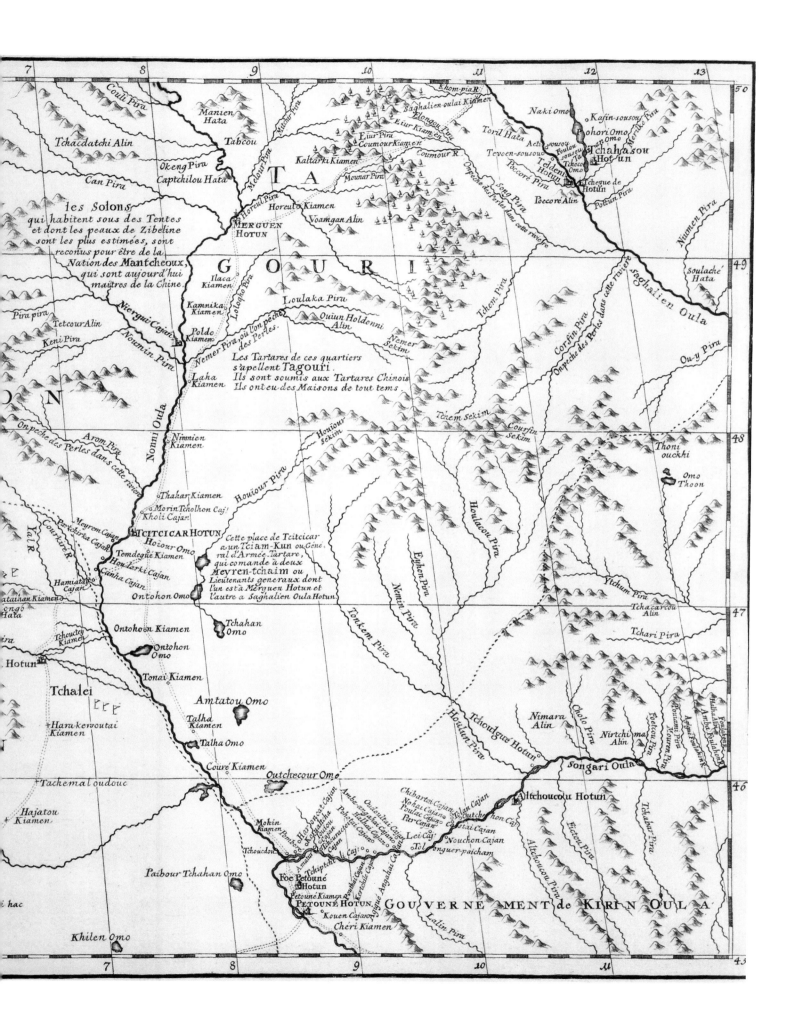

les Solons
qui habitent sous des Tentes
et dont les peaux de Zibeline
sont les plus estimées, sont
reconus pour être de la
Nation des Mantcheoux,
qui sont aujourd'hui
maîtres de la Chine.

T A G O U R I

Les Tartares de ces quartiers
s'apellent Tagouri.
Ils sont soumis aux Tartares Chinois
Ils ont eu des Maisons de tout tems.

Cette place de Tcitcicar
a un Tciam-Kun ou Géné-
ral d'Armée Tartare,
qui comande à deux
Meyren-tchaim ou
Lieutenants generaux dont
l'un est à Merguen Hotun et
l'autre a Saghalien Oula Hotun.

On pêche des Perles dans cette riviere

On pêche des Perles dans cette riviere

Onpêche des Perles dans cette riviere

G O U V E R N E M E N T de K I R I N O U L A

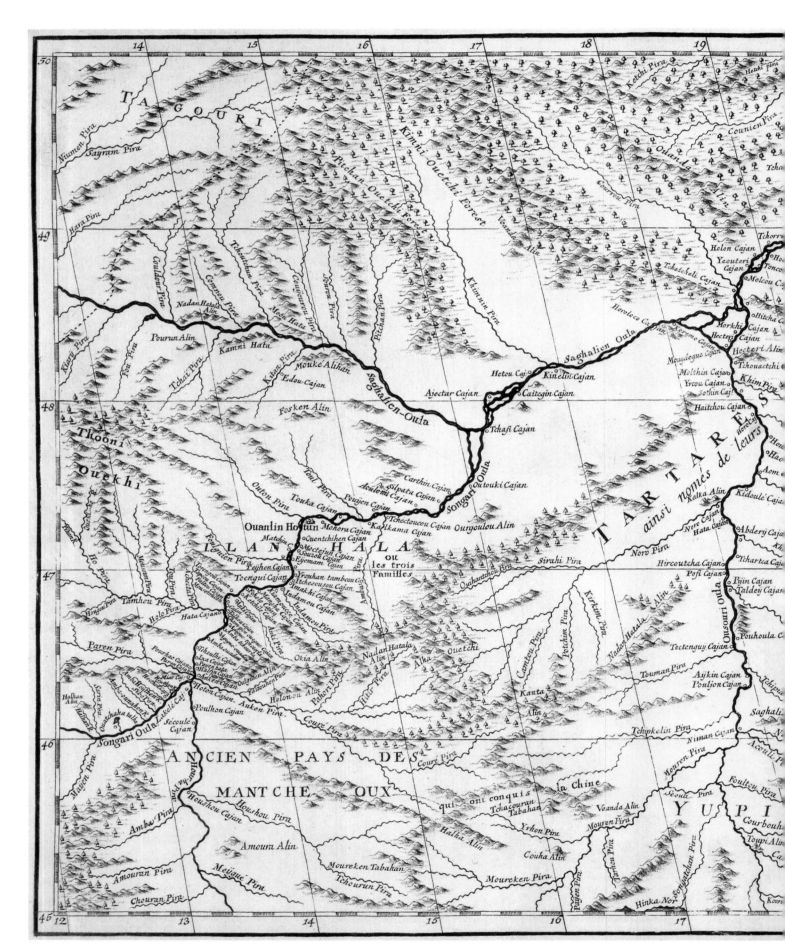

MAP 24. Sixth detailed page [of Chinese Tartary]

K E T C H E N
Nation qui a un langa-ge particu-lier
nomme FIATTA

Parall Pira

Tchala Cajan
Norrypille
Connen Caj
mi Cajano
da Cajano
ur Cajan
Cajan
n Cajan
Cajan
lé Cajan

Sangou Cajan
Tchoulaty Cajan

Kaltiki Cajan

Tondon Cajan

Tha Cajan
Cajan Cajan
Houlé Cajan

Mouzou Cajan
Oucroumi Cajan
Yrcoulou Cajan
Tchonnsceou Cajan
sati Cajan

Tondon Pira

UPI
de peau de poisson
its

Horo Pira

Pijin Pira

Amnou Pira

ury Alin

oumo Alin

Elé Pira

Yozé Pira

Bois très épais

Couvert d'un

Tout cet Pays est

les rivieres qui ont leur embouchure sur cette côte

Perles dans

On peut pécher des

VI.ᵉ Feuille particuliere
de la
TARTARIE CHINOISE,
contenant
le Pais des Tartares
YUPI et ILAN-HALA
qui est
de l'ancien Pais
MANTCHEOU.

Lys ou Stades Chinois.
50   100   150   200   250

Lieües communes de France.
5   10   15   20   25

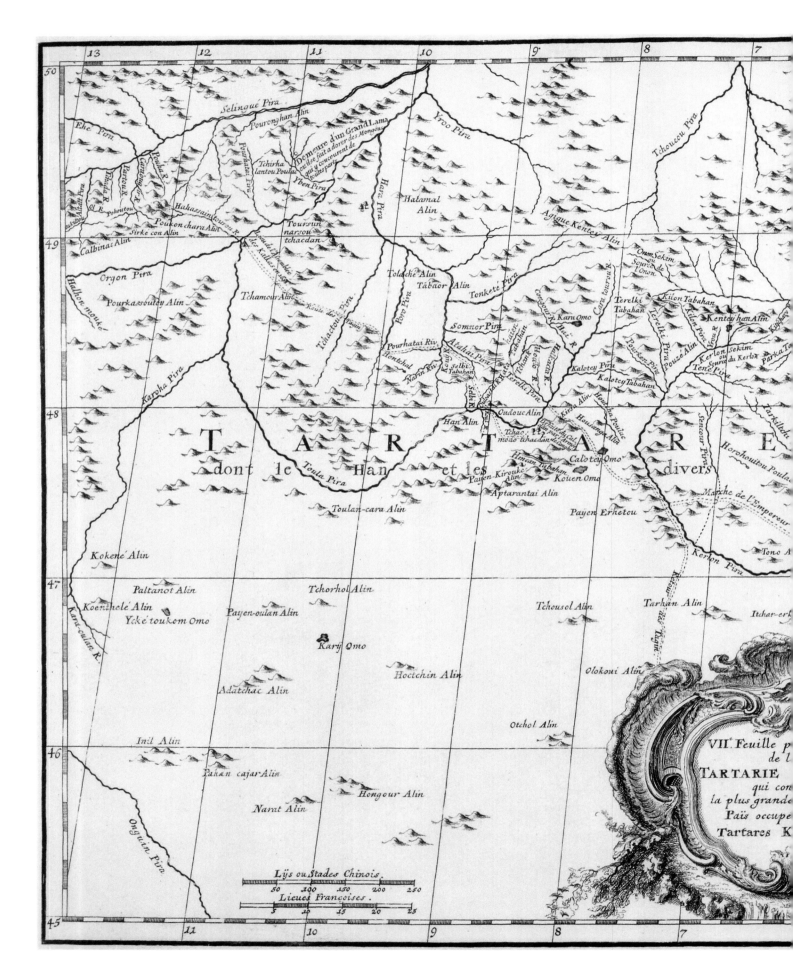

MAP 25. Seventh detailed page [of Chinese Tartary]

6 5 4 3 2 1 0

50

Abatchou Pira

Palii Pira

Onon Pira

Houleoton poulac

Olon Omo

Obodou Omo

Onon vel Saghalien Oula

49

Koursou Pira

Houtou baijdou

Esmouna R.

Herbot Alin ou Montagne du chameau

Tchiraki

Courban podocto

Tchilan kar tchaha

Para Hotun *Touré Omo* *Kerlon Pira.*

pour tenir

l'Assemblée des Etats Kalkas sur l'Orgon.

S *Telberki Poulac* *Kouroumé Omo* *Route des Tagin*

Tchour houtchou *Taben tolohoei*

Kouré Omo *Kedou*

48

Erome Alin

Kere pouritou

Chirde sibeké

K A L K A

Erden Tolohoei

Princes *le soumirent l'an 1691, et qui composent*

en allant à la rencontre

Ecoure'haiha *Courban perlon Alin*

XIII Bannieres ou Etendarts.

Poulac

Ordem tolohoei

Retour de l'Empereur *Kalkas pour se tenir*

Terme Alin

Matas mataha Alin

Houplou

Taben tolohoei *Yentou pouritou chery*

Yentou Alin

Louc sirha Alin

Oulan-tapsou Omo

Holostai poulac

re ocho *Portaiha Alin*

Hinkan-tchap dactchin Alin

47

Tarha tchaidam-Omo

Cou toutchol Omo

Tchortchi kebour

Ilan-touraha Alin

Coutoul Poulac

Ashatou Alin *Aduntsilo arou Poulac*

Tari canga

Tchone R.

Tourin chery

Oughestchiue

Tchahan Poulac

46

Chibartai Chery

Ou-ouen Tchotoloc Alin

Houlastai

uliere

Sira pouritou Omo

Ongon elesou

NOISE,

tie du

es

KAS.

Kara-manni abirhan chery *Sentinelle*

Houloussoutai-tchahan Omo

Limites entre les Mongous et les Kalkas

sourhoutou poulac

Tchahan-tchilo Alin

Inscription Chinoise sur l'expedition de l'Empereur Yong lo contre les Mongous

Soudetou chery

5 4 3 2 1 0 45

Route de Peking à Niptchou

MAP 26.   Eighth detailed page [of Chinese Tartary]

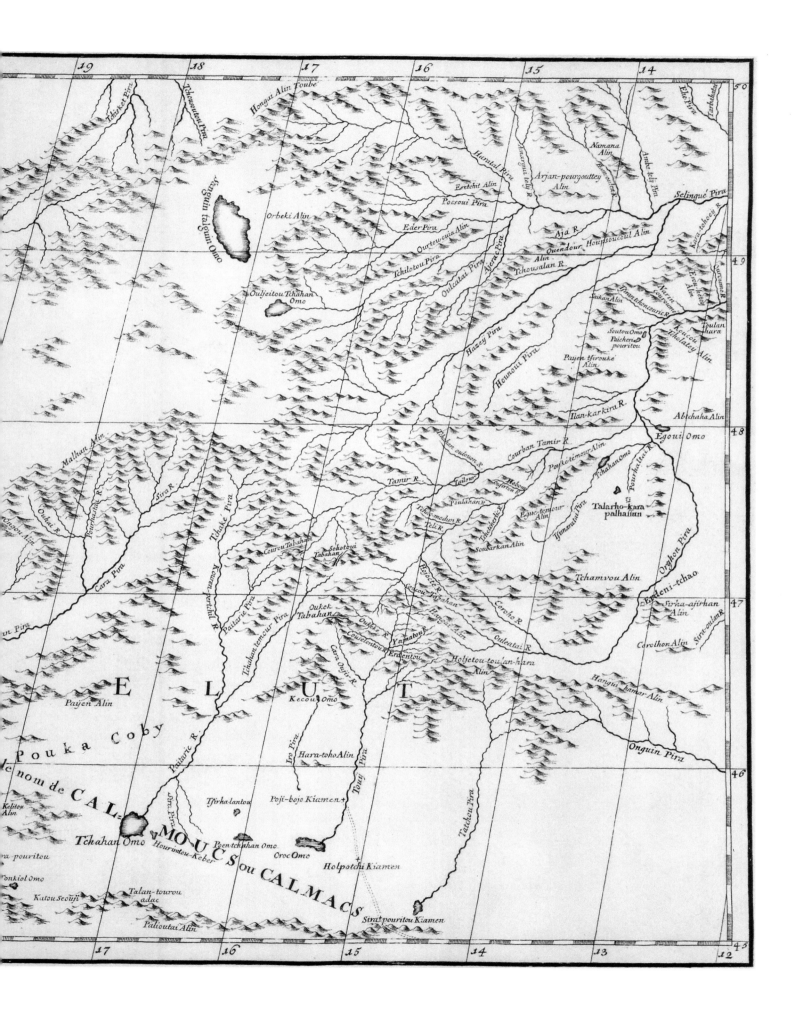

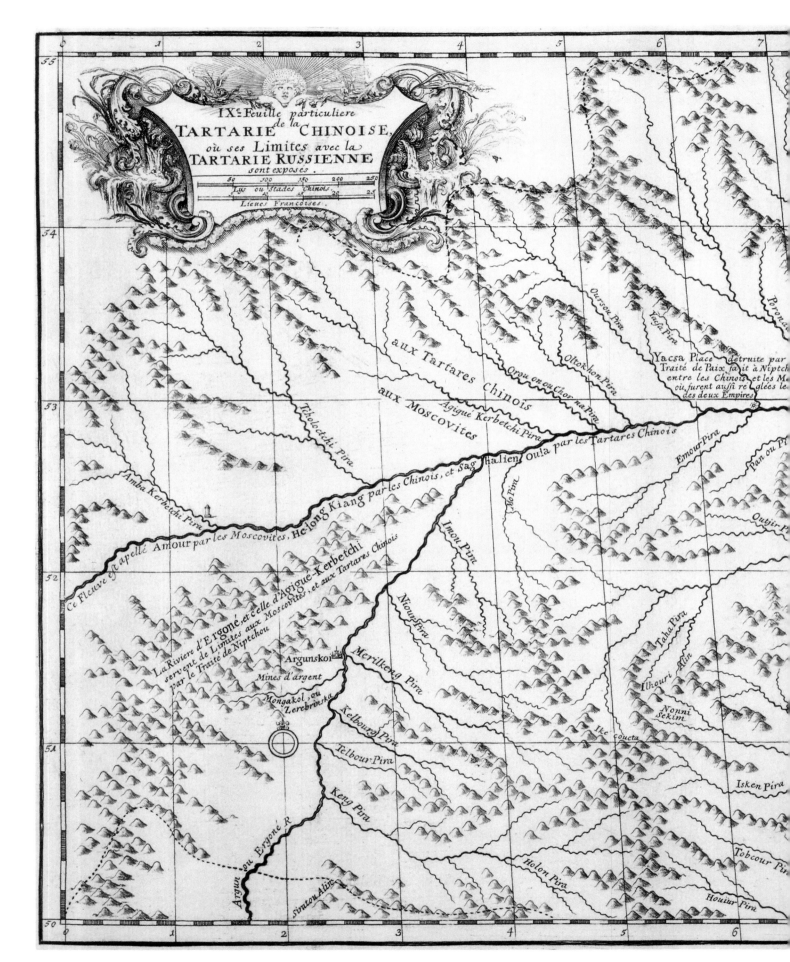

IX.e Feuille particuliere
de la
TARTARIE CHINOISE,
où ses Limites avec la
TARTARIE RUSSIENNE
sont exposés.

Lis ou Stades Chinois.

Lieues Francoises.

aux Tartares Chinois

aux Moscovites

Agigué Kerbetchi Pira

Tchoketchi Pira

Ce Fleuve est apellé Amour par les Moscovites, He-long Kiang par les Chinois, et Sag halien Oula par les Tartares Chinois

Amba Kerbetchi Pira

Orou on ou Chor na Pira

Oltok-hon Pira

Yaca Pira

Oursou Pira

Porona

Yacsa Place détruite par
Traité de Paix fa it à Niptch
entre les Chinois et les M
où furent aussi re glées le
des deux Empires

Emour Pira

Pan ou Pi

Outjir Pi

La Riviere d'Ergoné, et celle d'Agigue-Kerbetchi
servent de Limites aux Moscovites, et aux Tartares Chinois
par le Traité de Niptchou.

Ja Pira

Imou Pira

Niou-Pira

Argunskoi

Mines d'argent

Mongakol, ou
Zerebrinska

Merilkeng Pira

Kelbourg Pira

Telbour Pira

Keng Pira

Argun ou Ergoné R.

Siraton Alin

Holon Pira

Ike coucta

Taha Pira

Ilkouri Alin

Nonni
Sekim

Isken Pira

Tobcour Pir

Houlur Pira

MAP 27. Ninth detailed page [of Chinese Tartary]

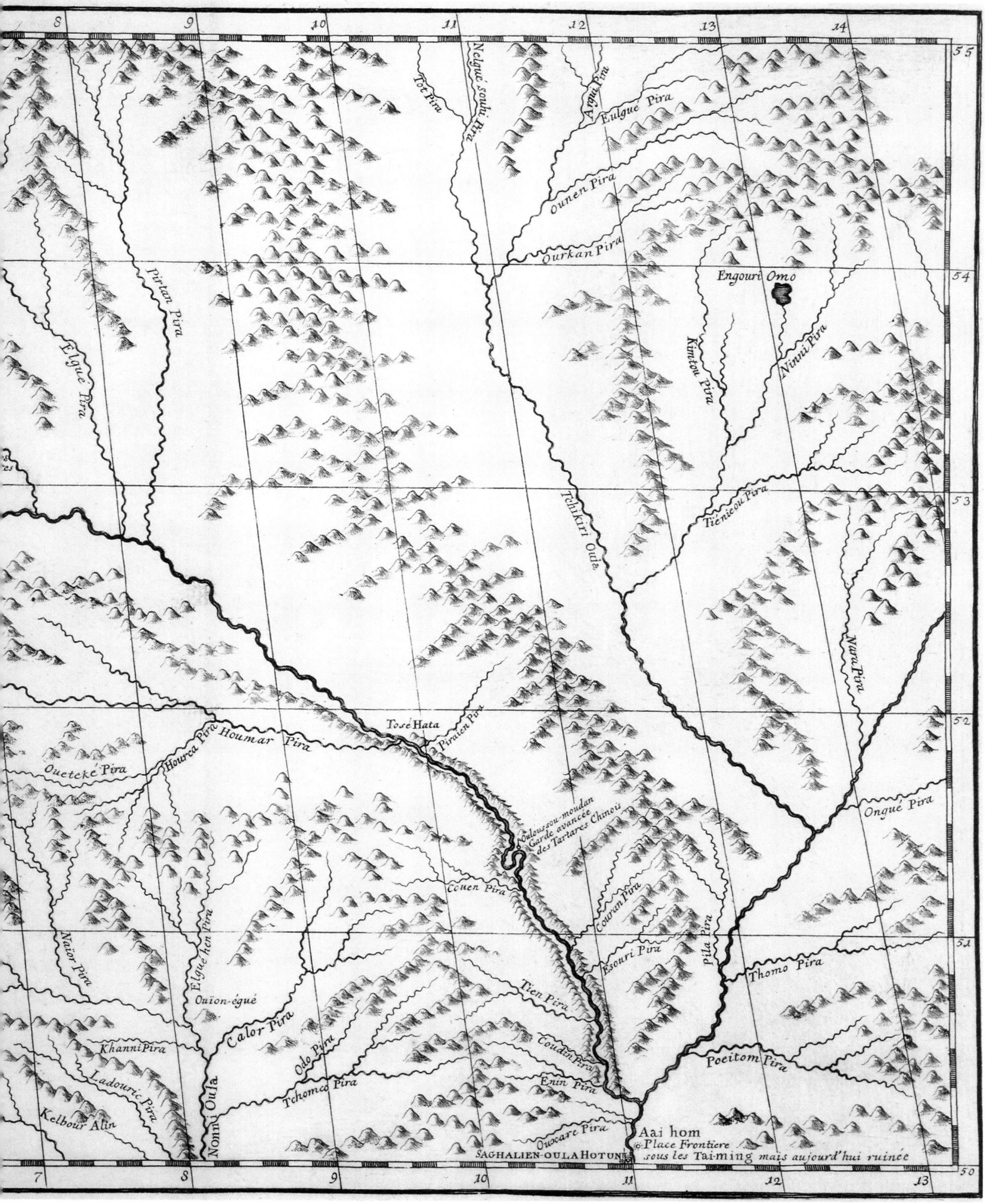
8
9
10
11
12
13
14
55
54
53
52
51
50
7
Tot Pira
Nelguі souhi Pira
Argui Pira
Eulgue Pira
Ounen Pira
Ourkan Pira
Engouri Omo
Kimtou Pira
Ninni Pira
Pirtan Pira
Elgue Pira
Tchikiri Oula
Tienieou Pira
Nara Pira
Tosé Hata
Piraien Pira
Hourca Pira
Houmar Pira
Oueteké Pira
Ongué Pira
Oulousou-moudan
Garde avancée
des Tartares Chinois
Couen Pira
Couran Pira
Pila Pira
Esouri Pira
Thomo Pira
Naior Pira
Elguéhen Pira
Ouïon-égué
Tien Pira
Calor Pira
Khanni Pira
Coudin Pira
Poeitom Pira
Ladouric Pira
Odo Pira
Tchomco Pira
Enin Pira
Nonni Oula
Kelbour Alin
Ouxare Pira
Aai hom
Place Frontiere
sous les Tai-ming mais aujourd'hui ruinée
SAGHALIEN-OULA HOTUN

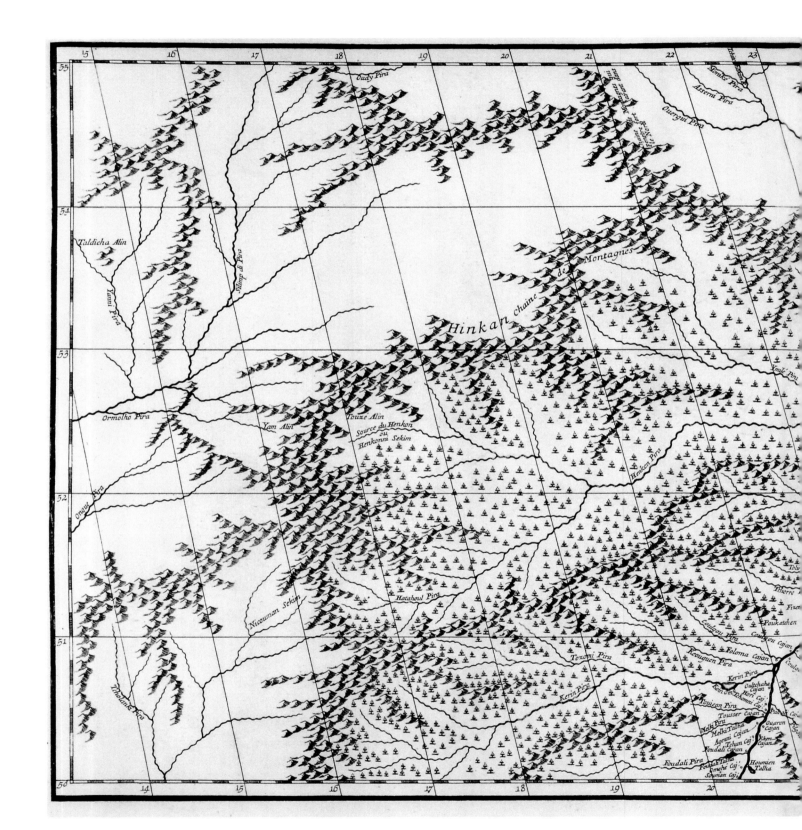

MAP 28. Tenth detailed page [of Chinese Tartary]

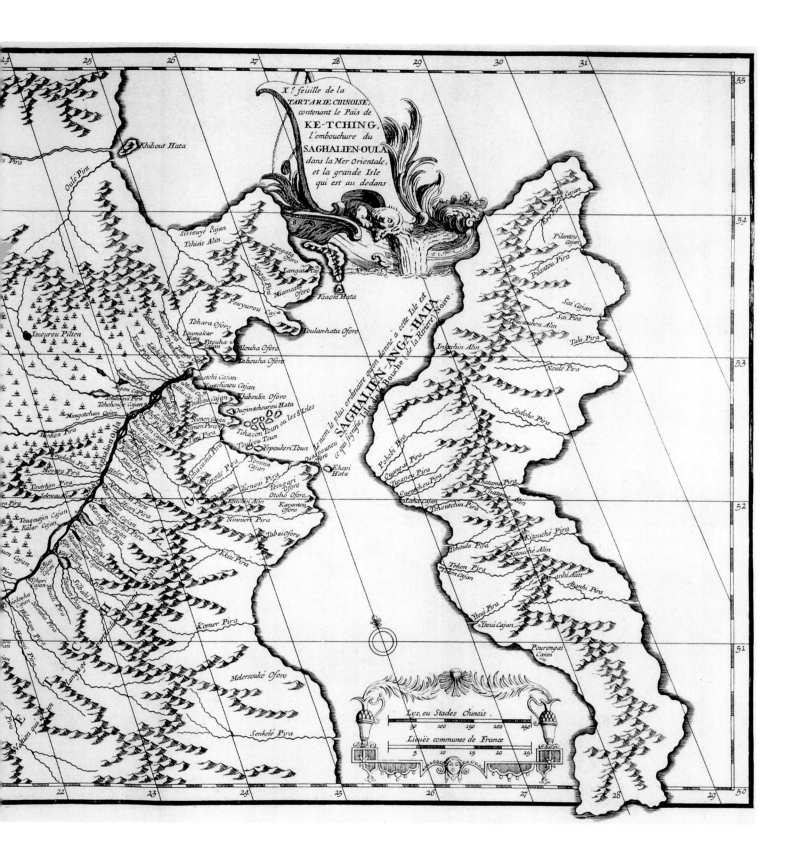

X.^e feuille de la
TARTARIE CHINOISE,
contenant le Païs de
KE-TCHING,
L'embouchure du
SAGHALIEN-OULA,
dans la Mer Orientale,
et la grande Isle
qui est au dedans

Khibout Hata

Oulé Pira

Siscouyé Cajan
Tchiric Alin

Langata Oforo
Langata Pira
Miameatn Oforo
Kiaoki Hata

Pouyurou Cajan

Tchara Oforo
Isumakar Hata
Fitpuha Cajan
Mouha Oforo
Houlan-hata Oforo
Tahouha Oforo

Isceurou Pilten

Mangatchan Cajan

Henken Pira

Ouctchi Cajan
Yaptchineu Cajan
Khiboulin Oforo
Ouejin-tcheurou Hata
Nimen Cajan
Nimen Pira
Eni Pira
Tchacon Toun ou les 8 Isles
Teulcou Toun
Yepoukeri Toun

SAGHALIEN-OULA

SAGHALIEN-ANGA-HATA
le nom le plus ordinaire qu'on donne à cette Isle est
ci qui signifie, Isle de la Bouche (de la Rivière) Noire

Quatsouneu
Ehepi Hata

Pohobi Pira

Cuangui Pira
Tiganek Pira
Cuendhou Pira
Lahai Cajan
Tchoutchun Pira

Moyeu Pira
Toutchin Pira
Toleucou Alin
Yeuqeutjin Cajan
Kalar Cajan
Thacama Pira
Kerete Pira
Henai Pira
Teingari Oforo
Otoho Oforo
Khitchin Alin
Kayantou Oforo
Ninnuei Pira
Tabai Oforo
Tikai Pira

Komer Pira

Melersouké Oforo

Senkelé Pira

Tchari Cajan
Tarli Pira
Hindouha Pira
Nenitha Pira

Inktchin Alin

Noulé Pira

Godoho Pira

Thatama Pira
Thatama Alin

Tchoula Pira
Token Pira
Teken Cajan
Ytevi Pira
Ytevi Cajan

Kitouché Pira
Kitouché Alin
Aranhi Alin
Aranhi Pira

Pourongai Cajan

Er Cajan

Pilantou Cajan
Pilantou Pira

Sai Cajan
Sai Pira
Tuchouhou Alin
Talu Pira

Lys, ou Stades Chinois.
50   100   150   200   250
Lieües communes de France
5   10   15   20   25

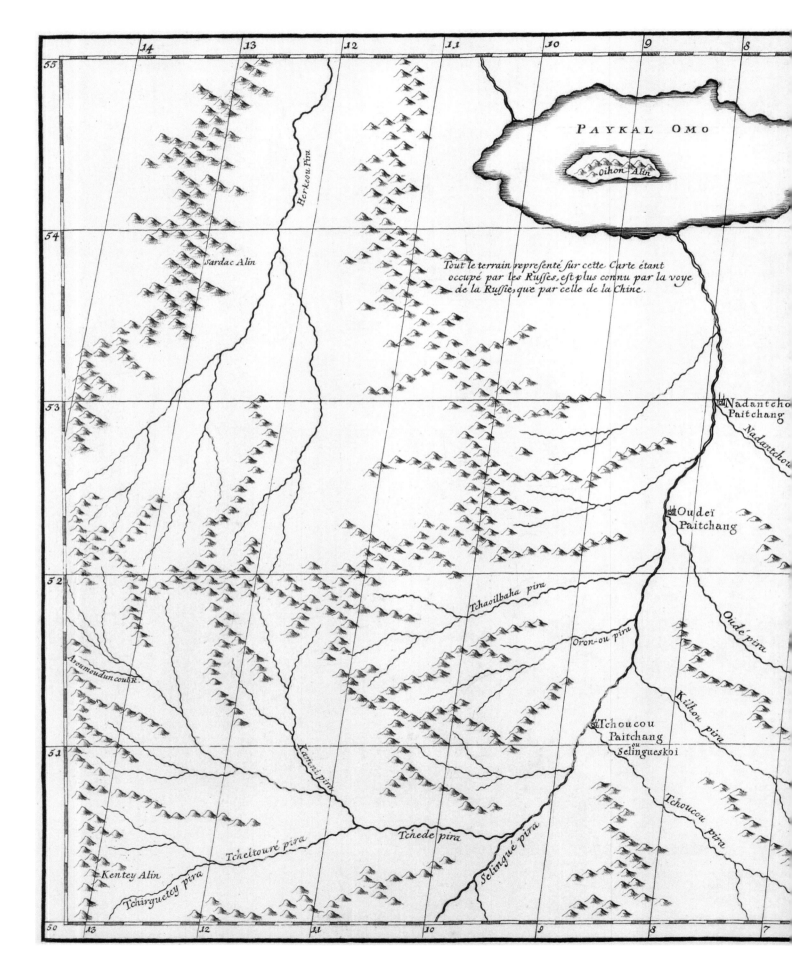

Text visible within the map:

PAYKAL OMO

Oihon Alin

Herkeou Pira

Sardac Alin

Tout le terrain representé sur cette Carte étant occupé par les Russes, est plus connu par la voye de la Russie, que par celle de la Chine.

Nadantcho Paitchang

Nadantchou

Oudeï Paitchang

Tchaoilbaha pira

Oron-ou pira

Oudé pira

Aoumoudun couli R.

Kilhou pira

Tchoucou Paitchang ou Selingueskoi

Karnail pira

Tchoucou pira

Tchede pira

Tcheitouré pira

Selingué pira

Kentey Alin

Tchirguetey pira

MAP 29. Eleventh detailed page [of Chinese Tartary]

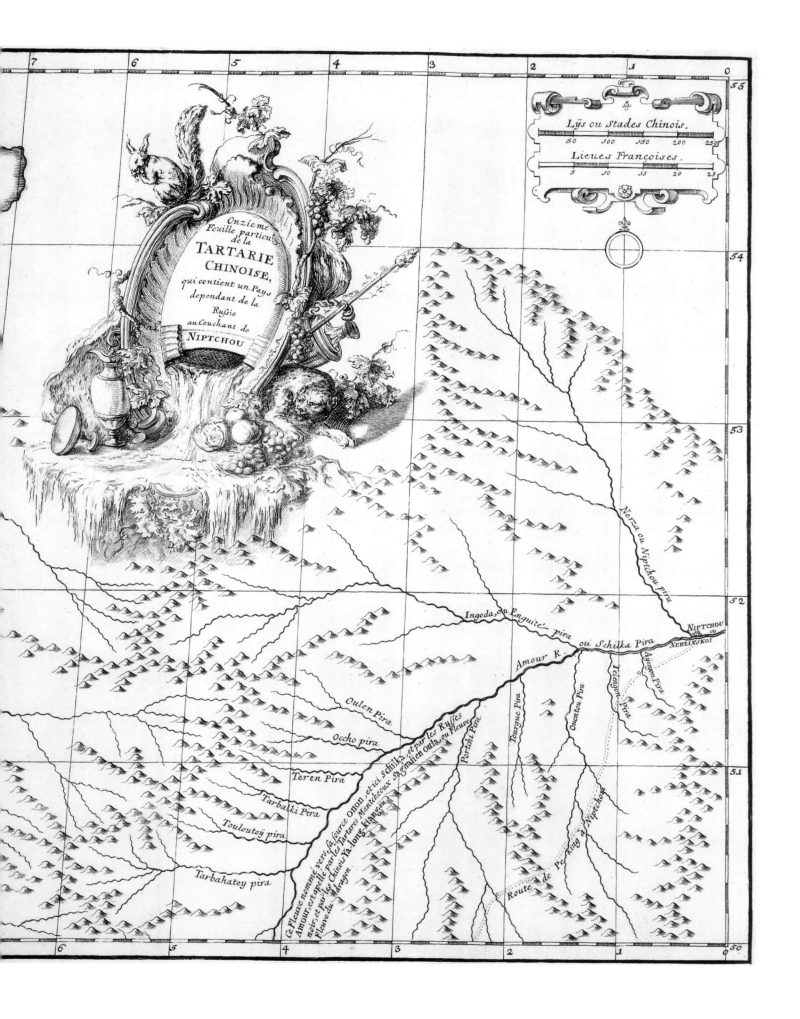

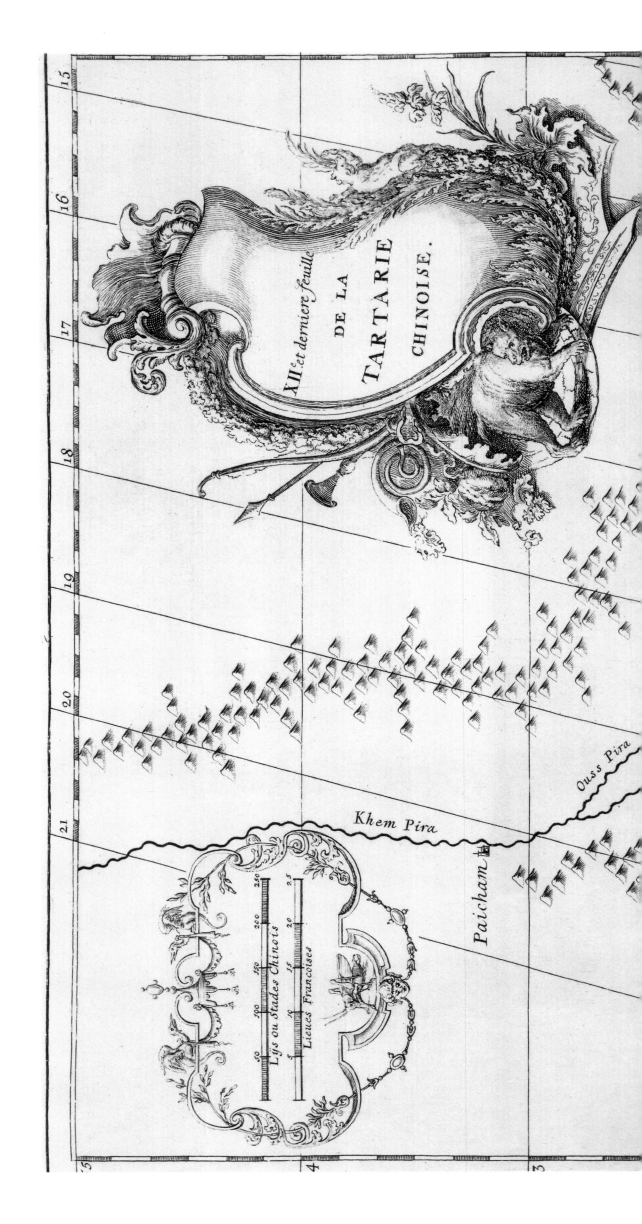

XIIe et derniere Feuille

DE LA

TARTARIE

CHINOISE.

Khem Pira

Ouss Pira

Paicham

Lys ou Stades Chinois

Lieues Francoises

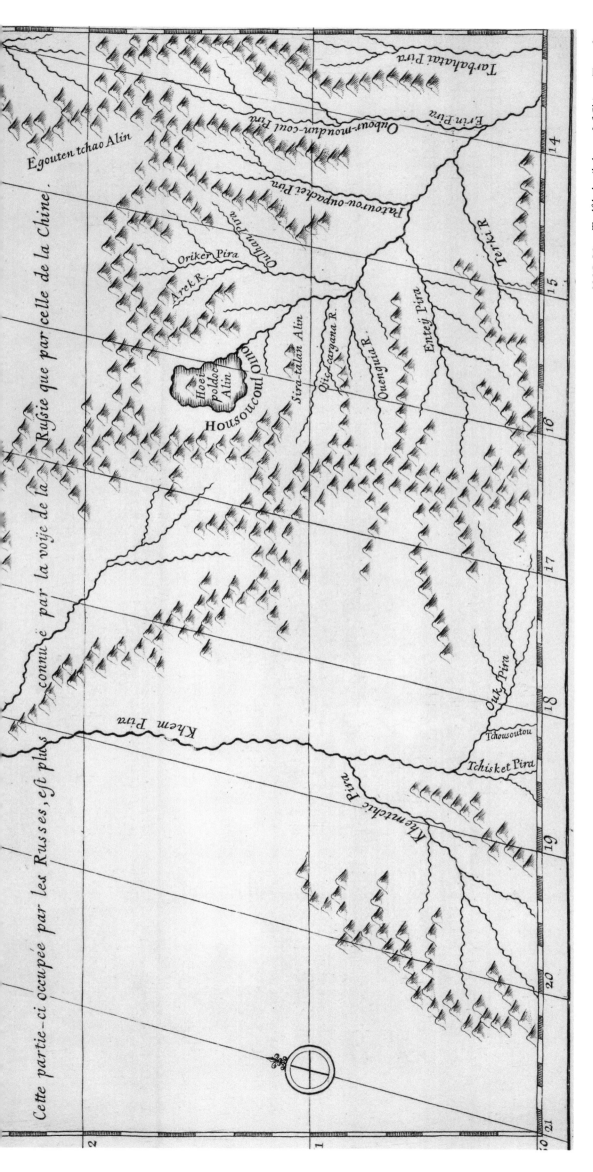

Cette partie-ci occupée par les Russes, est plus connuë par la voïe de la Russie que par celle de la Chine.

Egouten tchao Alin

Tarbahatai Pira

Erin Pira

Oubour-moudun-coul Pira

Patourou-ououdei Pira

Oriker Pira

Oulïan Pira

Arek R.

Hoei poldoc Alin.

Housouccoul Omno

Sira-talan Alin

Oic-caxyana R.

Ouenguïa R.

Entei Pira

Terki R.

Khem Pira

Outi Pira

Tchousoutou

Tchisket Pira

Khemtchic Pira

MAP 30.   Twelfth detailed page [of Chinese Tartary]

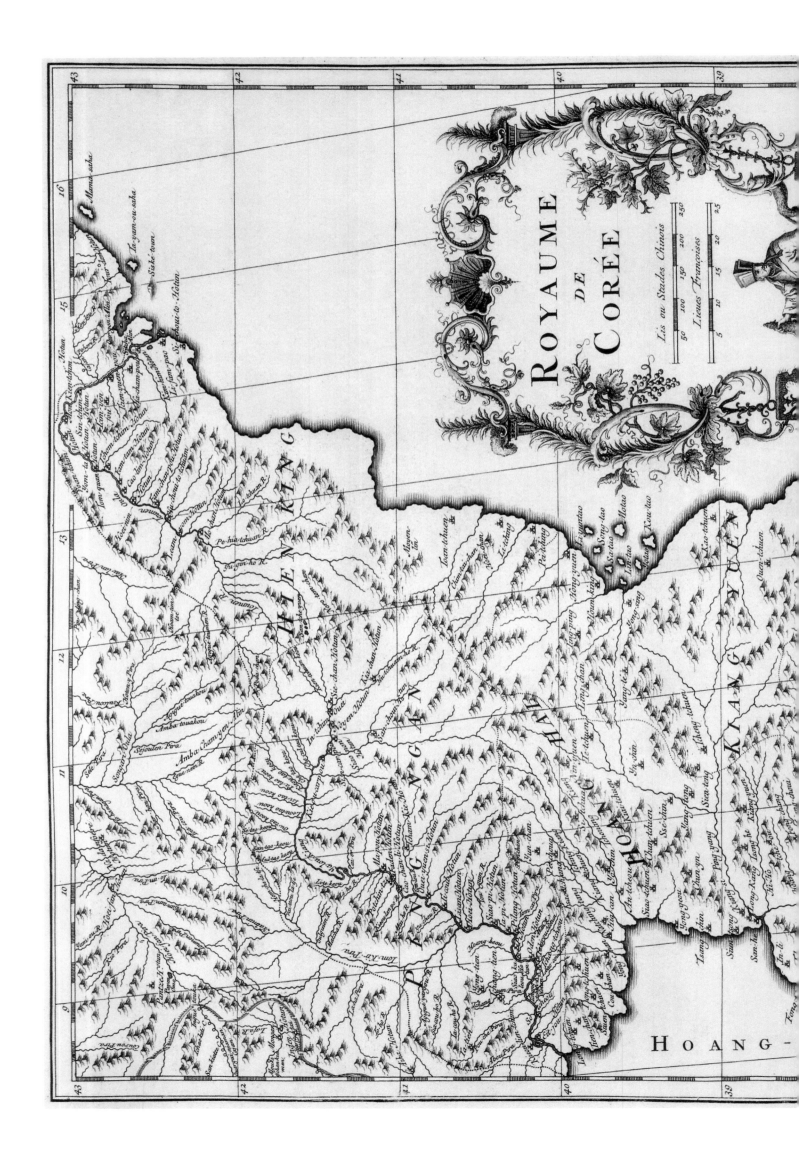

ROYAUME
DE
CORÉE

Lis ou Stades Chinois
Lieues Françoises

MAP 31.
The Kingdom
of Korea

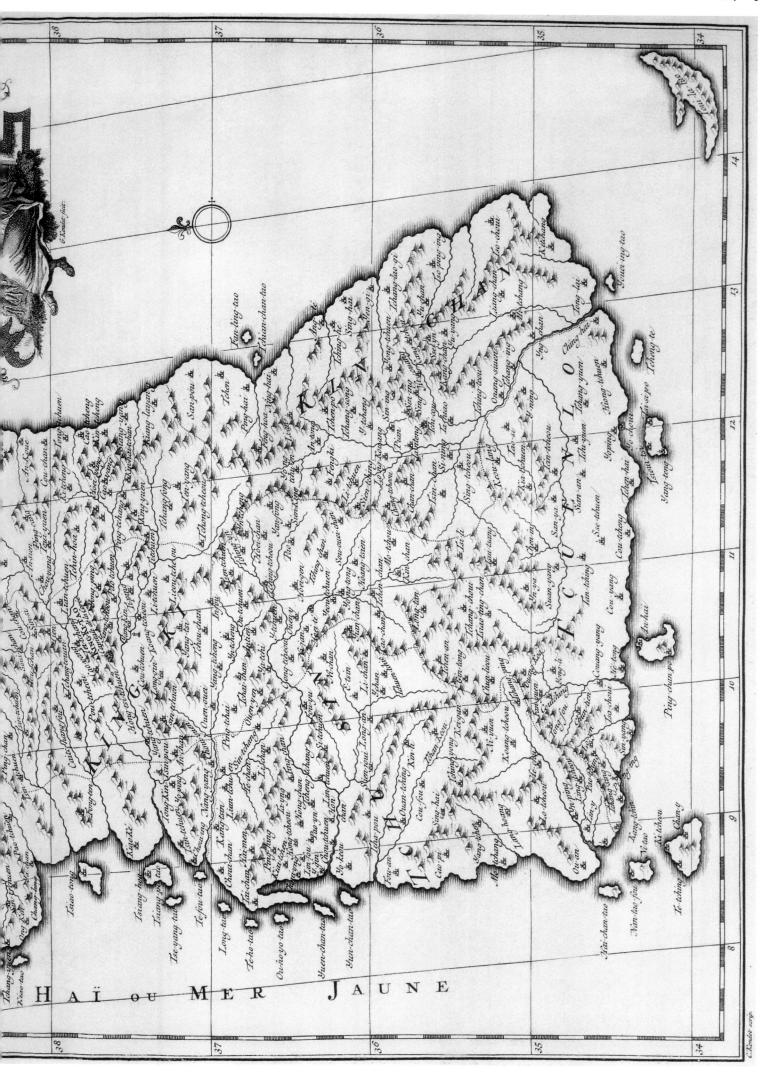

HAÏ ou MER JAUNE

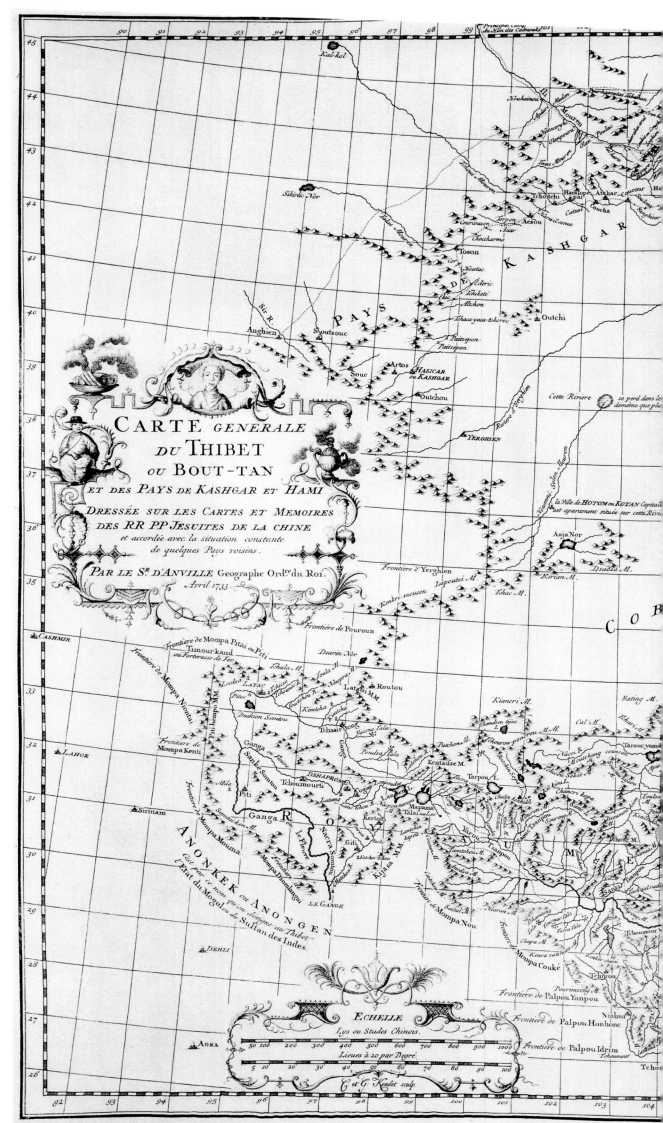

MAP 32.
General Map
of Tibet

Poro-opou

Kimsé

Tounel

Soroto-anga

Tchaca-por

Pilio

Minca

Honin-oso

Toboron

Churmatai

Kitaki

Morol

Moucour-pion

Norse-pion

Souhaitou

Porotchoui

Hara-oso

Cor

Pasta-noma
Cobi

Coucchetou

Catao

Chaca-hamar

Ercouseti

Routchetou

Oronhi

Cachun Seghien Yolotou Hotun

Opto-kiltekan

Alac-tchoutchi

Actas Hotun

Ourton Poulac

Orto

Olan-oso

Hapircan Poulac

Par col
Par col

Orto
Poulac

Mohaito

Courmetou

Orto Hotun

Torpol

Semtchin
Hotun

Tchictama

Sira Hami

Tchaca-hamar

Pou rol

Tagouric

Lemtchin

Otor-ketcheme

Asaralic ou
Asarlic Hotun

Tchacteli

Pitchan

Hong

Cobi-hontchin

Tekelit

Tchaca

Tohotchic Hotun

Talpia

Egimec

Tchacar

Astac ou Astané
Hotun

Tchac-lactagi

Laptchou Hotun

Somen char Hotun

Ilcon

HAML
HOTUN

Hatamtam

Couselento

Asartou

Hara-oussour

Hara-toube

Sira-ouloso

Tala-Oso

Eltemor ou Eldemor

Ontchi Pou

COBI   DESE

Polte

Lop Omo

Keser yanton

Kanio

Paha-cachon

Annhirto, ou Anghir

Ike-cachon

Cachon

Pachi ou Pagi-houtos

Tamé-oso

Talai-hotoc

Orton

Nere-okouei-hatac

Tchonou-hotoc

Ilhon

Yapar-hotoc

Toson-hotoc

Olan-tcharim

Hotoc-oso

Tala oso

Couptchen Poulac

Ohoulang

Torpetchin

Souichonto

Manitou

Ocol

Tchaca-tchontchi

Soroto

Olosotai

Hara-Omo

Hara-oso

Tchaca-tohoi

Emer-yapar

El cong-ming

Choua

Coucou-tchacsac

Pour-hato

Cha tcheou

Tas-poulsa

Payan-mouren

Pouro-tchontchi

Sipgicon-couten

Sirkatchi ou

MAP 33.   First detailed page [of Tibet]

20　　　　　19　　　　　18　　　　　17　　　　　16　　45

Lys ou Stades Chinois.

Lieues Françoises.

chi Atchi

honnotei

ké noma
Cobi

Setereng

E.tereng

E.tereng

44

Eké

Noÿen-hara Alin

Maila Poulac

Onekon

43

Sira-oso　　Soukouc Omo

T　　　o　u　　　　C　H　A　-　M　O

Cholong-kotoc

Houpatar Paitchang

Sopou ou Sobou Omo

Hapircan ou Hapiracan

Koutoulé pira

Tchi-tchouam

42

Tchaca-tchontchi

Chao-ma-ing

Chao-ma-ing　Hotun

Iᵉ FEUILLE
Comprise dans la
Carte Générale du
THIBET
qui contient en par
ticulier
L'Extrêmité Occi
dentale du grand
DESERT de SABLE
et le
PAYS AUX EN
VIRONS DE
HAMI.

lic

ura-oudouc　Chaca-teryaso

Mao-mo

Tchang

manni Poulac

Ouei-yuen

Toraito

Tien-tsang

Yang-hong-tou

Hoa-tsiang

Polonhir-Pira

Pourol

Co-hong

Oua cong-jn

Alac Omo

Tapson or

ori

CatchiPoulac

Tchi-ke-tching

Etchine Pira

a-hai

Ouei-lo

Tarito

Keta tching

Pong

19　　　　　18　　　　　17　　　　　16　　　　　15　　　　　14　　40

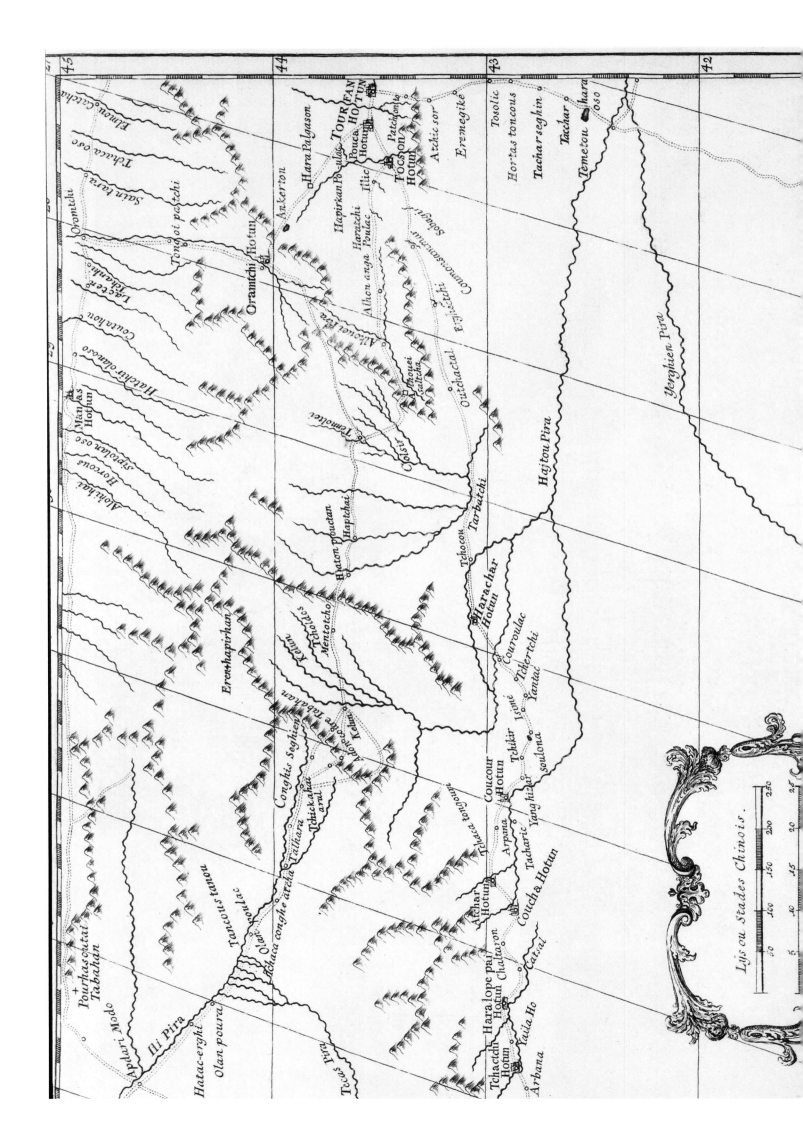

Lijs ou Stades Chinois.

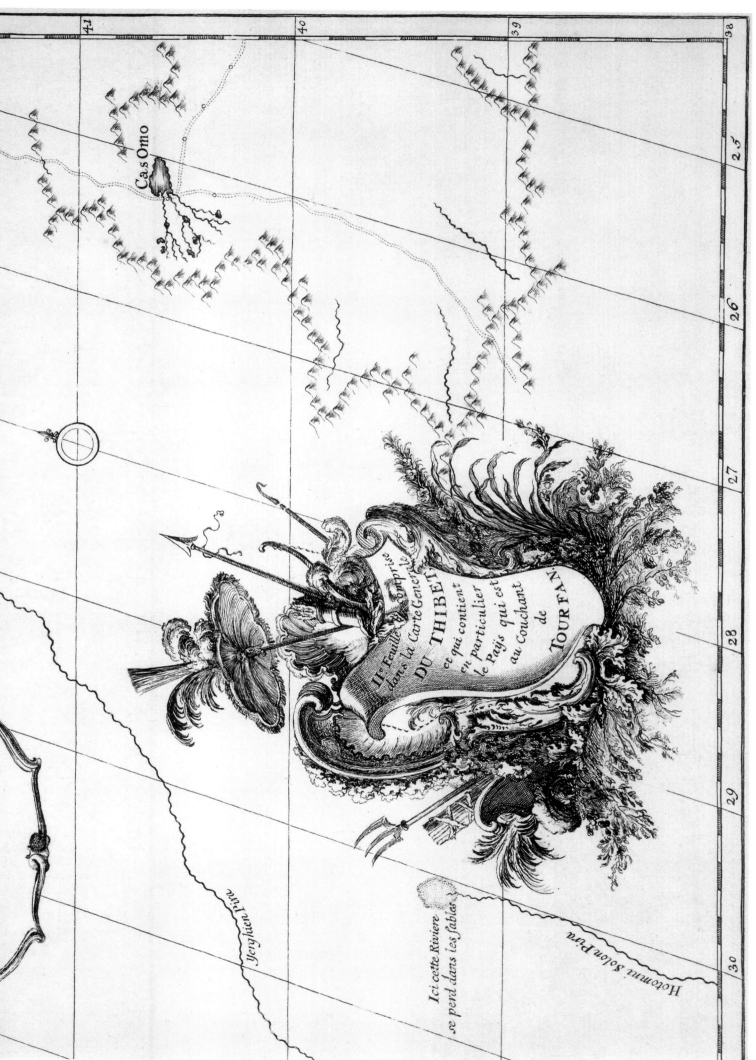

MAP 34.
Second detailed
page [of Tibet]

41

40

39

38

25

26

27

28

29

30

Cas Omo

II.ᵉ Feuille comprise
dans la Carte Generale
DU THIBET
et qui contient
en Particulier
le Pais qui est
au couchant
de
TOURFAN

Yerghen Piru

Ici cette Riviere
se perd dans les sables

Hotonnu selon Piru

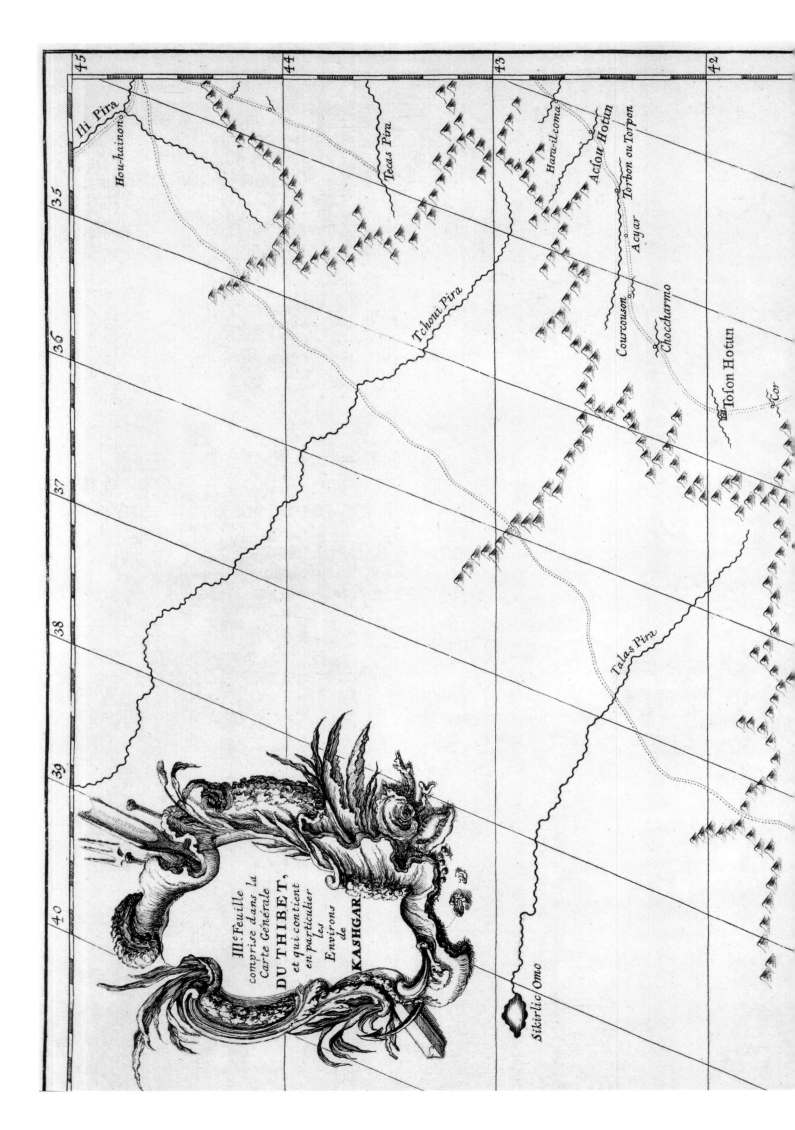

45

44

43

42

35

36

37

38

39

40

Ili Pira

Hou-hainono

Teeas Pira

Tchoui Pira

Haru-ilcoma

Acíou Hotun

Torbon ou Torpon

Acyar

Courcouson

Choccharmo

Tofon Hotun

Cor

Talas Pira

Sikiurlic Omo

IIIᵉ Feuille
comprise dans la
Carte Générale
DU THIBET,
et qui contient
en particulier
les
Environs
de
KASHGAR

MAP 35.

Third detailed
page [of Tibet]

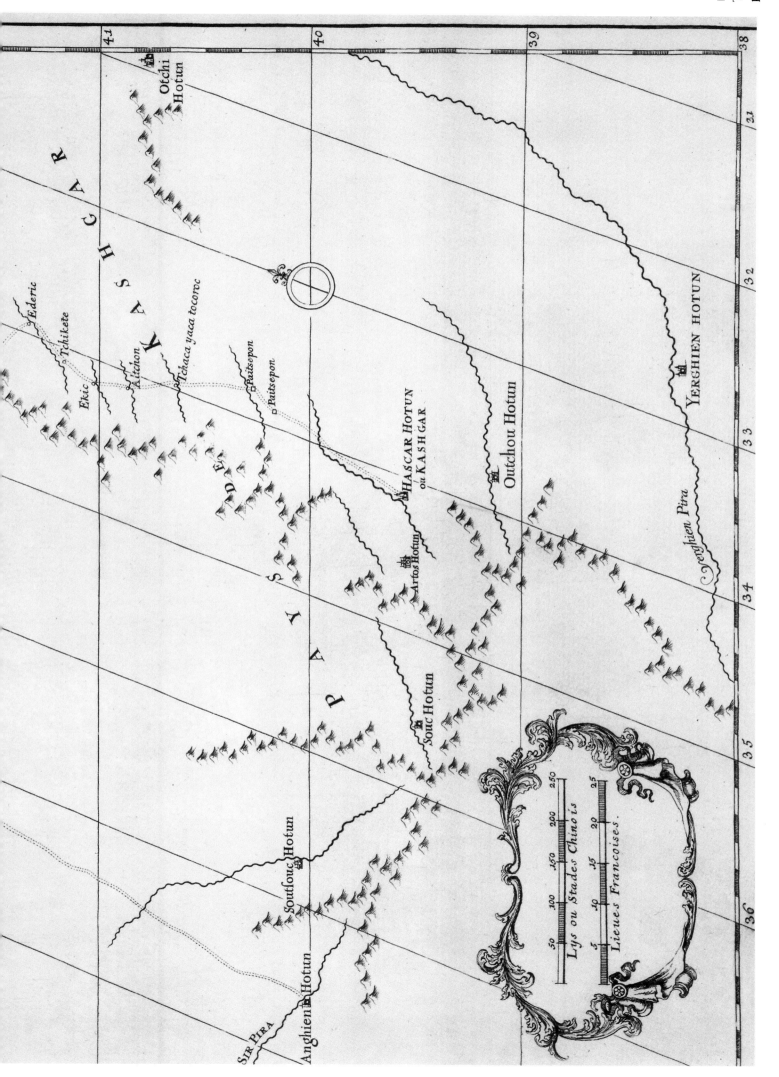

41

40

39

38

31

32

33

34

35

36

K A S H G A R

Otchi
Hotun

Ederic

Tchikete

Altchon

Ekic

Tchaca yaca tocoroc

Paitsepon

Paitsepon

Paitsepon

D E L

S

P A Y S

HASCAR HOTUN
ou KASH GAR

Artos Hotun

Souc Hotun

Outchou Hotun

YERGHIEN HOTUN

Yerghien Pira

Soutfouc Hotun

SIR PIRA

Anghien Hotun

Lys ou Stades Chinois

250

200

150

100

50

Lieues Francoises.

25

20

15

10

5

25　24　23　22　21　20

40

Poropitong *opo houta sou*　*Iletertei*　*Tc haca oso*

Hara Hata　*Ike houbang*

Paha houtang　*Oulan Habalan*

Houtong　*Itche*

39

Serteng

IV.ᵉ. *Feuille*
Comprise dans la Carte gene-
rale du **THIBET**, *et*
qui contient en particu-
lier le Pais des
TARTARES
de
HOHO-NOR

38

COBI ᴏᴜ **DESERT DE SABLE**

Horloue Omo

Hara O

37

F.M.LaClave Sculp.

Elason Omo

Talo Tc

Tchaiteng Pira

36

Ici cette riviere
se perd dans
les sables.

T A R T A

Alac Omo

35

Paha tom kot

Tcharing Omo

23　22　21　20　19

MAP 36.　Fourth detailed page [of Tibet]

19   18   17   16   15   14

40

Touha poulac
Ourcastai
Cong tchouha
Kia yu quan
Sotcheou   *Choun tcin pou*   *Tching pou*
Etshine Pira
PROVINCE
Tcin choui pou
Ting ngnan pou
Kaotai so
Hong tchoui pou   *Cha ho y*
Li yuen pou

Lys ou Stades Chinois
50   100   150   200   250
Lieues communes de France
5   10   15   20   25

Kan tcheou
Long tcheou pou
Chan tan ing
Nan cou tching
Hong chouing
Yung coutchin
Tuma ing
Kao cou tchin
Yang tchang oei   *Cha ho y*
Ngin yuen pou
Yong ngin pou

39

Hatou palbou Pira
Toulai Pira
Fitcheni Pira
CHEN-SI
Leangtcheou
Tcho urouke Tabahan

Ta ho y

Olan mouren Pira
38

ghe mo
Coulan Tabahan
Koutchiniy Tabahan
Miao ou Pagode
Tze horgi Pira
Cococ Pira
Tatzu Tabahan
Ke olan hoc ho Pira
Tchin kiang in

Pouca Pira
Paha omo
37

Cor Omo
HO-HO-NOR
Temba
Oei yuen pou
Tai tong Ho
Tchaha hata
Couisun Toulouhai
Poro tchonke Pira
Tolun Pira
To pa
Por Omo
Tapson Omo
Tchin ha pou
Sining oei
Lao a ya pou
Poulonkir Pira
Coutchuen pou
Ping siao y
CHEN

u Tabahan
Naran saro Tabahan
Conke
Sira toro cheri

36

RES   *HO-HO-NOR*
Tct du chan
ashang nin y
Corten sira cheri
Ho ang Ho
Hofcheou
in Shue
SI
rin antsai
Cheu hpu Pira
Ta hia pou

Toson Omo   *Toure Omo*

35

18   17   16   15   14   13

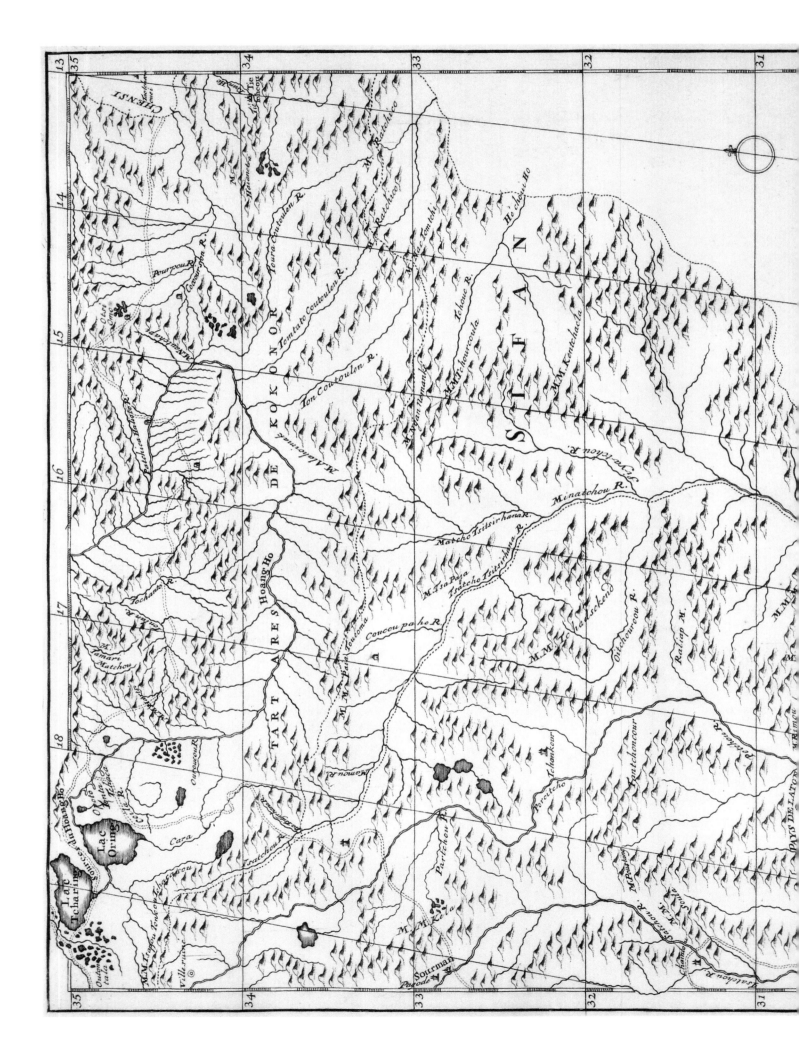

MAP 37.

Fifth detailed page
[of Tibet]

V. feuille
qui est proprement
la premiere
DU TIBET,
et qui contient
LE SI-FAN
et Païs
Limitrophe.

Lijsou Stades chinois.
50   100   150   200   250

Lieües communes de France.
5   10   15   20   25

30

29

28

27

13

14

15

16

17

18

CHU-ES

Ta-tien Leou

Parma tchou ou
Douane

Tanker tong

Toutsi tchamrialong

Mitcho R.

M.Pouitatang

M.Toura

M.Champtan

M.Tara

Contehoud'ong

Metchantou

 g

oula

Mi. Charoutrou
Nantincou

Sompil

PG
M.Kioutrenatam

Payr tichar tactam

Metchou R.

CAARKENTING

Mili

ou kiau

Ti-ha-Fan
Tonker tong

Petchou R.

PAYS DE POMSARA

PAYS DE DSANCLO

Tchou R.

TERRES DES LAMAS
DE
MONG FAN

Vou leang Ho

Kin-tcha Kiang
ou Sable d'Or

Lan tsan Kiang

CYONG NING TOU FOU

LI KIANG TOU FOU

YUN - NAN

Nou Kiang

YA-OUA-KOUÉ
ou
Royaume d'AVA

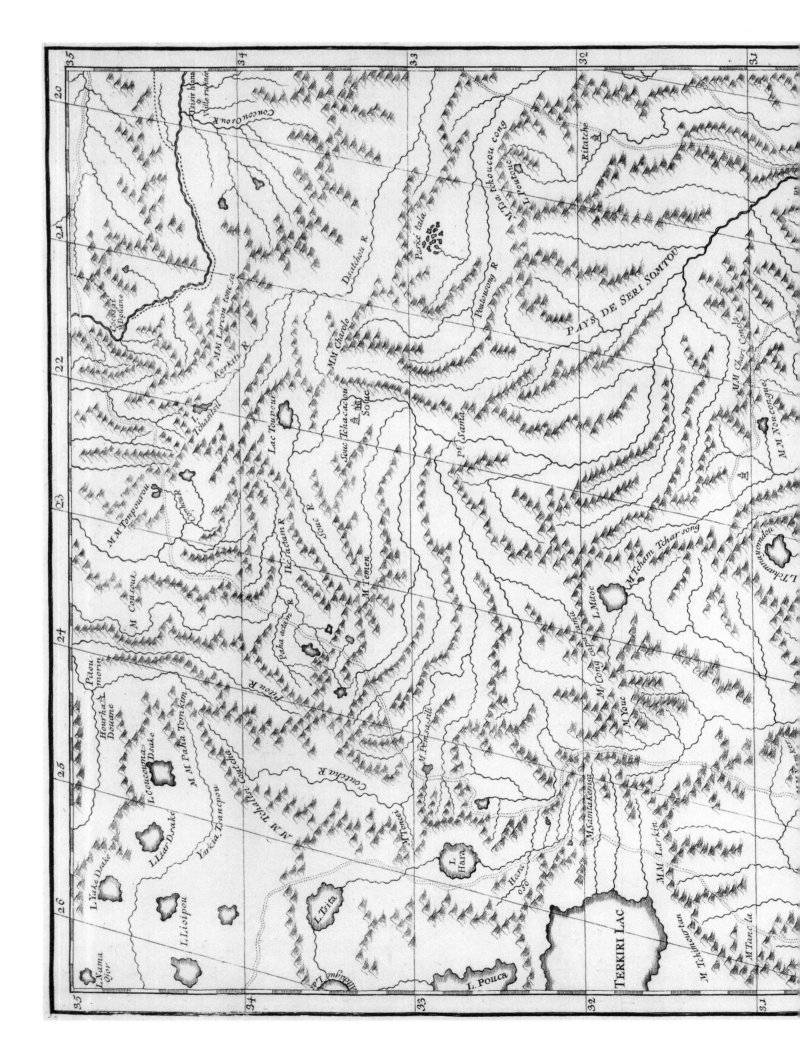

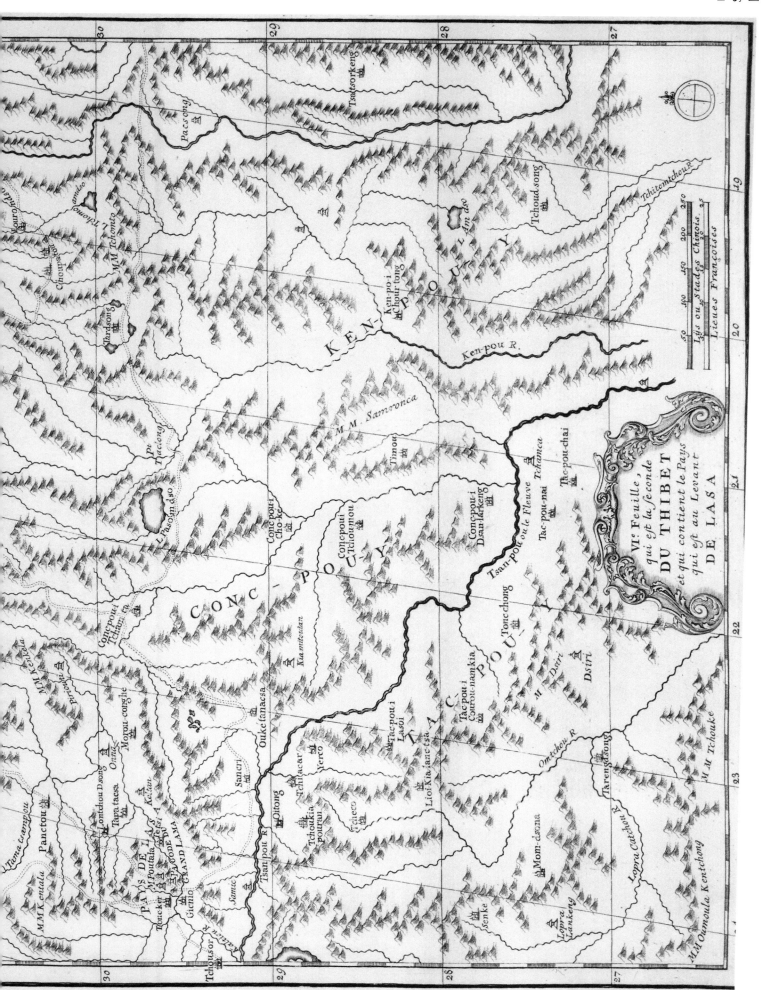

MAP 38.

Sixth detailed page
[of Tibet]

VI.ᵉ Feuille,
qui est la seconde
DU THIBET
et qui contient le Pays
qui est au Levant
DE LASA.

KEN-POU-Y

CONC-POU-Y

TAC-POU-Y

PAYS DE LASA

Tsatsorkeng

Ken-poi Tchour tong

Ken-pou R.

L. Am dso

Tchoud-song

Tchitemtchou R.

M. M. Samronca

Timou

Concpou i Dsan-larkeng

Tchamca

Tac-pou-chai

Tac-pou-nai

Tsan-pou ou le Fleuve

Concpou i Tchoumou

Concpou i Choke

Tac pou i Courot-nankia

Ton-chong

M. Dsri

Dstri

Omtchou R.

Ka mteitan

Tac-pou i Lasoi

Lioi-Kia-larc-tsa

Ouke lanacsa

Yerco

Mom-csana

Lopra Catchou R.

Tarengdsong

Lopra Lienkeng

M. M. Tchouke

M. M. Oumoula Kentchong

Tchoukia pourun

Echeo

Tchllacar

Senke

Oitong

Tsan-pou R.

Samie

Gichio GRAND LAMA

PAGODE DU

Toucker M Poutala

Loitchou Dsong

Tapataesa

Ona

Kelan

Moroui-congke

Piroule

M. M. Kentela

M. M. entala

Panctou

V. Tiana tcempou

Sancri

Tchousor R.

Tchousor R.

Concpou i Tchang

Pu Tiaiong

L. Pason dso

M. M. Tchomto

Thardson

Chouparon

L. Tsomo il I.

Passong

amdso

Lieues Françoises

Lis ou Stades Chinois

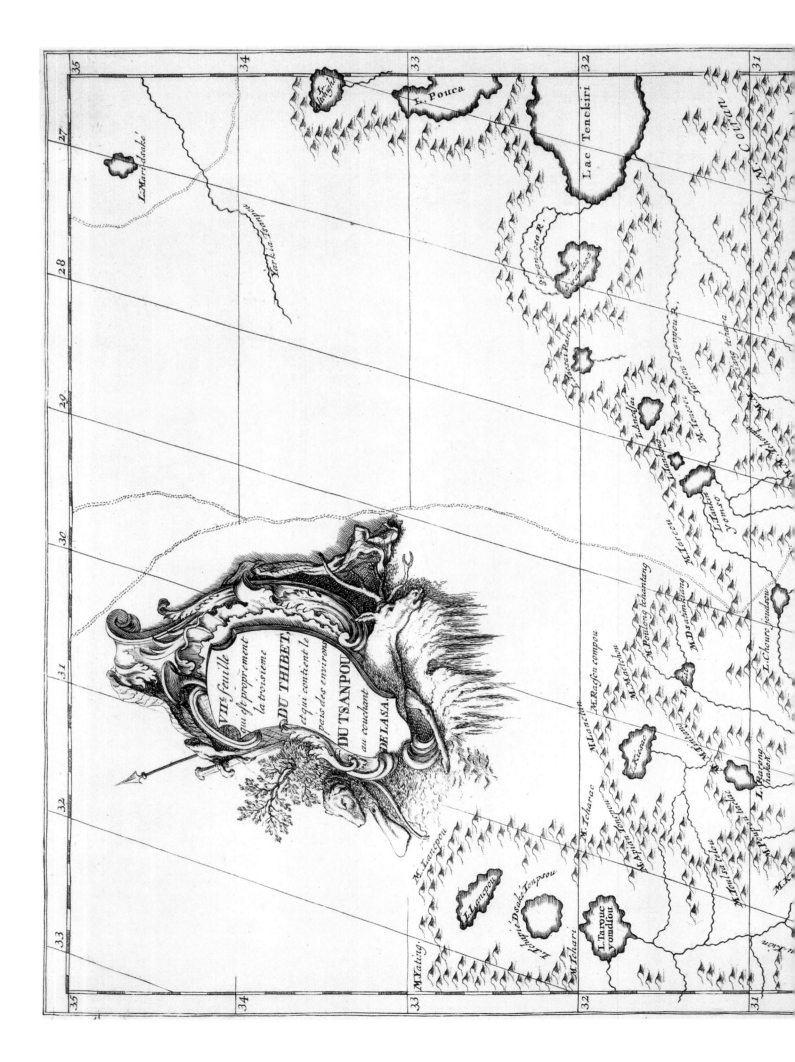

VIII.ᵉ feuille
qui est proprement
la troisième
DU THIBET,
et qui contient le
pais des environs
DU TSANPOU
au couchant
DE LASA.

L. Aichighi
L. Pouca
Lac Tenckiri
La Marjednake
Yar-Kia Tsanpou
Siban-losa R.
Coïran
Teonkoso
Tosai Poteki
L.Ancissai
Lidantsing
M. Tencou Yar-ou Tsanpou R.
L. Itang te-tcha
L. Tanken Yomso
M. Hercou
M.Dsabomtsiang L.
M. Peulong Tchantang
L. Choure Youdeou
M. Poulong Tchantang
M.Bokiari
M. Matchou
M.Apian Toupou
L.Reagong
L. Choure
Thibet
M.Laictun M.Ragon conpou
M. Kione
M.Yating.
M.Laocpou
M.Tcharac
M.Laocpou
L.Chighi Dsake Tonpsou
I.Laocpou
M.Tchari
L. Tarouc
Yomdfou
M.Peup
M.Teulsa telou
M.Yting
M.K.

MAP 39.
Seventh detailed
page [of Tibet]

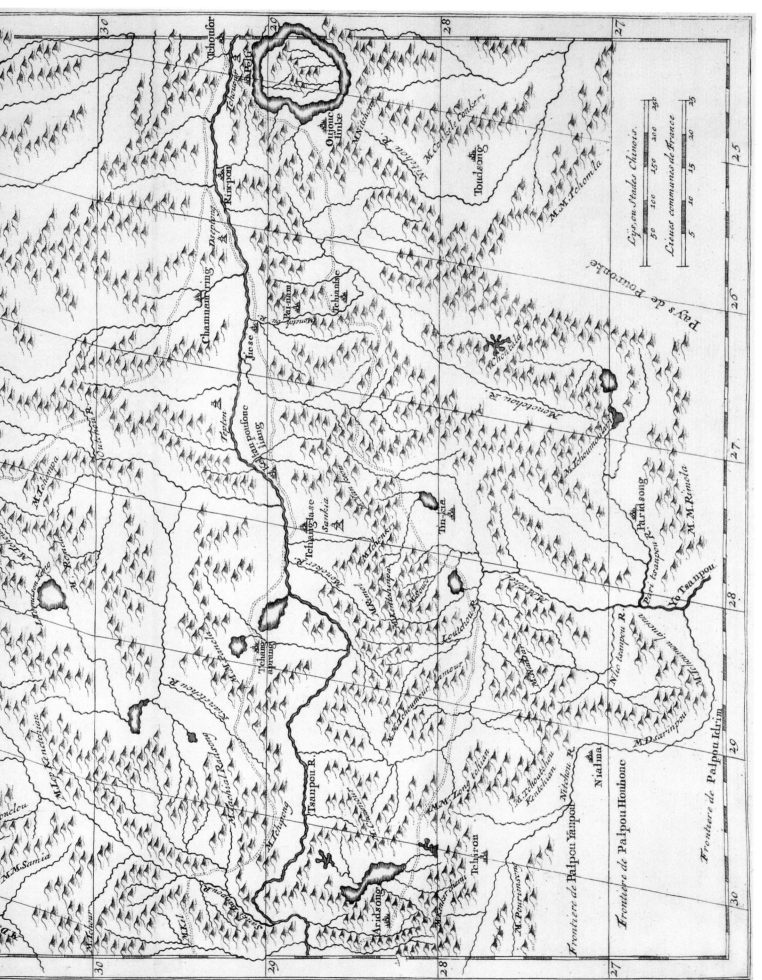

Tchonsor

à Petit

Tchaume R

Rincpou

Dsrphra

Chaune R ring

Jiese

Taptin

Ouitita P.

M Tchompa

M Remela

Lorum dom Kong

Michelou

M M Samia

onclou

Mki

M Lop Kentchian

Magchian Rado

Kiantchou R.

Tsampou R.

M Tchping

Kouora

Tchang spring

M M Tchomla

Oujouc
linke

M Nitchou

M Couhli Coulzri

Toutsong

Michou

Pai-nam

Tchanise

Monday on R.

Tsan poufouc
liang

Tchangla se

Sankia

Tan Sea

R. Tchang

Monderir R.

M Tchenku

M Ramo

Mitchahnga

Aidoue R.

Tin-sta

Leuichou R.

M Kentchian

Pays de Poutouke

Ljis ou Stades Chinois.

50   100   150   200   250

Lieues communes de France

5   10   15   20   25

Monichou R

Tchontala

M Tchoumoulashi

M Renela

Paridsong
Part Tsanpou R.

To Tsaupou

M M Renela

Nio tsmpou R.

M Tchi

Nitchou R.

M Dsarinpou

Nialma

M Tchoutthau
Kentchian

Tehjron

M M Long tchlian

M Tchoumouin lanour

M Poutonson

Aridsong

M M Ser chang

Frontiere de Palpou Yampou

Frontiere de Palpou Houhone

Frontiere de Palpou Idrim

25

26

27

28

29

30

27

28

29

30

30

20

28

27

25

26

27

28

20

30

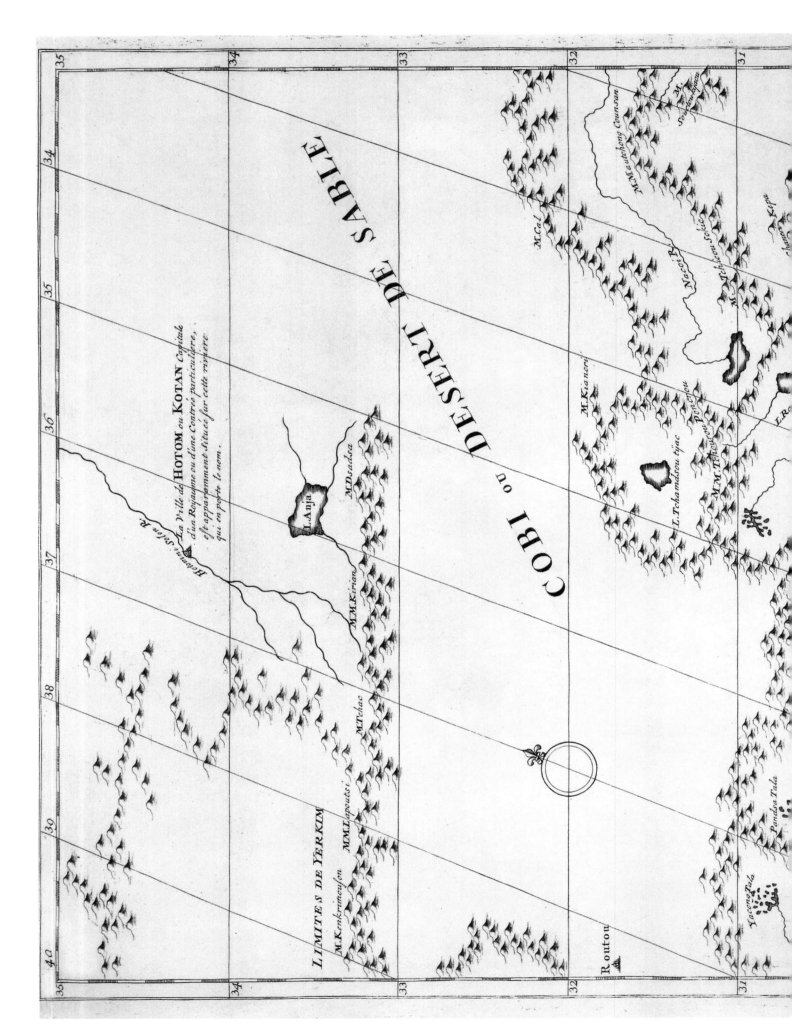

COBI ou DESERT DE SABLE

LIMITES DE YERKIM

La Ville de HOTOM ou KOTAN Capitale
d'un Royaume ou d'une Contrée particuliere,
est apparemment situeé sur cette riviere
qui en porte le nom.

MAP 40.

Eighth detailed
page [of Tibet]

VIII.e feuille
qui est proprement
la quatrième
DU THIBET,
et qui donne l'origine
DU TSANPON et DU GANGE,

FRONTIERE DE MOMPA-COUKE

FRONTIERE DE MONPA-NOU

PAYS DE NACRA
(SONTOU ATCHAN)

Ganga R. qui va dans le Mogol

Lys ou Stades Chinois.

50   100   150   200   250

Lieües communes de France.

5   10   15   20   25

M.r Kentaisse

L.
Mapama

L.
Lauken

L. Tarpou

Naouc Tsanpou R.

Artchou R.

Kianc.Ria Somta R.

Yarot Dsancpou ou Tsanpou R.

Matchou R.

Kerton

Pourimi
Tacla

Jiti ou Gitti

Ketchar-tchou

Tsantchia Kipou

Dsanfrong
ou
Tchalprong
Latang

Cogue
Lonpudse

MM. Choula

Tchantong
Tir.la

Tronumbecke

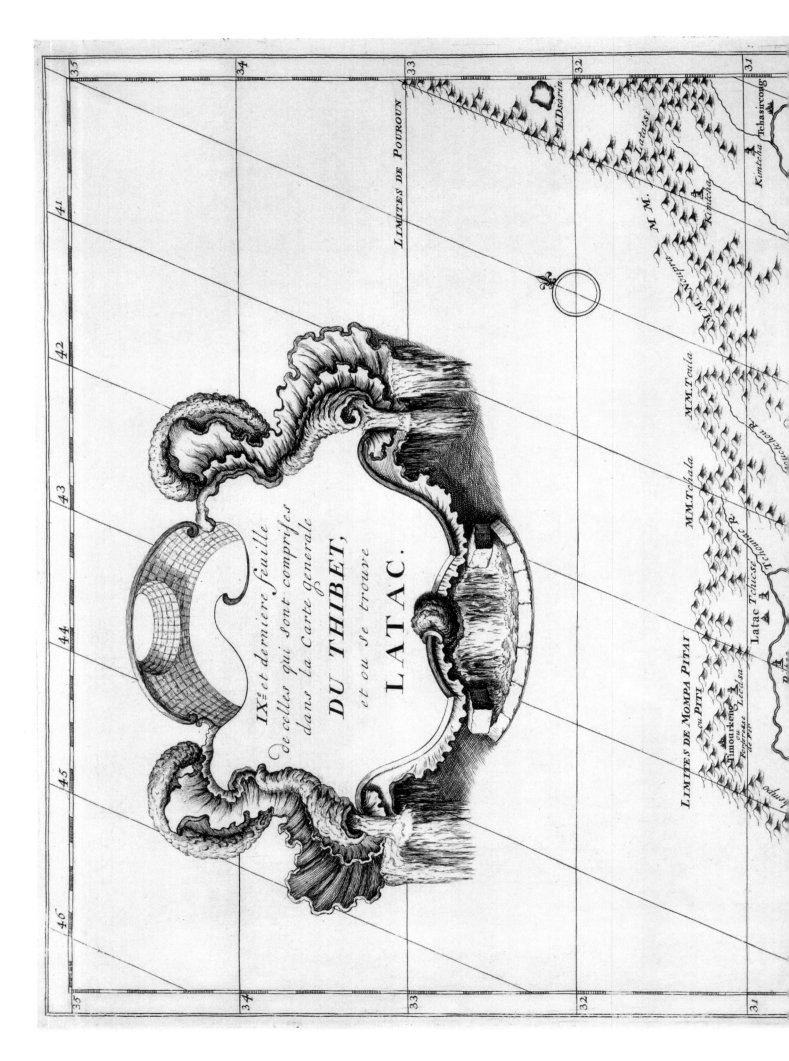

LIMITES DE POUROUN

L.Dsartie

Latatsi

M. M.

MM.Noupra

Kamtcha

Kimteha Tchasreoug

MM.Toula

MM.Tchala

LIMITES DE MOMPA PITAI
ou PITI

Timourkeng
ou
Forteresse
de Fer

Lcculsa

Latac Tchuese

IXe et derniere feuille
De celles qui sont comprises
dans la Carte generale

DU THIBET,
et ou se trouve

LATAC.

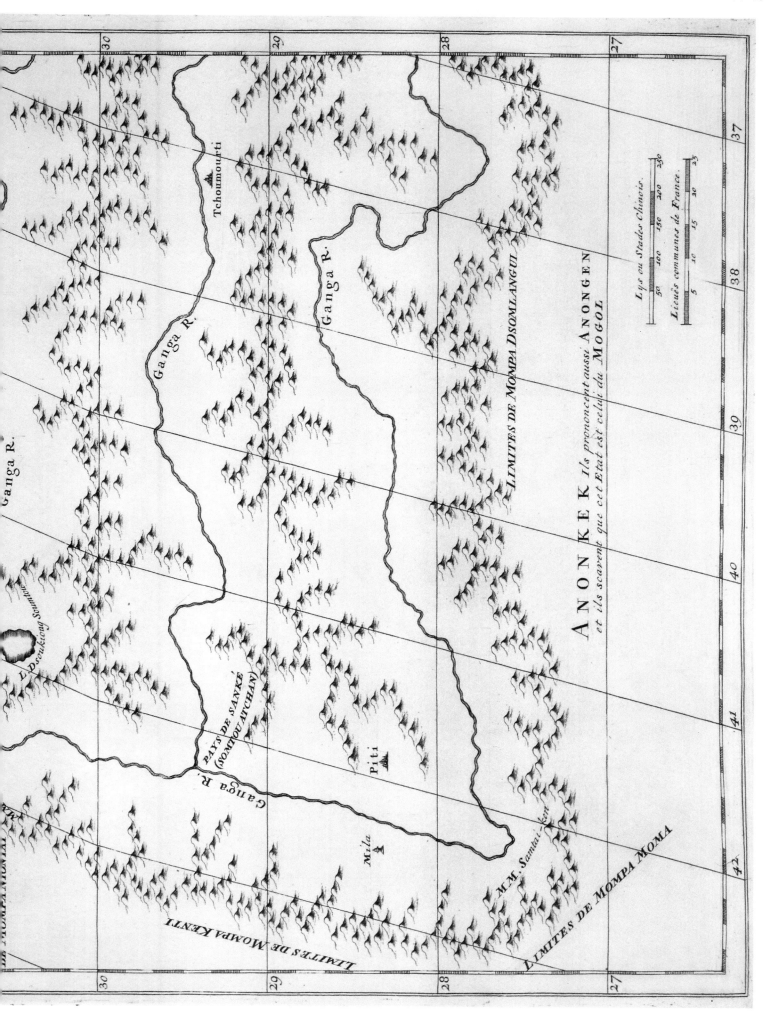

MAP 41.
Ninth detailed
page [of Tibet]

30

29

28

27

37

38

39

40

41

42

Ganga R.

Ganga R.

Ganga R.

Ganga R.

Ganga R.

Tchoumourti

L. P. Dsoukioy Soumbou

PAYS DE SANKÉ
(SOMHOUAITCHAIN)

Mila

Piti

M. M. Samtai-keri

LIMITES DE MOMPA DSOMLANGUL

LIMITES DE MOMPA KENTI

LIMITES DE MOMPA MOMA

A N O N K E K Ils prononcent aussi A N O N G E N
et ils sçavent que cet Etat est celui du M O G O L

Lys ou Stades Chinois.
50   100   150   200   250

Lieuës communes de France.
5   10   15   20   25

30

29

28

27

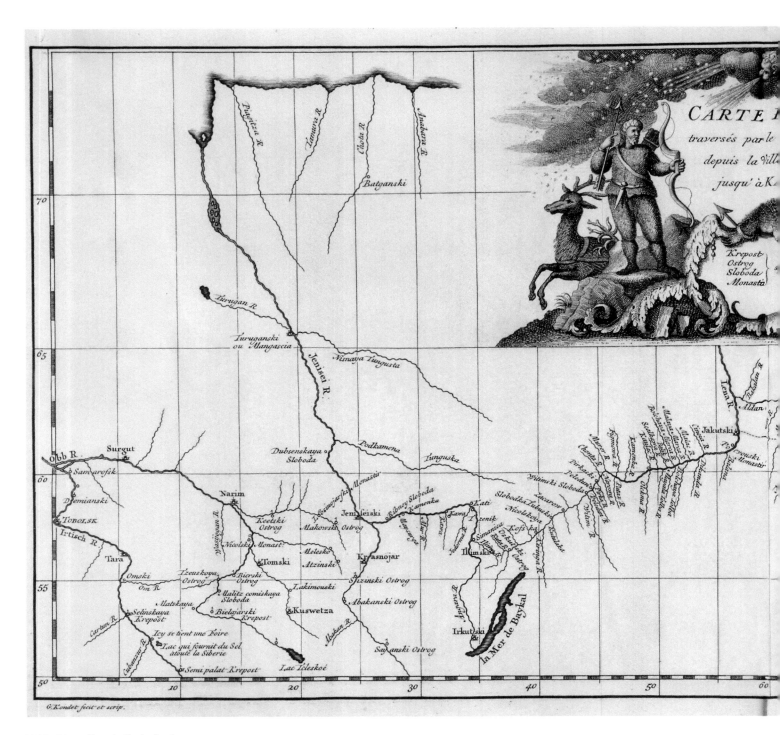

MAP 42. Captain Bering's trip

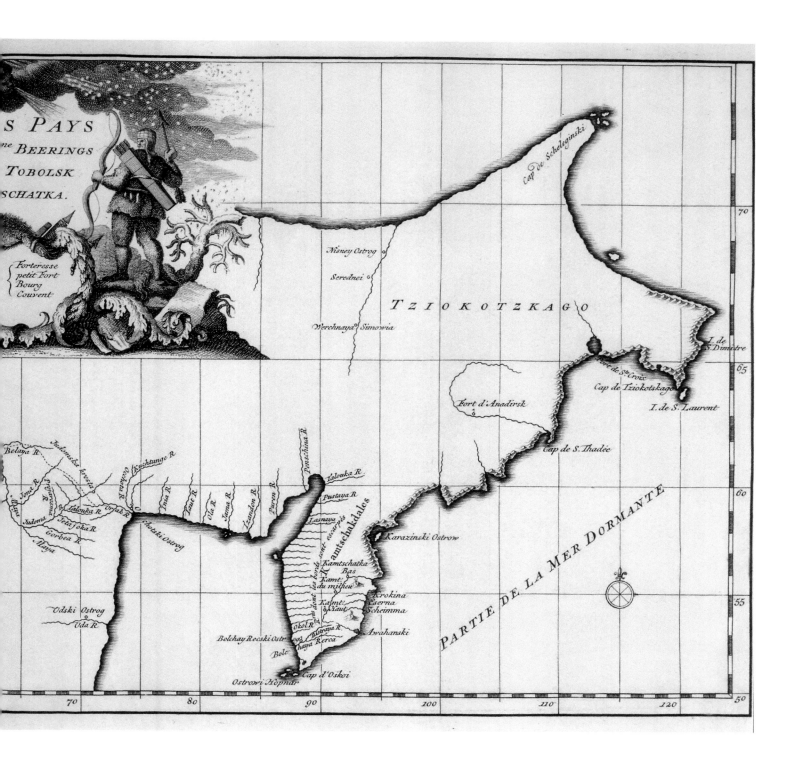

S PAYS
ne BEERINGS
TOBOLSK
SCHATKA.

Forteresse
petit Fort
Bourg
Couvent

Cap de Scheleginski

70

Nisney Ostrog

Serednei

T Z I O K O T Z K A G O

Werchnaya Simowia

I. de
S. Dimetre

65

Fort de S. Croix

Cap de Tziokotskago

Fort d'Anadirsk

I. de S. Laurent

Cap de S. Thadée

Belaya R.
Indomskie krisete
Kuchtunge R.

Jona R.
Inna R.
Taui R.
Ula R.
Jama R.
Ixendon R.
Paren R.
Ponschina R.
Talouka R.

Yalouka R.
Jelesoka R.
Byak R.
Pustaya R.

PARTIE DE LA MER DORMANTE

60

Judoma R.
Gorbea R.
Maya
Chatski Ostrog
Lasnaya

Kamtschatkdales

Karazinski Ostrow

Kamtschatka
Bas
Kamt:
du milieu

Udski Ostrog
Uda R.

Krokina
Eserna
Scheimma

55

Kasmt:
Ciuit

Okol R.
Bolchay Recski Ostrog
Bistraya R.
Rerca
Awahanski

Bolc
haya R.

Cap d'Oskoi

Ostrowi Hopnar

70   80   90   100   110   120   50

LIST OF CONTRIBUTORS

MARIO CAMS is a Ph.D. Candidate in Early Modern Sino-European Contacts, at the Katholieke Universiteit Leuven (Belgium).

JOHN W. O'MALLEY, S.J., is University Professor in the Department of Theology at Georgetown University, and editor of the "Early Modern Catholicism and the Visual Arts Series," published by Saint Joseph's University Press, Philadelphia.

R. PO-CHIA HSAI is Edwin Erle Sparks Professor of History at Pennsylvania State University, University Park, PA.

HAN QI is Professor in the Institute for the History of Natural Sciences, Chinese Academy of Sciences, Beijing.

ROBERTO M. RIBEIRO is former Director of The Beijing Center for Chinese Studies.

INDEX

A

Académie des Sciences (estab. 1666), 39

administration, imperial, 26

Alaska, United States, 69n

Anton, Ronald, S.J. (founder Beijing Center for Chinese Studies), 2–3

d'Anville, Jean-Baptiste Bourguignon, S.J. (1697–1782) (French Jesuit, cartographer), 2–3, 37, 40–47, 48–49n, 59, 65, 68

    works:

        Mémoire de M. d'Anville, Premier Géographe du Roi, Des Académies Royale des Belles-Lettres, & des sciences. Sur la Chine (1776), 48, 62n

        Traité des mesures itinéraires anciennes et modernes (1769), 62n

Aquinas, Thomas, O.P., St. (1225–74) (Italian Dominican, philosopher, theologian), 30

Amsterdam, Netherlands, 46

Amur River, Russia, 32, 67, 69n

ancestors, 33–34

Antu, Ming (c. 1692–1763) (Mongolian astronomer, mathematician, topographer), 57

Arabic, 43

Archives departementales de l'Orne, 42, 48n

artists, 31, 56

Asia, 25, 28, 37, 47

Astracan, Russia, 44

astronomy, 1, 26–27, 30–31, 43, 46, 51, 53–54, 57, 61n; astronomers, 27, 39, 57–59; instruments, 12, 53

atlas, 1–2, 37–42, 44–47, 48n-49n, 51, 58, 60, 66, 69n

Atlas général de la Chine, de la Tartarie chinoise, et du Thibet. Pour servir aux différentes Descriptions et Histoires de cet Empire (1790), 49n

Altas général de la Chine; pour servir à la Description générale de cet Empire (1785), 49n

Atlas Maior (1655), 14–15

Augustinians (estab. 1244) (Ordo Sancti Augustini), 34, 57

B

ballistics, 28

Bavaria, 29

Bazhou, China, 55

Beerings, Cpt. (Swedish officer, cartographer), 41, 69n

Beijing, China, 1–2, 18, 25–29, 32, 34, 39, 43–45, 47, 52–56, 60n, 67–68

Beijing Center for Chinese Studies, Beijing (estab. 1998), 2–3, 9–10, 14–16, 18–19

Belgium, 29

Bernard of Clairvaux, St. (1090–1153) (French Cistercian abbot, theologian), 30

Bibliothèque du Roy, 62n

Bibliothèque Nationale de Paris (estab. 1368), 62n, 42, 48n

Blaeu, Joan (1596–1673) (Dutch cartographer), 14–15

Bohemia, 29

Bonjour, Guillaume Fabre (1667/70–1714) (French Augustinian missionary), 57, 67

books, 26, 29, 41, 55, 69n; Arabic, 43; calendar, 58; Greco-Roman, 30–31; historical, 40; Jesuit, 2, 29, 62n; liturgical, 30; mathematical, 30; religious, 30; route, 42–43; scientific, 30, 53

Borgia, Francis, S.J., St. (1510–72) (4th Duke of Gandia, 3rd Superior General of Society of Jesus), 30

Bouvet, Joachim, S.J. (1656–1730) (French Jesuit, missionary, sinologist), 32, 52–53, 56–57, 67

Breviarium Romanum (1674), 30

Buglio, Ludovico, S.J. (1606–82) (Sicilian Jesuit, mathematician, theologian), 30, 51

Bukhara, Uzbekistan, 44–45, 68, 69n

Bureau of Mathematics, 57

C

calendar, 52, 54, 57–58; imperial, 26–27

Calendar Case (1665), 27–28

Calendar Office, 26

Camull, China, 69n

cannons, 32

Cardoso, Joao Francisco, S.J. (1677–1723) (Portuguese Jesuit, cartographer), 57, 67

cartography, 1–2, 37–38, 40, 46, 48n, 51–56, 58–59; cartographers, 2, 26, 37, 40–43, 47, 56, 59, 61n

cartouches, 41, 45

Caspian Sea, 44, 68

Cassini, Giovanni Domenico (1625–1712) (Genoese mathematician, astronomer), 58–59

Castiglione, Giuseppe, S.J. (1688–1766) (Milanese Jesuit, missionary, court painter), 30

Catholic Church, 34

Cave, Edward (1691–1754) (English publisher), 46, 62n

cemetery, 13

certification, imperial, 34–35

Changchunyuan (Chinese imperial villa), 57–58

charts, 41, 43, 52

China, 25, 31–32, 34, 37, 40, 45, 47, 51, 55, 67, 69n; geography, 2, 53, 56, 59; language, 1–2, 28–31, 37, 60n, 69n; maps, 2–3, 38–43, 47, 56, 59–60, 68; Ming, 2, 25–26; patron saint, 30; Qing, 25, 30–33, 37–38, 42–43, 51, 60, 69n; science, 26–27; Valignano, 1; see Chinese Mission

China Illustrata (1667), vi, 7–8

Chinese Lunar Calendar, 27

Chinese Mission (1582–1800), 1, 25–26, 28–30, 33–35, 39, 45, 51, 55

Chinese Rites Controversy (17th–18th c.), 28, 33–34

Chongzhen Calendar Compendium, 26

Chongzhen Emperor (1611–44) (16th Ming emperor), 26

Christianity, 1, 26–27, 31, 33, 35

Chu-er-qin (Tibetan lama, mathematician), 57

Cicero, Marcus Tullius (106–43 B.C.) (Roman philosopher, orator), 31

Cicigar, 69

Clarke, Jeremy, S.J., 12–13

Clement XIV, Pope (1705–74) (Franciscan cardinal, suppressed Society of Jesus), 34

clergy, 28–29

clockmakers, 26

colleges, 28

communications, 2

communities, Christian, 29, 34

Complete Map of the Imperial Territory, 37

Complete Map of the Kangxi Reign (1708–17), 51, 56

Comprehensive Gazetteer of the Qing, 52

Concise Introduction to the West (1669), 51, 54

Confucianism, 27, 29

Confucius (551–479 B.C.) (Chinese teacher, philosopher, politician), 9–11, 29, 33–34

Confucius Sinarum Philosophus (1687), 9–10, 29

Congregation for the Propagation of the Faith (estab. 1622) (Propaganda Fidei), 28

converts, 1, 26, 33

copperplates, 38, 41–42, 48n, 59, 62

Costa, Inacio da, S.J. (1603–66) (Jesuit missionary), 29

council, regency, 31

Couplet, Philippus, S.J. (1622–93) (Belgian Jesuit, missionary, Procurator of China Jesuits, Rome), 9–10, 18, 29

court, imperial, 26–28, 33, 39–40, 42–43, 53, 57–58, 60–61n

Court of Colonial Affairs (estab. 17th c.) (supervised Mongolian dependencies), 57

courtiers, 29, 31

Credo, 30

culture, 1–2, 31–32

cultural exchange, 1, 42, 47, 48n

D

Daoists, 33

Da Qing Yitongzhi (1686), 52

De Amicitia (1595), 31

Delahaye Workshop, 41

Delisle, Guillaume (1675–1726) (French cartographer, First Royal Geographer), 39–40, 43, 46–47

Delisle, Joseph-Nicolas (1688–1768) (French astronomer to Russian court), 39

Description geographique, historique, chronologique, politique et physique de l'Empire de la Chine (1735), 2, 19, 22, 62n

Description geographique, historique, chronologique, politique et physique de l'Empire de la Tartarie Chinoise (1736), 23, 39, 59

A Description of the Empire of China and Chinese-Tartary . . . (1738–41), 62

dialogue, 1

diplomacy, 31–33, 47

Directorate of Astronomy, 26–27

Dominicans, see Order of Preachers

Dondon River, 69n

E

Eborensis, Andreas, 31
  works:
    Sententiae et Exempla, 31

eclipses, 56, 58, 60n, 67

Edict of Toleration (1692), 33–35

Elemens de Géometrie, 53

Elements (4ᵗʰ c. B.C.), 1

emersions, 58–59

Enchiridion, 31

engineering, 32; engineers, 26

engravers, 26, 41, 68

envoys, 26, 43

Epictetus (55–135 A.D.) (Greek Stoic philosopher), 31

Ershiwu yan (1605), 31

Essential Principles of Mathematics, 57

d'Estrees, Cesar, Cardinal (1628–1714) (Bishop of
    Laon, French diplomat to Papal States), 18

Euclid (4th c. B.C.) (Greek mathematician), 1, 30
    works:
        Elements (4ᵗʰ c. B.C.), 1
        Enchiridion (4ᵗʰ c. B.C.), 31

Europe, 1–2, 25–29, 30, 32, 37–43, 45–47, 52–53, 59

European Astronomy (1687), 26

Exact Meaning of the Pitch-Pipes, 57

evangelization, 25–26, 28–29

excommunication, 34

excursions, 53

F

Far East, 1

First Historical Archives of China, 59–60n

Fontaney, Jean de, S.J. (1643–1710) (French Jesuit,
    mathematician, missionary), 32, 35n, 52, 61n

Fort Nerchinsk, Russia (estab. 1654), 32

Foucquet, Jean Francoise, S.J. (1665–1741) (French
    Jesuit, missionary), 57

Four Books (c. 300 B.C.), 29

France, 2, 29, 33, 38–39, 41–42, 46–47, 52, 58–59,
    60n, 62n; French, 28–29, 33, 69n

Franciscans (estab. 1209), 34

Fridelli, Ehrenbert Xavier, S.J. (1673–1743) (Austrian
    Jesuit, missionary, cartographer), 57, 67

friendship, 1–3

frontispieces, 7, 11, 14

Fujian Province, China, 34, 57, 59, 62n, 67, 87

Fuzhou, China, 30

G

Gallicanism, 34

Gaubil, Antoine (1689–1759) (French Jesuit, Beijing
    missionary), 39, 41–44, 46, 47n

gazetteers, 38

*The General History of China. Containing a geographical,
    Historical Chronological, political and physical descrip-
    tion of the Empire of China, Chinese Tartary, Corea
    and Thibet. Including an Exact and Particular account
    of their customs, manners, ceremonies, religion, arts and*

*sciences. The whole adorn'd with curious Maps, and
    variety of copper-plates* (1736), 62n

*Geographia nubiensis: id est accuratissima totius orbis in
    septem climata divisi descriptio, continens praesertim
    exactam vniuersae Asiae, & Africae, rerumq[ue] in ijs
    hactenus incognitarum explicationem* (1619), 43, 48n

geography, 29, 37–38, 40, 43, 47, 48n, 51–53, 56, 60,
    62n, 67, 69n, 2; Arabic, 43; books, 43; ecclesiastical,
    29; geographers, 26, 39–40, 57, 65, 68; Italy, 40;
    Jesuit, 2, 26; names, 45

geometry, 27, 30

Geometry (c. 300 B.C.), 30

Gerbillon, Jean-François, S.J. (1654–1707) (French
    Jesuit, interpreter, diplomat Chinese court), 32, 48n,
    52–53, 68

Germany, 29, 47

globes, 53

gnomon (Gk one that knows, part of sundial), 27

Gobien, Charles le, S.J. (1653–1798) (French Jesuit,
    Superior of Parisian Province), 33

Gong'e, 58

Gonzaga, Aloysius, S.J., St. (1568–91) (Mantuan Jesuit,
    student Roman College), 30

González de Santalla, Tirso, S.J. (1624–1705) (Spanish
    Jesuit, General of Society of Jesus), 33

Gou-gu (Chinese—Pythagorean theorem), 54–55

Granada, Luis de, O.P. (1505–88) (Spanish Dominican,
    spiritual author), 30

Gravier, Charles (1717–87) (French diplomat), 47

Great Wall, 8, 26, 57, 67

Green, John (alias Bradock Mead), 46

Grimaldi, Philip, S.J. (1638–1712) (Italian Jesuit, math-
    ematics tutor to Emperor Kangxi), 31

Grosier, Jean-Baptiste (1743–1823) (French cleric), 2

Guangdong Province, China, 27–28, 57–59, 62n, 67, 102

Guangdi, Li, 54–55

Guangqi, Paul Xu (1562–1633) (Chinese mandarin,
    Christian convert), vi, 1, 7, 22, 26, 30

Guangxi Province, China, 57, 59, 62n, 67, 104–5

Guangxian, Yang (1597–1669) (Confucian scholar,
    mandarin), 27, 51

Guizhou Province, China, 59, 62n, 67, 109

Guodong, He, 57–58

Guozong, He, 57

H

Hague, Netherlands, 45, 59, 62, 66

du Halde, Jean-Baptiste, S.J. (1674–1743) (Parisian
    Jesuit, Chinese historian), 2, 19, 22–23, 38–47, 59,
    62n, 66, 68–69
    works:
        *Description geographique, historique, chronologique,
        politique et physique de l'Empire de laChine*
        (1735), 19, 22–23, 39, 59, 62n

du Halde, Jean-Baptiste, S.J. (*continued*)
  A Description of the Empire of China and Chinese-Tartary . . . (1738–41), 62n
  The General History of China. Containing a geographical, Historical Chronological, political and physical description of the Empire of China, Chinese Tartary, Corea and Thibet. Including an Exact and Particular account of their customs, manners, ceremonies, religion, arts and sciences. The whole adorn'd with curious Maps, and variety of copper-plates (1736), 62n
Hall of Military Glory, Beijing, 58
Hami, China, 67, 69n
Han Chinese, 31, 59
Hangzhou, China, 13, 29–30, 32
Heilongjiang, China, 57
Henan Province, China, 57–59, 62, 67; map, 16–17, 92–93
Heshaotun, China, 55
Hinderer, Romain, S.J. (1668–1744), 57
Hsia, R. Po-chia, 1
Huangyu Quanlantu (1708–17), 37, 51, 56, 58–60, 61–62n
Hubei Province, China, 69
Huguang Province, 57, 59, 62n, 67, 69n, 91
Humblot, M., 41
Hunan Province, China, 69n
hydraulics, 27, 30

I

immersions, 58–59
Imperial Board of Astronomy, 57–58
Imperial Commissioned Calendrical Sciences, 57
India, 28, 39
Industan, 68
instruments, scientific, 12, 53, 55–56, 58, 60n
interpreters, 32
Intorcetta, Prospero, S.J. (1625–96) (Italian Jesuit, sinologist), 9–10, 29
Italy, 29, 43; Italians, 1, 25, 29, 31, 33, 38, 59

J

Jacques, Jean-Baptiste, S.J. (1688–1728) (French Jesuit, missionary), 47n
Japan, 1, 28, 43, 68
Jartoux, Pierre, S.J. (1669–1720) (French Jesuit, cartographer), 38–39, 56–59, 61n, 67–68
Jesuitica Sinica (collection of Beijing Center for Chinese Studies), 2, 9–10, 14–16, 18–19
Jesuits, see Society of Jesus
Jiangnan Province, China, 57–59, 62n, 67, 71, 83
Jiangxi Province, China, 57, 59, 62n, 67, 85
Jiao River, China, 55

Jiaoyou lun (1595), 31
Jilin, China, 57
jing tian (Chinese—respect heaven), 34
Joseph, St. (d. 1st c. A.D.) (foster-father of Jesus), 30
Juecheng, Mei, 57
Jupiter (planet), 58–59

K

Kalun, China, 53, 60n
Kangxi, Emperor (1654–1722) (2nd Qing emperor), 1–2, 27–28, 30–35, 37, 51–60, 61n
Kangxi yuzhi wenji, 60n
Kechintase, 67
Khalka, 67
Kircher, Athanasius, S.J. (1602–80) (German Jesuit, scholar, polymath), 7–8
  works:
    China Illustrata (1667), vi, 7–8
Korea, 38, 41–43, 47, 56, 59, 65–68, 72, 139
Kostka, Stanislaus, S.J., St. (1550–68) (Polish Jesuit novice), 30
Kumul, 69n
Kunmo, 69n
Kunyu Quantu (1674), 52
Kunyu Wanguo Quantu (n.d.), 52

L

laity, 29
Lam, Anni, 60n
lamas, 33, 57, 61n
languages, 1, 29, 59; Chinese, 1–2, 28–31, 37, 60n, 69n; German, 62n; Latin, 28, 31–32, 43; Manchu, 31, 41–42, 69n; Persian, 69n; Russian, 46, 62n; Turkic, 69n; Uyghur, 69n
latitudes, 45, 53, 55–56, 58–59, 61, 67
Le Comte, Louis-Daniel, S.J. (1655–1728) (French Jesuit, missionary), 11, 33, 52
Le-de-hong, 52
legations, 32; legates, 34
legislation, 35
Lettres édifiantes et curieuses (1702–76), 2, 35n, 38–39
Liaodong Province, Manchuria, 57, 67, 69n
Liaoning, China, 57
Lifanyuan (Imperial agency with oversight of Mongolian dependencies), 57
literature, 51, 55
liturgy, 29–30
London, England, 46
longitudes, 53–56, 58–59, 61n
Louis XIV (1638–1715) (King of France, House of Bourbon), 33, 52

Louis XV (1710–74) (King of France, House of Bourbon), 40

Low Countries, 2

Loyola, Ignatius, S.J., St. (1491–1556) (founder Society of Jesus), 25

Luli Yuanyuan (n.d.), 57

Lulu zhengyi (n.d.), 57

M

Macao, 25

Magalhaes, Gabriel de, S.J. (1610–77) (Portuguese Jesuit, Chinese missionary), 18, 51

magnets, 53

Maigrot, Charles (1684–1709) (bishop, Doctor of Sorbonne, Vicar Apostolic of Fujian), 34

Manchu , 26–27, 31–32, 67, 69n; language, 41–42, 69n

Manchuria, 38, 69n

mandarins, 26, 33; Jesuits, 27

Manuale ad sacramenta ministranda juxta ritum S. Romae Ecclesiae (1675), 30

manuscripts, 18, 42–43, 48n; see books

maps, 2–3, 35, 37–39, 48n, 52, 56–59, 61–62n, 66–68; Beijing, 18, 39; Beizhili, 67, 80; Captain Bering's trip, 160; Caspian Sea, 44, 68; China, 2–3, 15, 38–43, 45, 47, 56, 59–60, 67–68, 74; Chinese Tartary, 38, 40–41, 43–45, 47, 52, 59, 66, 68, 74, 110–36; Dutch, 45–46; Europe, 53, 69n; France, 58, 60n; Fujian, 62n, 86; Guangdong, 59, 62n, 102; Guangxi, 59, 62n, 104; Guizhou, 59, 62n, 108; Henan, 16–17, 59, 62n, 92; Huguang, 59, 62n, 90; Japan, 68; Jiangnan, 59, 82; Jiangxi, 59, 84; Korea, 38, 41–43, 47, 65–68, 138; Liaodong, 67; Manchuria, 38; mapmakers, 38, 42, 45, 47; Martini, 2; Mongolia, 38, 67; Ricci, 52; Shandong, 59, 62n, 67, 94; Shanxi, 59, 62n, 96–98; Shengjing, 62n; Sichuan, 59, 100; Tibet, 38, 40–45, 47, 66, 68, 74, 140–58; Turkestan, 38, 42; Western, 53; Wula, 62n; Wusuli Jiang, 62n; Yunnan, 59, 62n, 106; Yupik, 67; Zhejiang, 59, 88; Zhili, 59, 62n; see d'Anville, Jean-Baptiste; cartography; du Halde, Jean-Baptiste

Martini, Martino, S.J. (1614–61) (Italian Jesuit, missionary, cartographer), 1–2, 13–16, 34

mathematics, 26, 27, 30–31, 51, 54–55, 57, 61n, 65;

mathematicians, 30, 52, 54, 57

Matteo Ricci and Xu Guangqi (1667), vi, 7

Mead, Bradock, 46, 49n

medicine, 31–32

Mémoire de M. d'Anville, Premier Géographe du Roi, Des Académies Royale des Belles-Lettres, & des sciences. Sur la Chine (1776), 45, 62n

Mémoire sur la Chine (1776), 45

Memoirs and Observations about China (1697), 11

Mengyangzhai , 57

MEP, see Paris Foreign Mission

Mergen, China, 67

measurements, 2, 38, 40, 42, 53–56, 58, 60n

meteorology, 27

microscopes, 53

Ming Dynasty (1368–1644), 2, 25–26

Mingren, Zhong, S.J., 13

Mingxuan, Wu (Chinese Muslim, astronomer), 27

Ministry of Rites, 26, 52

Ministry of Works, 54–55

Missale Romanum (1670), 30

missionaries, 1, 25, 29, 31, 33, 38, 41, 52–53, 57, 65, 67

missions, see China Mission

Mongolia, 38, 57

Mongols, 67

Morales, Juan Bautista de, O.P. (c. 1597–1664) (Andalusian Dominican, missionary to Philippines, China), 33–34

mountains, 29, 45, 46, 52, 56–57

Moyriac de Mailla, Joseph-Anne-Marie de, S.J. (1669–1749) (French Jesuit, cartographer), 45, 57, 67

music, 27, 30–31; musicians, 26

N

Nahai, 58

Nanjing, China, 32

National Library of France, see Bibliothèque Nationale de Paris

Neifu yuditu (n.d.), 62n

Nepomok, John, St. (c. 1345–93) (Czech cleric, martyr), 30

Newton, Isaac (1642–1727) (English physicist, mathematician), 59

Ningbo, China, 52

Nobel, Filip, 69

Noel, François, S.J. (1651–1729) (French Jesuit, missionary), 61n

Nouvel atlas de la Chine (1718), 2, 37, 59, 62n

Nouvel atlas de la Chine, de la Tartarie chinoise, et du Thibet (1718), 45

Nouvelle relation de la Chine (1688), 18

Novus Atlas Sinensis (1655), 14–16

O

observatory, 3, 12, 58

Order of Preachers (estab. 1216), 33–34

orders, mendicants, 28, 33

d'Orleans, Louis (1702–52) (Bourbon Duke of Orleans), 40

Orry, Louis-Francois, S.J. (French Jesuit, treasurer of China mission), 39

orthography, 45

Ostend, Belgium, 42, 48n

P

painting, 30–31

Palace of Heavenly Purity, Beijing, 53

papacy, 30, 34; decrees, 25, 34; legates, 34

Pardies, Ignace-Gaston, S.J. (1636–73) (French Jesuit, mathematician, scientist), 53
  works:
    Elemens de Géometrie (1671), 53

Paris, France, 2, 38, 40–47, 66, 69; Jesuits, 33, 38–39, 44, 46, 48n

Paris Foreign Missions (estab. 1658–63) (M.E.P.), 28

Parrenin, Dominique, S.J. (1665–1741) (French Jesuit, missionary, cartographer), 56–57

patronage, 26, 31, 38, 46, 47n

Pereira, Thomas, S.J. (1645–1708) (Portuguese Jesuit, music tutor to Emperor Kangxi), 31–32, 53

persecution, 32

Perspectiva pictorum (1706), 31

Philippines, 28, 33

philosophy, 31

physicians, 26, 32

Plan de la ville de Pekin Capitale de la China (1688), 18

Poland, 29

Pole Star, 53–54, 57–58, 60n

Portugal, 18, 29, 33; enclaves, 25; Jesuits, 30, 32–33, 35, 53; legations, 32; merchants, 25

Pozzo, Andrea, S.J. (1642–1709) (Italian Jesuit brother, painter, architect), 31
  works:
    Perspectiva pictorum (1706), 31

prayers, 30

printers, 2, 41, 62n

printing press, 29, 62n

propaganda, 33

Protestantism, 25

Provinces, Chinese, 29, 35, 41–43, 57–58, 67, 69; Fujian, 34, 57, 59, 62n, 67, 87; Guangdong, 27–28, 57–59, 62n, 67, 102; Guangxi, 57, 59, 62n, 67, 104–5; Guizhou, 59, 62n, 67, 109; Henan, 16–17, 57–59, 62, 67, 92–93; Hubei, 69; Jiangnan, 57–59, 62n, 67, 71, 83; Jiangxi, 57, 59, 62n, 67, 85; Shaanxi , 57–59, 62n, 67, 98; Shandong, 57, 59, 62n, 67, 94; Sichuan, 58–59, 62n, 67, 101; Yunam, 67; Yunnan, 58–59, 62n, 67, 72, 107; Zhejiang, 53, 57–59, 67, 71, 89; Zhili 55, 57, 59, 62n

Pythagorean theorem, 54–55

Q

Qianlong Emperor (1711–99) (4th Qing emperor), 35, 60n

Qing Dynasty (1644–1911), 25, 30–33, 37–38, 42–43, 51, 60, 69n

Qinruo Lishu, 57

Qiqihar, China, 67, 69

quinine, 32

R

Ratio Studiorum (1st ed. 1599), 31

rebellion, 31–33

recruitment, 28

Régis, Jean-Baptiste, S.J. (1663–1738) (French Jesuit, missionary, cartographer), 58–59, 61n, 67, 42–43, 56–57

residences, Jesuit, 25, 29, 30

rhetoric, 31

Rho, Giacomo, S.J. (1592–1638) (Milanese Jesuit, mathematician), 26

Ricci, Matteo, S.J. (1552–1610) (Maceretan Jesuit, Founder of Chinese mission), vi, 1, 7, 22, 25–26, 28, 30–31, 34–35, 52
  works:
    Ershiwu yan (1605), 31
    Jiaoyou lun (1595), 31

Ripa, Matteo (1682–1746) (Italian secular priest, engraver), 38, 59

rites, 33–34

Rome, Italy, 18, 28, 33–34

rosary, 30

Rougemont, Franciscus de, S.J., 9–10

Ruggieri, Michele, S.J. (1543–1607) (Neapolitan Jesuit, founder China mission), 25

Ruo, Hong (Chinese name—Jean de Fontaney), 52

Russia, 38–39, 41, 47; language, 62n; Russians, 32–33, 46

S

sacraments, 29

Saghalien-Oula (Manchu - Amur River), 69n

Saint-Petersburg, Russia, 39, 43, 46–47

Saint-Petersburg Academy of Sciences (estab. 1724), 47

salvation, 25

sanfan (Chinese—Three Feudatories), 52

sanjiaoxing (Chinese—triangle), 55

Sanson, Nicholas (1600–67) (French cartographer), 61n

Sapientia Sinica (1662), 29

Schall von Bell, Adam, S.J. (1592–1666) (German Jesuit, astronomer), 1, 22, 26–27, 33

scholars, 3, 27, 29, 31, 41, 60

Schreck, Johann, S.J. (1576–1630) (German Jesuit, mathematician), 26

science, 2, 26–27, 29, 31, 52, 58, 60n; scientists, 26, 29, 35

Seneca, Lucius Annaeus (4 B.C.-65 A.D.) (Roman Stoic philosopher, statesman), 31

Sententiae et Exempla, 31

Seventeen Questions (1643), 34

Shaanxi Province, China, 57–59, 62n, 67, 98

Shandong Province, China, 57, 59, 62n, 67, 94

shangdi (Chinese—God), 34

Shanghai, China, 29

Shanxi, China, 57, 59, 62n, 67, 97

shen wei (Chinese—seat of the spirit), 34

Sheng-zhu (Tibetan lama), 57
Shixue (1729), 31
Shoujing, Guo (1231–1316) (Chinese astronomer, engineer, mathematician), 58
Shoushi Calendar, 58
Shuli Jingyun (n.d.), 57
Shunzhi Emperor (1638–61) (1st Qing emperor), 27
Siberia, 69n
Sichuan Province, China, 58–59, 62n, 67; map, 101
Slavíček, Karel, S.J. (1678–1735) (Czech Jesuit, astronomer to Chinese court), 39, 58
Society of Jesus (estab. 1540) (Societas Iesu), 1, 25–27, 34, 37, 51–52, 59, 68; anti-Jesuit, 34; artists, 30–31; Belgian, 26, 32, 51–52, 55; China Mission, 1, 2, 26, 28–30, 33–35, 39, 45, 51, 54–55; colleges, 28; confessors, 40; courtiers, 29, 31; diplomacy, 31–32, 34; dissolution, 25; French, 2, 31–33, 35, 38–39, 47, 52–53, 58–59, 62n; interpreters, 32; Italian, 1, 25, 33; Macau, 35n; missionaries, 1, 25, 29, 31, 33, 38, 41, 52–53, 57, 65, 67; Paris, 33, 38–39, 44, 46; Portuguese, 30, 32, 53; printing, 29–30; propaganda, 33; residences, 29; scientists, 2, 26–27, 29, 35; Swiss, 35; texts, 2; translators, 29; Visitator, 1
Songgotu (1636–1703) (Manchu nobleman, uncle of Kangxi's primary spouse), 32
Souciet, Etienne, S.J. (1671–1744) (Parisian Jesuit), 48n
Source of the Pitch-Pipes and Calendar (n.d.), 57
Spain, 29
Spanish Netherlands, 29, 32, 45, 59, 62n
standards, 53, 55–56
stipend, imperial, 26
strategy, 1
Studio for the Cultivation of Youth, 57
Suanxueguan, 57
Summa Theologica (written 1265–74), 30
Suozhu, 58
surveys, 2, 38, 40, 43, 51–59, 61n, 65, 67–68;
surveyors, 38, 47n, 55
Swiss, 35

T

Taiwan, 52, 57
Tartre, Pierre-Vincent de, S.J. (1669–1724) (French Jesuit, missionary), 57, 67
Taschereau de Linières, Claude Bertrand, S.J. (1658–1746) (French Jesuit, royal confessor), 40
Tatars, 65, 68
telescopes, 53
temples, 33
Teresa of Avila, St. (1515–82) (Spanish Discalced Carmelite, reformer, mystic), 30
Thomas, Antoine, S.J. (1644–1709) (Belgian Jesuit, missionary), 52, 55–56, 60–61n

Three Feudatories (Chinese rebellion 1673–81), 32, 52
tian (Chinese - God), 34
Tianzhu shengjiao nianjing zongdu (1628), 30
Tibet, 38, 40–45, 47, 57, 59, 65–66, 68, 71–72; maps 74, 140, 142, 145, 147–48, 151, 153, 155, 157, 159
Tongzhou, China, 55
topography, 2, 56
Tournon, Charles-Thomas Maillard de (1668–1710) (Savoyard cardinal, papal legate to China); 34
Traité des mesures itinéraires anciennes et modernes (1769), 62n
translations, 1–2, 11, 30–31, 38, 43, 46
Treaty of Nerchinsk (1689), 32
triangles, 55, 67
Tribunal of Mathematics, 68
Turkestan, 38, 42
tutors, 30–31, 40
The Twenty-Five Sayings (1605), 31
Typus eclipsis lunae (1971), 20

U

Universal Map (1674), 52
Universal Map of Ten Thousand Countries, 52
Uzbekistan, 44

V

Valignano, Alessandro, S.J. (1539–1606) (Neapolitan Jesuit, Visitator to Jesuit missions), 1
Verbiest, Ferdinand, S.J. (1623–88) (Belgian Jesuit, Director of Directorate of Astronomy), 1, 12, 20, 22, 26–28, 31–33, 51–52
works:
European Astronomy (1687), 26
Virgin Mary, 30
Visdelou, Claude de, S.J. (1656–1737) (French Jesuit, missionary to China), 52
Visitator of Society of Jesus, 1,
Von Strahlenberg, Philipp Johann (1677–1747) (Swedish officer), 44–45

W

Wanli Emperor (1563–1620) (13th Emperor, Ming Dynasty), 26
war, 32, 47
West, 1–2, 31, 51, 54; astronomy, 26–27; geography, 51, 53; literature, 51, 55; teachings, 27
Wild-Court, London, 62n
Witek, John, S.J. (d. 2011) (American Jesuit, professor Georgetown University), 3
woodblocks, 38, 41–42, 46, 48n, 60n
Wujingdian (Chinese -Hall of Military Glory), 58

X

Xavier, Francis, S.J., St. (1506–52) (Navarrese Jesuit, missionary), 25, 30
Xifang Yaoji (1669), 51
Xinjiang, China, 69n
Xiyang chouren (Chinese—mathematician from West Ocean, Antoine Thomas, S.J.), 54–55
Xiyao, Nian, 31
Xu, Candide (1607–80) (granddaughter of Paul Xu), 22
Xu, Paul (1562–1633) (Chinese mandarin, Christian convert), vi, 1, 7, 22, 26, 30

Y

Yangtze River, China, 53, 57
Ying, Li, 58
Yingtang, Bai, 58

Yinzhi, Cheng (1677–1732) (Chinese prince, third son of Kangxi Emperor), 54–55, 57
Yongzhen Emperor (1678–1735) (3rd Emperor, Qing Dynasty), 35
Yunam Province, China, 67
Yunnan Province, China, 58–59, 62n, 67, 72, 107
Yupik (indigenous peoples of Alaska and Far East Asia), 67, 69n
Yupitase, 69
Yushu, Zhang (1642–1711) (Chinese grand minister), 55

Z

Zhaoha, China, 58
Zhejiang Province, China, 53, 57–59, 67; map, 71, 89
Zhili Province, China 55, 57, 59; maps, 62n
Zhou Dynasty (c. 1046–256 B.C.), 54, 56